THE KINGDOM OF CHRIST

OR

HINTS TO A QUAKER

RESPECTING THE

PRINCIPLES, CONSTITUTION, AND ORDINANCES

OF THE

CATHOLIC CHURCH

BY

FREDERICK DENISON MAURICE, M.A.

IN TWO VOLUMES

VOL. II.

THIRD EDITION

London
MACMILLAN AND CO.
1883.

CHARLES DICKENS AND EVANS,
CRYSTAL PALACE PRESS.

CONTENTS.

———— — ——

Part II.—(Continued.)

CHAPTER IV.

Section II.—The Creeds.

Section III.—Forms of Worship.

Section IV.—The Eucharist.

CONTENTS.

CHAPTER V.

ON THE RELATION OF THE CHURCH AND NATIONAL BODIES.

INTRODUCTORY.

SECTION I.—OBJECTIONS OF THE QUAKERS.

SECTION II.—THE PURE THEOCRATIST.

SECTION III.—THE SEPARATISTS.

A*

Part III.

THE ENGLISH CHURCH AND THE SYSTEMS WHICH DIVIDE IT.

CHAPTER I.

INTRODUCTORY.

HOW FAR THIS SUBJECT IS CONNECTED WITH THOSE PREVIOUSLY DISCUSSED.

CHAPTER II.

THE ENGLISH SYSTEMS.

PART II.—(CONTINUED.)

OF THE CATHOLIC CHURCH AND THE ROMISH SYSTEM.

THE KINGDOM OF CHRIST.

CHAPTER IV.—(CONTINUED.)

THE SIGNS OF A UNIVERSAL AND SPIRITUAL SOCIETY.

SECTION II.—THE CREEDS.

IN the last section I defended my view of Baptism as the sign of admission into a Spiritual and Universal Kingdom, grounded upon our Lord's incarnation, and ultimately resting upon the name of the Father, the Son, and the Holy Spirit, against the different Quaker, Protestant, Philosophical, and Romanist theories, which are current respecting it. But I have very much failed of my purpose, if I have not led the reader to observe that Baptism, according to this idea of it, is also the justification of many of those Quaker, Protestant, Philosophical principles, which were considered in the first part; one step towards the satisfaction of that great idea of a Church, one, indivisible, and imperishable, to which the Romanist clings with such honourable tenacity.

That man is a creature prone to sense, rising above

it by virtue of a union with an invisible Teacher, is the doctrine of Quakerism. Baptism embodies that doctrine, and converts it, as Fox wished that it should be converted, from a mere doctrine into a living fact. The only foundation, says the Calvinist, for faithful action and for sound hope, is the belief that we are God's elect children. Baptism offers to men that foundation; it tells them that they are chosen of God, and precious. It makes this foundation, what Calvin and all earnest Calvinists have felt that it ought to be, not dependent upon our feelings, apprehensions, and discoveries, but on the will and word of God. At the same time the distinction which it draws between the new and the old man, the man in Christ who alone can be raised and glorified, and the old man which is to be utterly abolished, is a far finer, clearer, more practical distinction than any which the *exclusive* Calvinist has been able to reach. It denounces the unclean living into which the believer in an absolute separate election for him is in such danger of falling, as absolutely incompatible with the knowledge and enjoyment of God which is eternal life; and yet it does not treat any living man as lying beyond the pale of God's covenant. Philosophers say that man can only be that or do that which is according to his constitution; he cannot be made by some miraculous process something else than he is; or, if he can, that power must be an injurious one. Baptism declares man's true and right constitution to be that of union with God, and separation from Him to be a violation of that only order according to which, as reason and experience alike shew, he can live. It is a fact that men are living anomalously; it is their own testimony that in doing so they are following their natures.   Baptism declares that those who will are taken out of that inconsistent condition to which they are prone, and are taken into a reasonable condition, in which they may live so long as they remember the covenant of God.   Finally, Romanism demands that by some direct, visible, permanent token, which all may acknowledge, it shall be felt that God has established the true, Divine, Catholic body upon earth; that it is the same from age to age; that the members are brought under a condition of Divine and spiritual discipline, are invested with mighty privileges, are laid under mighty responsibilities, are trained for a high and glorious condition. Of this demand, Baptism is the accomplishment, in a larger, fuller sense, than the Romanist will at all admit.   By this sign we claim him, and hundreds of thousands in the East and West, whom he has anathematized, to be members of the Church and body of Christ; by this sign we protest against him and them, when by any acts or any theories they degrade the spirituality, or narrow the universality, of that fellowship into which they have been admitted, and so (as far as in them lies) make void the covenant and the purpose of God.

I wish now to consider whether there be any other notorious facts which can only be explained on the same principle as this of the existence of Baptism; facts appearing on the face of them to import that there is a spiritual and universal constitution of society for mankind; facts denied to have that significance by a number of warring parties; facts which establish their claim to be what they seem to be, by the help which they afford us in justifying and realizing the leading principles of each of these parties, and in reconciling them with each other. The first which presents itself is this :—

There is actually found at this present day, in every Christian country, a certain document called a Creed. It is not necessary to inquire minutely at what time it was formed. Let it be admitted that there is an obscurity over its origin; that we cannot say who put it into that shape in which we now see it. From whatever quarter it may have come, here it is. It has lasted through a great many storms and revolutions. The Roman empire has passed away; modern European society has risen out of its ruins. Political systems have been established and overthrown; religious systems have been established and overthrown. Even the physical world has undergone mighty alterations, and our conception of its laws is altogether changed. The very languages which were spoken in all parts of the world when the Gospel was first preached, have given place to others; but this, "I believe," remains. It is substantially what it was, to say the very least, sixteen hundred years ago. During that time it has not been lying hid in the closet of some antiquarian. It has been repeated by the peasants and children of the different lands into which it has come. It has been given to them as a record of facts with which they had as much to do as any noble. In most parts of Europe it has been repeated publicly every day in the year; and though it has been thus hawked about, and, as men would say, vulgarized, the most earnest and thoughtful men in different countries, different periods, different stages of civilization, have felt that it connected itself with the most permanent part of their being, that it had to do with each of them personally, and that it was the symbol of that humanity which they shared with their brethren. Reformers who have been engaged in conflict with all the prevailing systems of their age, have gone back to this old form of words, and have said that they lived to reassert the truths which it embodied. Men on sick beds, martyrs at the stake, have said that because they held it fast, they could look death in the face. And, to sink much lower, yet to say what may strike many as far more wonderful, there are many in this day, who, having asked the different philosophers of their own and of past times what they could do in helping them to understand the world, to fight against its evils, to love their fellow-men, are ready to declare that in this child's creed they have found the secret which these philosophers could not give them, and which, by God's grace, they shall not take away from them.

Now a man who has noticed these facts, and has settled it in his mind that, whatever they mean, they must mean something, would certainly wish to inquire into the nature of this document which has been diffused so widely, has lasted so long, and has seemed to so many different persons of so much value. He will find, I think, that it differs from all the digests of doctrines, whether religious or philosophical, which he has ever seen. A man is speaking in it. The form of it is, I believe. That which is believed in is not a certain scheme of divinity, but a name—a Father, who has made the heaven and the earth : His Son, our Lord, who has been conceived, born, and died, and been buried, and gone down into hell, who has ascended, and is at the right hand of

God, who will come to judge the world : a Holy Spirit who has established a holy universal Church, who makes men a communion of saints, who is the witness and power whereby they receive forgiveness of sins, who shall quicken their mortal bodies, who enables them to receive everlasting life. The Creed is evidently an act of allegiance or affiance ; and since it has ever been connected with Baptism, one must suppose that from Baptism it derives its interpretation. If by that act we are acknowledged as spiritual creatures, united to a spiritual Being, by this act we claim our spiritual position, we assert our union with that Being. The name into which we are adopted there, is the name we confess here. Those acts which, having been done for all mankind, were the warrant for our particular admission into the covenant, are the acts which we here proclaim to be the warrant of our faith and our fellowship. So far the form is consistent with its apparent object. But is it also consistent with the idea of Christ's kingdom which the Bible develops to us ? There we found the primary postulate of such a kingdom to be a condescension of God to man, a cognizance taken of the creature by the Creator ; the second, an apprehension of God by men, a recognition of the Creator by the creature. By *grace* are ye saved ; by *faith* are ye saved. The position is freely given ; a position of union and fellowship with another, a position of self-renunciation ; the power is given wherewith to claim it : then comes the claim itself. Such seems to be the testimony of Scripture : and the relation in which the Creed stands to Baptism, and their common relation to that name and that kingdom which Scripture is revealing, surely expounds, in a remarkable way, that testimony.

But there is another creed possessing apparently equal authority with the one of which I have spoken, adopted perhaps into earlier use in the Eastern part of Christendom, and recognised by the Western ever since the age of Constantine. If it should be found that these two creeds clash with each other, or that they are not constructed upon the same principle, or that they do not both connect themselves with the idea of which we have spoken, the evidence from the preservation of either would certainly be weakened. Or if, these differences not appearing, it should seem that one could be conveniently substituted for the other, that there is nothing distinct and peculiar in each, one might be puzzled to account for the existence of both, at least as universal symbols. To see whether any of these objections apply, I would urge the reader to a thoughtful comparison of the two documents. First I would ask him whether in reading that which we call the *Apostles' Creed*, considering it as a declaration of the name into which he is baptized, he do not feel that it is meant to proclaim the distinct personality of the Father, the Son, and the Spirit, as signified by certain relations in which they have been manifested to *men?* Then whether another question do not arise in his mind, which he may perceive from history has arisen also in other men's minds:—Is there not a more mysterious and awful relation implied and prefigured in these? Does not the name express such a relation? Is not the knowledge of this, as the ground of those relations, part of the revelation which has been vouchsafed to us ; one of the deep things which cannot indeed be understood (for who understands the mystery of his own ordinary human relations?) but which lies so immediately beneath those facts which most concern us all, is so needful as the interpretation and reconciliation of those facts, has been so eagerly felt after in all ages, that if it be not disclosed to the heart and reason of man, they will be tormented with such dreams and imaginations concerning it, as must make the acknowledgment of the Divine Unity impossible?

Now the *Nicene Creed* agrees with the Apostles' altogether in its form and principle. It is still *I believe*; it is still belief in a name, and not in notions. It differs in this, that it unites with a declaration of the Divine relations to men, a declaration of the relations in the Godhead.

To every peasant and child it speaks of this marvellous subject. Certainly a strange fact, doubly strange when one knows how much it has been the tendency of teachers and priests in all ages to believe that only a few initiated persons are fit to know anything which concerns the name and nature of God; and how much this tendency did actually mingle itself with the awe and reverence of those ages by which these creeds have been transmitted to us. That the doctors of the Church should have allowed the Apostles' Creed to be heard in every cottage is strange; that they should not have said that this deeper creed, though embodying the principles and data of the other, was only for theologians, is scarcely credible: yet so it was. Now if it were the purpose of God that His name should be revealed to men ; if His name, which seems to most of us to be connected with the highest and most esoteric abstractions, be really the only ground of a universal society, we can interpret these facts. What other explanations have been found for them, I wish now to consider.

OBJECTIONS.—*The Quaker.*

To the Quaker it seems quite evident that the invention of creeds is one manifest symptom of the working of that mystery of iniquity which has been always arising to counterfeit and to destroy the kingdom of Christ. The faith which a Christian man exercises in the Divine Invisible Teacher is entirely of an inward spiritual kind. Here it is thrown outward, turned into propositions, made the language of a whole body or congregation, reduced into a nullity.

One side of this objection I considered when I was speaking of the differences between the Quaker and the Lutheran. It is precisely the objection to the acknowledgment of the *manifested* Word, and arises from a desire, more or less consciously entertained, to divorce the idea of a spiritual object from that of an actual person.

There is, however, mixed with this radical dislike, a feeling of a most different kind—a feeling that mere conceptions, opinions, notions, are most inadequate to the wants of a spiritual being, mere pictures and poor pictures of that which is real. To this doctrine I assent most heartily; there is none which I have been so anxious to maintain throughout this book.

The problem how we may be delivered from opinions and notions, how we may rise out of them into another region, is the very one which I am investigating. The history of Quakerism I have found most helpful to me in the inquiry, at least in a negative way; for it shews us, I think, that there is no such certain and direct road into mere notionality, as that of rejecting all common and united forms of utterance. The apprehensions and conceits of each man's mind, being those which he regards as alone sacred, become his tyrants; and so far as he is able to give expression to those apprehensions and conceits, they become the tyrants over the minds of others. In no society are there so many traditional phrases which have had a meaning once and have lost it, or are rapidly losing it, as in the Quaker society; in no society is there greater bondage to these phrases, a greater dread of exchanging them for any equivalents. And, therefore, without pressing the point again, that by this means all universality is lost, that a body which professed to be for mankind became in a very few years the narrowest and most peculiar of sects, I maintain that the experiment of dispensing with a Confession as a means of promoting spirituality has been made, and has failed utterly. Once more I claim our strongest opponents as witnesses in our favour. By the character of their arguments, and by the results of their practice, they have increased the probability that if there is to be a kingdom of Christ on earth, a creed, which should present a living object as revealed in living acts to the *faith* of all men, would be one of the divinely-appointed means of its preservation.

Modern Protestant Objections.

But the moment we use the phrase, *divinely-appointed means,* the modern Protestant, or Evangelical, steps in, and demands how we dare to claim such a dignity as this for a mere human composition, a mere ecclesiastical tradition? The Bible is the Divine document; it is a gross intrusion upon the rights of the Bible to assert that character for any other.

I would beseech the person who proposes this objection, to ask himself whether he seriously believes that the Bible is the only document, the only thing, which has been preserved to men by Divine care and providence? If he will say boldly, " I do think this," all debate is at an end. We are reasoning with a person who is separated by the very narrowest plank from absolute Atheism; a plank so narrow and so fragile, that in a very short time, it will be broken down. For, that he should believe this, and yet continue for any length of time to acknowledge a book which is characterised by nothing so much as its strong assertion, that whatever men possess they are to attribute to God's care and providence, is impossible. But supposing he disclaims, as he no doubt will, very indignantly, any such wicked hypothesis, I would beg him next calmly to consider what assertion of mine it is which offends him. Have I said that the creed is a substitute for the Bible? Have I urged that the creed is necessary, because it supplies information which the Bible does not supply? Have I said that the creed corrects or qualifies anything which the Bible asserts? I have maintained none of these

propositions. I have said, "I find a document which has
lasted for sixteen centuries or more. It is a document
which explains to me the meaning and purpose of the
Bible, which shews me that it has done what it proposed to do. As a declaration of the name of God, it
proclaims that that which the Bible undertakes to
reveal, has been revealed; as an act of faith on the
part of men, it proclaims that that faith by which the
Bible affirms we are saved, can be exercised."

Is the doubt, then, why the creed, seeing that it
only affirms the principles and facts of the Bible,
should be necessary to those who already possess the
Bible? The history of Protestantism gives the
answer. The Bible, in the hands of its orthodox
teachers, was reduced into a set of dry propositions,
about the limitations of which they were perpetually
fighting. The Bible, in the hands of its Unitarian
and Rationalistic teachers, was reduced into a set
of dreary truisms, not worthy to be fought about.
You talk about the Bible, and the Bible only; but
when you are brought to the proof, you give us, in
place of it, dry husks of logic or pompous inanities,
dignified with the name of simple truths. We want
the Bible as it is, in its life and reality; and experience shews that we shall not have it, if we have not
some witness of the principles which it embodies.

Again, the doctrine that faith justifies is, as Protestants affirm, the *articulus stantis et cadentis ecclesiæ*.
So said Luther, and looked to the creed as the great
witness of what he said; as that "confession of the
mouth unto salvation," in which "the heart's belief
unto righteousness" is expressed and fulfilled. Such
language seems to the modern Protestant dry, cold,

and carnal; what is the warm, juicy, and spiritual language, which he has substituted for it? History replies, endless controversies about the nature, mode, effect, signs, attributes, qualifications of a living or dead faith; controversies in which nothing is forgotten, save the object of the faith and the person who exercises it; controversies which fill the hearts of humble Christians with bewilderment and despair; controversies in which the exercised dialectician detects on each side great acuteness, admirable ingenuity, but regrets that in both the favourite argumentative figure should be the *petitio principii.* Am I then wrong in claiming the pure Protestant as a witness that this Catholic creed is an essential sign of the kingdom of Christ?

Rationalistic Objections.

The rationalist denies that the creed can be a permanent symbol of human fellowship, because it rests upon the acknowledgment of certain events. "Now, assuredly," he says, "these events could not have met with so much credence, if they had not pointed to certain great principles or ideas which are characteristic of us as members of a race. They do point most clearly to the sense which there is in all men of a something Divine; to the possibility that this should overcome evil, sorrow, and death; to the feeling that it must submit to sorrow and death as a way to that victory. This, which is the essence of the creed, is no doubt universal; it may be traced in heathen and Jewish records; it has survived all the fables with which, in both, it is encompassed.

There is therefore every probability that it will survive what are called the facts of Christianity likewise. And this is the more likely, because every day the documents in which those facts are recorded, are subjected to a more sifting analysis, and because every day the evidence in their favour seems to be less decisive."

In the former part of this book I have considered the general meaning and effect of this argument. I have endeavoured to show how true the assertion is upon which it is grounded, that the belief of a divine humanity has existed in all ages, that it has taken innumerable forms. I have maintained that all these forms have presumed the existence of some more perfect form; that they never have compassed the end at which they aimed; that they have not revealed THE MAN, the head of the race, while nevertheless they have testified, one and all, with more or less distinctness in proportion as the light which they endeavoured to concentrate was more or less clear, that such a one there must be. When a great man assumed to be this, he became a tyrant and oppressor; in our Lord's words, a thief and a robber, not the assertor of humanity, but the denier of it. You do not therefore advance one step in weakening the authority of this creed, by producing instances of this worship from ancient or modern history, or by dwelling upon the tendency which they so manifestly indicate. The more you can produce of them the better; the more they are examined the better. They prove that there is such an idea in humanity as you speak of; they prove just as strongly, that with the idea humanity can never be satisfied; they declare that the idea is the idea of an actual living Being, of a perfect Being; of one who should prove his perfectness by entering entirely into the lowest condition into which man has ever entered, and actually rising into the highest of which man has ever dreamed. If these two elements of the lowest humiliation, of the greatest exaltation, be not combined, if they are not combined in acts, the idea is not fulfilled, it waits to be fulfilled; that is to say, we wait for a person who shall do precisely those acts of which the creed speaks. Any others will not avail; any others will not be universal enough, will not be the testimonies that He who performs them is *the Man*. We are asked then for the evidences of the creed. Our answer is this— You have shewn why it has been believed, what need there was in the deepest heart of mankind that it should be believed. It was believed, not upon the evidence of documents, but upon the simple proclamation of men who had the whole universe against them. They said to men, Christ must be; Christ you have been asking for in every land, through every age: Jesus the crucified is the Christ. The answers were three : The first was,—" There are a thousand Christs ; every kingdom and district has its own." This answer would have been satisfactory, if men had not listened to that other proclamation; " You are members of *one* body, and therefore you need one Head." But they did listen to it; they felt it to be true; therefore the thousand could not prevail against the one. No wonder this answer should be revived now; no wonder that when the sense of being one body has so practically forsaken us, the principle which is its counterpart should be so readily abandoned. But

I hope I have shewn that there never was so strong
a cry for a universal and united fellowship as in this
day of division; a cry proceeding from so many
opposite corners of the earth, from so many different
kinds of men. This reply, then, if it failed once, will
not prevail now. The second answer was,—"There
is an ideal Christ under these different Christs; and
it is this, not they, you are to worship." The people
admitted the doctrine of the philosopher, but they
said, "This is the ideal Christ, and here He is manifested to us." That this argument should be repeated
in a day when abstract notions have been so much
substituted for living truths, cannot be surprising.
Yet we have seen, I think, that there was never more
impatience of these abstractions, or a more vehement
demand for realities, embodied realities, than at this
very time. If then there be an idea of a universal
Prince in men's minds, they will either continue to
believe that this idea has been realized in Jesus of
Nazareth, or they will seek a realization of it in some
other person. And thus we arrive at the third answer
which was made to the proclamation of the Creed in
the first ages, and which has been made so often
since: "This crucified man is not the perfect Being
we look for; we want a warrior, a philosopher, a poet,
possessing qualities altogether different from those
which are brought out in the Gospel narrative, though
we may acknowledge that these too have a certain
value of their own." Such has for twelve centuries
been the belief of a large portion of the world which
was once Christian. Another portion of it has declared that they see in the Cross the symbol of love
triumphing through suffering, in the Crescent only

of power claiming dominion over weakness; that
the first is a bond of mutual fellowship among the
members of a suffering race; the other the pledge
of a universal slavery. That the spirit of the Cross
prevails very little in the nations which still profess
to honour it; that self-sacrifice is very generally and
very systematically denied to be the law of our being,
—most of us are ready with shame to confess. And
therefore the expectation is surely very reasonable,
that the experiment which was so successful in the
nations of the East, will be made, under other conditions, in the West. We have had many preparatory
Antichrists, many sovereigns reigning by the strength
of mind and will, and scorning all other right; why
should we doubt that *this* image will be yet more
completely manifested?

May God preserve those who live in the day when
it is manifested to the world, and when the world
goes wondering after it! In that day when intellect
and will shall be utterly crushed under the car of the
idol which they have set up; in that day when the
poor man shall cry, and there shall be no helper, may
God teach his saints to proclaim these words to the
sons of men: *He was born of the Virgin; He suffered
under Pontius Pilate; He was crucified, dead, and
buried, and went down into hell; He rose again on the
third day; He ascended on high; He sitteth on the
right hand of God; He shall come to judge the quick
and the dead.* May they be enabled to say, *This* is
our God; we have waited for Him.

The Romish System.

Any one who maintains the creed to be an heirloom of the Church, which has been preserved to men by the providence of God, and which each generation of her members is bound to watch over, as an essential sign and necessary safeguard of her existence, may be said to acknowledge the authority and value of a Tradition. He must be, I should think, a rather feeble and cowardly thinker, who is afraid of the name after he has recognised the thing; the creed he believes has been handed down, and that which has been handed down is a tradition. But the Romanist is the great apologist for tradition: how in principle can one who attaches this kind of value to the creed differ from the Romanist?

It is not necessary to inquire to what extent any given Romanist would approve of language like the following: *That Scripture is not of itself sufficient to make known all the system which the Church requires; that the notions, opinions, and explanations of the doctors of the Church, partly as elucidatory of Scripture, partly as supplying that which is deficient and was meant to be deficient in it, are authoritative and necessary; that these together with Scripture constitute the ecclesiastical doctrine.* I say I shall not inquire whether any particular Romanist writer may have objected to this statement; it will be allowed, I think, that so far as he did, so far he was rejecting, not certain excesses or exaggerations of the Romanist theory, but a characteristic and integral portion of it.

I think if this statement be compared with the view which I have taken of the creed, it will be seen

that they are not *exactly* the same.   It will be
admitted that there are points of difference; that at
all events I do not choose to use the phrases which
Romanists use.   But is the difference one of terms only,
or is it a vital one, indicating an entirely different
conception of the purposes for which this document,
and the other documents bequeathed to us by antiquity,
exist?   I shall reply to this question by translating
my words, "The creed is the sign of a spiritual and
universal society," into others which I believe to be
equivalent—"*The creed is a document which has
served as a protection to the meaning of the Scriptures
against the tendency which the Church doctors in
different ages have exhibited to disturb and mangle
them.   The creed has served as a protection to the
humbler members of the Church against the inclination
which the Church doctors of different ages have manifested to rob them of their inheritance, and to appropriate it to themselves.*"

These propositions I have already illustrated, in
reference to the doctors of Reformed bodies.   I have
maintained that the Bible, left to their mercies, would
have been utterly deprived of its significance; and
that had we been left to their mercies, we should have
been fed with stones rather than with bread.   In
making these remarks, I speak only of an inclination,
at times a most predominating inclination, which has
been discernible in these teachers.   I do not mean
that there have not been many counteracting influences
at work both in their own minds and in the minds
of those whom they addressed.   I have asserted again
and again that there have been and are such
influences; and that the more we consider the

meaning and object of the Reformation, the more we shall discover of them. But I do assert that it is such an inclination as has needed a most strong and Divine power to resist it; and that power which delights to work by humble instruments, has, I believe, been exerted in a great measure through this child's creed. I will now endeavour to shew in what sense and under what limitations I conceive similar remarks are applicable to those early teachers whom the Romanist and we both profess to honour, as well as to the pontifical writers, whom he reverences, and whom we, I trust, do not despise.

It was the great glory of the greatest philosopher of antiquity to affirm, What man wants is a knowledge of that which *is;* he cannot be content with opinions and notions about that which *may be.* His being will not rest upon this. Society will not rest upon it. The ground of both must be a reality, an invisible spiritual reality; not any scheme or theory about this matter or that. The first Fathers of the Church had the strongest sympathy with this philosopher, precisely because he affirmed this. They felt that he was asking for the very thing which a revelation, if it were a revelation, ought to give. They felt, We have a revelation not of certain notions and dogmas about certain things, but a revelation of God himself. When I say they felt this, I mean that it was the deepest, strongest conviction of their minds, the one which their admirers have always acknowledged to constitute the great charm of their writings. To know God is eternal life. The Church is that society which rests upon the Name and Unity of God, and through which they are made known to man. I ask any lover of the

Fathers, whether he will not fix upon these as the two
great principles, which by their words and their lives
they are illustrating?

Now, surely, if this be so, the theology of the
Fathers must be most precious. They worked their
way through infinite confusions into the clear heaven
of these truths: *God is—He is one—and His unity is
not a dead material notion, but a unity of life and love,
the foundation of all unity among men.* If we have no
sympathy with them, with those who first saw the
light and rejoiced in it, above all, if we dare to mock
them, surely we must expect that it will become every
hour less clear to us and to our children. And what
if these fathers, having the idea of God ever before
them, rather merged those of man and of nature in it,
than perceived that each must be distinct, in order
that each may preserve its proper relation to the
other; may not this very fault of theirs be only an
additional help to us, if we will use it humbly and
faithfully? Their works are given to students; to
them expressly and exclusively. They are committed,
then, to men who have a peculiar vocation, a peculiar
responsibility; who need nothing so much as to be
taught how prone we all are to worship idols of the
cave and idols of the forum; to set up the notions
which are fashioned by our own peculiar temperaments,
or which are popular in our age, in place of great
principles, whereof they are the false likenesses; to be
taught this in order that they may perceive the glory
of that which is free and universal, and be delivered
from the preference which our devil-infected nature
conceives for that which is esoteric and self-exalting.
This lesson, if it be received at all, must be received

from the examples of good men, not of bad; of those whose light makes the darkness visible, not of those in whom all is dark. Why then should we deem the Fathers less valuable because they are capable of imparting it?

Alas! students did not make *this* use of the Fathers; but just that use which they could not have made if they had ever heartily admired that which was most precious in them, or had not lost the admiration of it through the vanity of possessing something in which other men did not share. They extracted notions, opinions, theories, from the writings of those saints who had declared that men are thirsting, not for theories or notions or opinions, but for the living God, and that they must have that thirst satisfied, or perish. Of course, then, the Bible became to the Patristic, as it did to the Protestant, student a mere congeries of notions; of course he also proclaimed, that to ascertain what these notions are was the great problem of human life, the necessary step to the attainment of everlasting salvation. But this necessary step could not be taken by men generally; they could not find out the true notions. The Fathers must help them. They must interpret the Bible, and supply its deficiencies. Still we are at fault. The Fathers are as unattainable as the Bible. What each of them affirmed, what they agreed in affirming, could be as little ascertained, as what each of the writers of the Bible affirmed, or what they agreed in affirming. There must then be an authority capable of pronouncing on this point, a living authority. Where was it? Was it the whole Church of any given age, or some particular member of it? The first doctrine was plausible, but impracticable; the last, therefore, was adopted. To find the commission was not difficult where the necessity for it was clear. A man was enthroned as the dogmatist of Christendom; he was appointed to say, and could say, what men ought to think. Thus was another stone added—not perhaps, the key-stone—to the *Romish system*. But the system was not all that existed in the ages which gave it birth, and brought it to maturity. There was another element at work. Men still repeated their Paternosters and Credos; eminent men felt, "*Here lies the deepest wisdom; no decrees and dogmas can reach the sense of the Scriptures, the sense of the Fathers, like this infantine lore.*" And so through the very heart of school divinity there ran a stream of simple faith, a silent acknowledgment that the truth had been revealed, and that the infinite complications of our minds, the various forms under which we are capable of beholding it, need not hinder us from knowing it and loving it. By degrees this faith became more and more obscured; opinion became all in all; then corruptions and infidelity grew and flourished by the side of increasing superstition and slavery. Still, there were holy and brave men, even in the later schools, who sought for a truth beyond opinions. The mystical writers spoke of beholding God, and dwelling in God. Ficinus and the Platonists, at the revival of letters, declared that there was a method of seeking the substantial and the real. But the "*I believe*" changed the glorious hope of the one, the philosophical idea of the other, into a fact for men. Then it became necessary for Pope Pius IV. to do that openly which had so long been done covertly—to set antiquity at defiance, and to

invent a creed of his own. Thanks be to God, he
could not do this work effectually! In the nations
which acknowledge his infallibility, not his creed,
but the Apostles', is still repeated by mothers and
nurses to their infants, still lisped by them in their
own language, still taught them by their priests.
The words, surely, are not *always* dead sounds; at
all events they may start, some day, into life. Protestants may discover that there is in them the very
heart of that Reformation doctrine which the systems
of Protestantism have been setting at nought; the
Churches which seek for a centre of unity by crouching
to Rome, may find in them at once the bond of their
fellowship and the charter of their liberation; the
Greeks may wake up to the conviction that centuries
of alienation have been unable to deprive them and
the West of these common symbols, it cannot be God's
will that they should be divided. What a day will
that be for the Catholic Church! what a day for the
Romish system!

Section III.—Forms of Worship.

Every traveller is ready to testify how different the
modes of worship are in the countries which he has
visited. They vary, he says, with every degree of
latitude. Within the same district he notices a persistency in certain practices and in the acknowledgment of the traditions which have given rise to them.
Nevertheless the effects of Time may, he remarks,
be traced almost as visibly as those of Locality. If
through an invasion, or by any other fortunate accident, the habits of a more cultivated people are

brought to bear upon an inferior one, the old customs acquire a more reasonable character; by and by, if the cultivation spread, and a particular class do not acquire the power of narrowing it to a certain point, a scepticism respecting old traditions becomes general. On the other hand, if a people be left to itself, without any of these influences, their minds become daily grosser, and the old superstitions lose all traces of the meaning and worth which they might have once possessed.

These remarks, which must be familiar to every modern reader, are undoubtedly derived from a true observation. Nor is their application at all limited to Pagan or Mahometan countries. I believe that where Christianity is found, the influence of locality and of periods is far more noticeable than elsewhere. There is a more strongly marked nationality in the different countries of modern Europe than in all the rest of the world at any moment of its existence; and that one century differs more from another in them than in the East, is a truism which it is almost foolish to utter. It is equally certain (as liberal writers so continually assure us) that the effect of this nationality and these changes in society upon religious opinion is most striking, and that there is no parallel to it in China or Hindostan.

But if it be so, is it not remarkable that certain forms of worship, actually of worship, have subsisted through all the revolutions to which Christendom has been subjected; have defied the restraints of national customs and languages; have stood their ground against all the varieties of opinion in reference to subjects human and Divine?

Is it not a strange thing, to take an example, that we in England in this nineteenth century should be using forms of prayer which were written by Greeks in the third and fourth? nay, that the whole conception of our liturgy from beginning to end; the assignment of particular services to particular seasons of the year; the use of Psalms; the ascriptions; the acts of confession, thanksgiving, adoration, should have been taught us by nations from which, by taste, by feelings, by political institutions, by the progress of civilization, by religious antipathies, we are divided? Think only of our northern character, our cloudy skies, our Teutonic independence, our vehement nationality, and then recollect that we are using, perhaps every day, certainly every week in the year, at the times which we believe to be most solemn, words which we owe to Hebrews and Greeks and Latins; and that in these words the simple folk of England, in spite of their narrow notions and local customs, are able to find solace and delight.

Now if the meaning of Baptism be that we are brought into God's family, and that we become therefore capable, with one mind and one mouth, of glorifying His name; if the creed be teaching us, as children of that family, severally and unitedly to acknowledge that name, and how it is related to us; we must feel that acts of worship should be, of all acts, those which most belong to our position, and in which our fellowship is most entirely realized. And this feeling is surely one which must be wrought out in us the more we read the Bible and enter into the sense of it. That all division comes through idolatry; that all union comes through the adoration of the one living and true God ; these are the two texts of the Bible, which, from the record of the dispersion at Babel, where men would build a tower whose top should reach to heaven, for the worship of natural things, down to the day of Pentecost, when the little band of Apostles in the temple were heard by the multitudes, each in their own tongue, magnifying God, it is illustrating and inculcating. If anything is to break down the barriers of space and time, it must be the worship of Him who is, and who was, and who is to come, whom the heaven of heavens cannot contain, and whose dwelling is with the humble and contrite heart ; if anything is to bring those at one whom these accidents of our mortality are separating, this must be the means. That men have turned worship to precisely the opposite use ; that they have made it the slave of their circumstances, the badge of their divisions, the instrument of their hatred, I have confessed. The question is whether there be any witness in the world against this tendency; whether God have given us any sign that these separations are the effects of our choice, not of His will. I say that these forms of worship, preserved through so many generations, adapted to every locality, are such a sign; I say, that using these, I have a right to believe that the blessings of the day of Pentecost have been given once, and never withdrawn ; that in the deepest and most practical sense there is a community which the distinction of tongues and the succession of ages cannot break.

OBJECTIONS.—*The Quaker.*

Against this conclusion the Quaker protests vehemently. Forms of worship are not only no signs of the existence of a spiritual commonwealth; they are positively incompatible with it. The Spirit bloweth where it listeth. Prayer is given by the Spirit. By these prepared forms we make it the utterance of the will and the reason of man.

Nothing can be truer than the last assertion. We do make prayer the utterance of the will and reason of man. We consider it their highest and most perfect utterance; that in which, and in which alone, they fully realize themselves. What the human Will is we can understand from no terms and definitions of logic. They can only express one half of its meaning, for they can only describe it by its intrinsic properties; whereas its essential characteristic is, that it is ever going out of itself. They can only describe it at rest; whereas it only *is* while it acts. But in prayer we can know truly and safely what the will is; prayer expounds to us its inmost nature; prayer substantiates it, and proves that to be the greatest reality which seems in language to be the greatest contradiction. The will gives itself up that it may be itself. It dies that it may enjoy life. In acknowledging another will as the only will, it attains its own freedom; even as in trying to have a being of its own, it becomes a slave. "Father, not my will, but thine." Where do we behold the human will in such perfection, in such distinctness of life and power, as in these awful words? And it is the same with that organ which beholds as with that which determines, with that which is the seat of wisdom as with that which is the source of action. This only knows itself when it forgets itself; this only sees while the sense of sight is lost in the object of it. Accordingly the Reason also finds its deepest meaning and expression in worship.

But do we therefore deny that the Spirit of God is the author of prayer, or, in Barclay's words, that all prayer is spurious which does not proceed from Him? No; but in affirming the one proposition we affirm the other. We believe that the Spirit of God is the awakener, the only awakener, of the spirit in man; that the will and reason not called forth by Him must remain for ever the torpid helpless victims of nature and sense. We believe that unless the Spirit of God give these powers their direction, they will only minister to that which they are meant to rule, only rivet the bondage which it is their privilege to break. We believe that whoever in past ages, either in heathen or Jewish lands, used them aright, was taught and enabled so to use them, and in proportion as he used them aright, confessed the inspiration. We believe that it is our privilege to exercise them as they could not be exercised by heathens, or even by Jews, because it is our privilege to know that there is a living Person actuating and governing them; and to know what manner of person He is, of whom He is the Spirit, from whom He proceeds, with whom He dwells. We believe that this knowledge is far more deep and awful than that which any one possessed who merely felt that he was the subject of *an* inspiration; but that being deep and awful, it is incompatible with excitement, with any distortions of manner or of voice, with the notion that we are merely the unconscious animal utterers of certain sounds which are imparted to us, instead of the living, conscious, voluntary, rational agents of One who, when He promised the Spirit to His disciples, said: "Henceforth I call you not servants, but I have called you friends, for the servant knoweth not what his Lord doeth; but whatsoever I have heard and learned of the Father, I have made known unto you." We believe that we must attribute every act of our minds, every exercise of our affections, every energy of our will, to this Spirit; if the purpose to which we direct them be wrong, still the gift and power are His, that purpose only ours; if it be right, we shall own that of it also He is the author. We believe again that every operation in nature, the growth of every tree, the budding of every flower, should be referred to the influence of Him who first moved upon the face of the waters; but we do not call this a spiritual influence, because, though wrought by a spiritual Being, it is wrought upon unspiritual subjects, upon things, and not upon persons.

Such are some of the inferences which follow directly from the idea of Baptism as a new birth, and of the Creed as the proper act of the new-born creature. That which is born of the Spirit is spirit, and seeks its spiritual home and Father, refers all its acts and movements to His inspiration, and thereby attains its own proper distinctness and freedom. That which is born of the flesh is flesh, and seeks the earth from which it came, acknowledging no influence and attraction but that. The contradiction of humanity is this—when the human spirit glorifies itself, and, as the necessary consequence and punishment of that sin, abdicates its own proper rights and throne, and sinks into the slave of the flesh, impregnating it with its own sin. The glory of humanity is this—when the human spirit renounces itself, and as its reward attains a knowledge of Him from whom it came, a victory over the flesh, and the power of communicating to it its own life.

The objection, then, which the Quaker makes to forms of prayer, that they proceed from man's reason and will, and not from the Divine Spirit, is one which involves a denial of the very nature and possibility of prayer. And this denial has been of the most practical kind. He acknowledges prayer to be a necessary act, at once the sign of moral health and the instrument in producing it. Yet he dares not pray unless he have a sensible impulse urging him to the exercise. I will not dwell upon the Quaker use of the word "sensible," though it seems to me very significant, indicating that those who most abhor all appeals to the senses in worship, who think that the sights and sounds with which God has filled the universe cannot be redeemed by the redeemed spirit to his service, do yet grossly confound impressions on the spirit with impressions on the sense. But the important point is that the idea of our life as a conflict, an idea continually present, one would suppose, to Fox's mind, is thus set at nought. If the Quakers understood that the true will and real self was ever at war with the mere sensible impulse, they would surely have believed that the reluctance of the natural man towards an act which we know to be good, and feel to be necessary, is one of the best proofs that it is prompted and encouraged by the Divine Spirit. But the truth is, that the idea of a constant living personal presence has practically deserted those who seemed at one time to make this belief the whole of their religion; that the notion of *an* influence, *an* inspiration, visiting certain persons at certain seasons, which is common to Christianity with Paganism, is nearly all that they have preserved. Is it wonderful, then, that they should be unable to understand how the Spirit should have taught men in distant generations to express their deepest wants in the same words, or how through these words they should enjoy secret and awful communion with each other, and with the Most High? But, if so, what better proof do I want that these forms are one of the clear and indispensable signs of a spiritual and universal fellowship?

The Pure Protestant.

The pure Protestants who have rejected the use of Liturgies sympathize but little in the Quaker's objections to them. They have no disposition to deny the voluntary nature of prayer or of any religious act. Because it has this character, they say forms are an intolerable bondage. " Each man should be able to express his own wants in his own way. In his chamber each man does or should lay bare his own feelings and wishes before God. This is the proper rule and standard of prayer according to our Lord's words, ' When thou prayest, enter into thy closet.' But since the minister, who is or should be chosen by the congregation, has a knowledge of the different circumstances of its members, and is looked up to by them as a person fit to preach the Gospel of Christ to them, it is very right that he should offer up prayers for himself and them, suggested by the feelings of the moment, probably a preparation for the sermon he is about to deliver, and therefore full of earnestness and unction. Forms of prayers are manifestly unsuitable for both these purposes; they cannot be adapted to changes of circumstances; they cannot be connected with the feelings either of the pastor or of the people; they are the impositions of another age, affronting to the understanding and painful to the conscience of those who use them."

Prayer to God is assumed in this statement to be, according to the primary notion of it, *individual.* A particular man wants to obtain certain blessings; he therefore asks them of Him who he believes can bestow them. To many persons this proposition seems self-evident; whoever doubts it is an enemy of common sense. Nevertheless it is, I believe, at war with the experience of every religious man. He learns soon that passionate eagerness to get some good thing for himself—be it fine weather for the sake of his crops, or the salvation of his soul—is not a help to prayer, but the greatest possible hindrance to it. Explain the fact as you will, but a fact it is, confessed by persons of different sentiments in different forms of language, continually presenting itself afresh to those who visit dying beds. The selfish object which we seek floats before our minds—if it be an earthly object, palpably; if an invisible unknown object, in hazy images, having more in them of terror than of beauty—but *the* object, He to whom our prayer is addressed, is afar off; of Him there is scarcely the least discernment. He is regarded as a Being who can inflict evil and may choose to confer a blessing; or if, through the teachings of our childhood, we have some better knowledge, the consciousness of self-seeking perverts it, and we rise up feeling that the sacrifice is not accepted; "we are very wroth, and our countenance falls." And how is it that this kind of prayer, so natural to every man, is changed for any other? "When thou enterest into thy closet," these are the words of our Lord to which the pure Protestant appeals, say, "Our Father which art in heaven, hallowed be thy name." O wonderful teaching! not how the selfishness of the closet may be carried into the temple, but how the breadth and universality of spirit which belong to the temple may be attained in the closet.

When thou art most alone thou must still, if thou wouldest pray, be in the midst of a family; thou must call upon a Father; thou must not dare to say *my*, but *our*. Dost thou desire to be very holy? Yet this must not be thy petition; thou must say, "Hallowed be *thy* name." Dost thou wish for some assurance of a heaven for thyself? Yet this must be thy language: "*Thy* kingdom come." Dost thou wish to get some favourite project accomplished? It must be sought in this manner: "Thy will be done on earth as it is in heaven." Dost thou want a supply of thy necessities, bodily or spiritual? Then thou must desire the same for all thy brethren, as well as for thyself: "Give us this day our daily bread." Dost thou want forgiveness for thy individual sins? The prayer is still, "Forgive us our trespasses," and the gift is only received when it is circulated, "as we forgive them that trespass against us." Do you feel that your fellow-creatures are your tempters? Yet you must acknowledge their temptations and yours to be the same; you must ask that they may not be led into the very temptations which they cause, else you will be their tempter as well as your own. And this be-

cause the evil from which you must pray to be
delivered is a common evil, an evil which is the same
in root and principle, though it may take innumerable
forms; that very evil of selfishness, of individuality,
which we are disposed to make our very prayers a
means of seeking, and which will encompass us and
possess us, if we do not learn to join in the ascription: "Thine is the kingdom and the power and the
glory."

I do not mean that many objectors to forms may
not have preserved these truths, and with heart and
soul entered into them; but I must maintain, that
just so far as they have done so, the reason of their
complaint ceases. If the individual prayer is not the
highest and most essential prayer, but rather is no
prayer at all, then the prayer of the congregation is
not an aggregate of such individual prayers, but the
prayer of a body, each member of which professes
to have renounced his own selfish position, that he
may come as one of a family to seek the Father of it.

In what sense, then, can extempore utterances
be said to be most declaratory of our wants? Of
what wants? Do the members of the congregation
feel that they have sinned, and do they wish to confess
their sins? Is this a local feeling, a feeling belonging to one set of circumstances, or to one period of
time? Or is it a human feeling, belonging to men as
men? "But each man has his own particular sin; his
own burden, of which he himself is conscious." Undoubtedly; and is not his sin and burden just this, that
he has chosen a scheme of his own, that he has followed
certain tastes and inclinations of his own, and so that
he has forgotten his Father in heaven and his brethren

on earth? Does not each particular sin spring from this root? And is it not this which interprets that sense of the individual character of sin, and the personal responsibility for it, upon which so much stress is—so rightly—laid? The load lies on the separate conscience of each man. It is the very nature and law of the conscience that it singles out each man, severs him from his fellow, makes him feel that the participation of the whole universe in his guilt does not make it less to him. But then the conscience *reproves* us for this very thing; for having chosen to be divided when we were meant to be one. And since it has reproved men for this sin ever since Adam's fall, and since it has taught every Christian man that this was emphatically and most awfully his sin ever since Christ died that we might be all one, as He is with the Father; there seems no reason why the language of one generation, in confessing this sin, should not be the language of all. No reason why it should *not* be; the greatest blessing, if by any means it could be; since by this means the sense of sonship and brotherhood would be realized and revived in the very act of acknowledging disobedience and selfishness.

Or does some member of the congregation desire to give thanks for a blessing which has been vouchsafed to him particularly—must this be a local temporary feeling, because it is called forth by a local temporary occasion? Does it not cease to be a true feeling if it is? If from the particular blessing the heart do not gain enlargement, be not drawn out into a contemplation of other blessings; if it be not led to dwell most upon those which are common and permanent, as being the greatest, though perhaps

only observed, when they are taken away or when
some startling novelty brings them into notice, the
purpose of God in bestowing that good thing is surely
not accomplished; the man has not really profited by
it. But if he have, his feelings become human feelings; they do not want a specific, self-chosen mode of
expression; he can find them in the Psalms of David;
he can utter them in the language of Christian men
who lived in other climes and periods. He can give
thanks for creation, preservation, redemption; for gifts
enabling him to enjoy this life and another, which
are bestowed upon his race as well as himself; he can
ask that they as well he may have, above all other good
things, a thankful spirit; his own special mercies
will then be understood and appreciated.

Or does a particular member of the congregation
long for some means, not of declaring his own sins, or
his own thankfulness, but of praising the name of
God, of glorifying Him for His great glory? Is this
a specific, local, temporary, individual emotion? Can
it have a specific, local, temporary, individual expression? Is it too humiliating, too limiting to the largeness of a modern intellect, that it should use the words
of other days, and say, "We praise Thee, O God;
we acknowledge thee to be the Lord!" or, "Glory
be to the Father, and to the Son, and to the Holy
Ghost: As it was in the beginning, is now, and ever
shall be, world without end"?

Or, lastly, does the same particular member of the
congregation feel his need of mercies spiritual and
temporal, and desire to ask for them? We have seen
by the Lord's prayer how he ought to ask them, if he
be alone in his chamber; how necessary it is that he

should not look for them as meant for him, otherwise than as the child of a Father, as one of many brethren. Are they temporal, the blessings of food and raiment? Does he dare to seek for these with a desire to appropriate them exclusively? Then his prayer becomes a sin. Are they spiritual? Then the blessing itself is that of more intimate communion with his Father, a larger communion with the family. Is it necessary that he should limit these by the particular notions and phrases of his own time? Is it a great hardship and bondage to be obliged to use a more general, and therefore, one would fancy, a more becoming language?

If it be said, " Every prayer must be composed in some age, why do you suppose that those which have come down from another time must possess those qualities which you attribute to prayer more than those which are composed in our own?" I answer, I do not say that they must be better, or why they must be better, I have merely been contending with those who say, because they come down to us from another time, they cannot be fit for our use. I do believe, however, that the prayers written in the first ages of Christianity are in general more free, more reverent, more universal, than those which have been poured forth since. I do not think the opinion is a singular one; and I would rather its soundness were tried by the feelings and sympathies of religious men in different periods and circumstances, but especially of men in times of great suffering, than by any theories or arguments of mine. Still I do not find it harder to explain to myself why this should be so, than why there should be a fresher, truer feeling respecting nature and the outward transactions of men in Homer, than in the poetry of the seventeenth or eighteenth centuries. If there were that feeling respecting God, as the source of all things and the end of all things, which I attributed in the last section to the age of the Fathers, it cannot be strange, I think, that their devotional outpourings should have been simpler, purer, more human, than those of men who were occupied, and, as I conceive, were by the order of Providence meant to be occupied, in subtle questions respecting the operations of their own minds, or with inquiries into the law and course of nature. Whether the succession and order of devotional acts may not have much to do with the history and circumstances of man, as well as with the nature and plans of God; and whether, therefore, other ages may not have thrown a light upon this subject, which the first did not possess, I will not say. To those who deny all order in devotion, who think it little less than a sin that offices of confession should be laid down as preparatory to offices of thanksgiving, these again to offices of prayer, and these to the higher communion, it can seem no great derogation from the honour of the primitive times, if we should admit that the apprehension of this spiritual sequence may only in part have belonged to them. And if such persons still require a further reason why we think that the particular acts of praise and prayer were more congenial to older times than to modern, the considerations which have been occupying us under this head involve the reply. There has been a constant tendency for several centuries towards greater individuality of thought and feeling. There is a true ground for this tendency, though it may have led to the most false results. But it is in itself, when unsustained by another tendency, unfavourable to the worship of God, as well as to fellowship among men. A vehement reaction against this tendency has begun in all parts of Europe. One of the fruits of it will certainly be an aversion from all those utterances which modern Protestants have dignified with the name of devotion; if another consequence of it be not a return to the old forms and a delight in them, we must expect a reign of atheism.

The Philosopher.

When the modern philosopher makes any objection to forms of worship, it is chiefly because they substantiate and perpetuate two mischievous superstitions. One is that a Being, who by His idea and law is unchangeable and perfect, can be swayed or led into better acts and purposes than His own by our petitions; the other is that it can please Him to receive the praises or commendations of His creatures. These complaints are usually put forth with most breadth and precision by disciples of the Utilitarian school. But it is evident that they are practically adopted, though with some varieties of expression, and in connexion with a different anthropological theory, by a large section of Rationalists.

Now in one phrase or another both these parties acknowledge, by every word which they speak, and every act which they do, either as philosophers or as ordinary men, that evil exists, and that it ought to be and may be by some means diminished. The Utilitarian traces it all to bad systems of government; the Rationalist refers it directly to man's ignorance of himself and his own powers. Each looks forward to his own Avatar, and to a millennial period of the species which shall follow. Each then does acknowledge an *Ideal*, with which men should be in agreement, with which they are not in agreement, into agreement with which they may by some process be brought. Wherein, then, do we and they differ? Not in the acknowledgment of actual inconsistency and contradiction : this has nothing to do with either of us; we simply own what we cannot deny. But in *this*, that our Ideal is a living Being; that we believe Him to have given all things their right type and order; that we believe them when in their relation to Him to be still very good; that we believe their disturbance and incoherency to be the result of a voluntary renunciation of allegiance to Him, by the only creature which could commit such an act; that we believe all disturbance and incoherency to be contrary to His will; that we believe the restoration to begin in the submission of those who have brought about the confusion. The submission consists in the confession that His will is the good will; one of the main acts and exercises of it is that of entering into His will, and beseeching that it may be put forth for the removal of those curses whereof the evil will has been the cause. This is the rationale—in cold and miserable words—of those ancient litanies which express to this day the thoughts and longings of the most earnest people in different corners of the earth. They are not founded on the notion that any thing is mutable in God. They are cries for the vindication and preservation of His immutable order. They are confessions that every act of His providence, from the first hour of the world, has had for its end the making this immutable order manifest, and the bringing the universe into conformity with it. But they are not founded upon the lying fancy that the world is right; that persons are fulfilling their proper relations to each other; that things are not discomposed and made evil by the sin of those who are meant to direct them. Man, they assume, is God's minister, acting for Him, able to perform His intentions towards His involuntary creatures; able, because he has a will, to set them at nought. His proper condition, in whatever place he were, would be that of dependence, of doing the will of another. His proper way of fulfilling that condition here, is by crying out for the rectification of that which is independent, which has lost its centre, which is struggling to stand by itself, and which therefore cannot stand at all; for the rectification of this, and therefore of whatever else has through this cause suffered decay and ruin.

But if it be said, "This supposes that a restoration has taken place already. These prayers are unmeaning, unless those who offer them believe themselves, on some pretext or other, to be in a better condition than those about whom they pray—" I answer, "Unquestionably; it is the very point which I have been pressing, that prayer *does* suppose a restoration; that the idea of prayer and the idea of a Church can never be separated, each implying the other; and that a Church which is not built upon the confession of a restored humanity is a contradiction in terms." But, observe, a restored *humanity*; and therefore those who offer their prayers do not put forth any claim of superiority to their race, nay, not to the worst member of their race. The very essence of their prayers is this—a cry that those sins which they feel in themselves, under which they are groaning, which they have committed, may not be, as they have been, their masters, and the masters of the universe. They who pray do not feel this less than other men, but more; they do not reject evils from themselves to cast them upon their neighbours, more than other men do; on the contrary, they identify their neighbours' sins with their own; they feel that they have them, and are responsible for them. Only as members of a redeemed race and family can they vindicate the privilege, which has been asserted for them, of being new creatures, of casting off the slough of their selfish natures, of disclaiming that misery which by their rebellion they have made their own, of entering into that blessedness which their Master by His obedience has obtained for all who will have their portion in Him. So that the Philosopher says well and truly, that this superstition of prayer, if it be one, has been maintained by forms, and without forms would be likely to die out. Not as if the sense and necessity of prayer could ever die out in man, but because the only condition under which it can be a true and reasonable service, that of its being presented by men, as members of a body or family, which continues the same from generation to generation, and which converts the notion of a human race from a dream into a reality, is in these forms embodied, and wheresoever they are neglected is nearly lost.

I have still to speak on the subject of praise, which seems to the Philosopher a thing so unworthy of men to offer or of God to receive. The ground of this conclusion is that the words praise and flattery are convertible; and that since flattery is offensive to an imperfect being, so far as he has right feelings, and is only so far tolerable as he is weak and vain, it must to a perfect Being, if He took cognizance of such folly, be altogether odious. Now I join issue with them upon all these points. Suppose praise to be offered to a fellow-man which he does not deserve, it is abominable because it is *false;* suppose that, being deserved, it is offered to him with the view of bribing him to bestow future favours, it is offensive, because it is *mean;* suppose him to deserve it, and that it is offered with no unworthy motive, it may be wrong, because it is *imprudent;* for men, through their imperfections, are made vain, by hearing themselves even rightly commended. But if we could suppose these circumstances absent, I confidently affirm, that there is not any occupation so elevating and delightful to a man, as that of praising and thanking his brethren. Generous men, in all ages and nations, have felt it so; when the motives of self-interest have been farthest from them, even respect for the object of their admiration, and fear of doing him hurt, have not availed to restrain them from expressing their sense of the favours which he has bestowed on them, or their delight in the beauty and harmony of his character. With no ignoble aim, these outpourings of the heart have often been directed to kings and great men; because the thankful and humble heart has felt their acts as a condescension, and has perceived a kind of special propriety and suitableness in their virtues. But they have been directed also to suffering friends, and poor scholars, and persecuted saints, and especially to the dead, from whom nothing could ever be ex-

pected, and to whom they could not be dangerous.
Wherefore the true and obvious analogy from human
experience is,—that if God have none of the imperfection which could make Him obnoxious to the
mischievousness of praise; and if there have proceeded from Him all the benefits which all His
creatures have received; and if there be in Him all
the goodness and truth, of which the goodness and
truth in man are the reflection,—there can be no act
so entirely suitable to man, so thoroughly joyful, as
that of thanking and blessing Him. In which act
if any one discovers a low and cringing desire to win
some good from the Being thus magnified, let him
know that whoever enters upon the work in this
spirit, and with this object, will be soon so struck
with its utter ridiculousness and incongruity, or else
so wearied with the heartless and hypocritical effort,
that no pains he can use will enable him to persevere
in it; or, at any rate, to persuade himself that he is
doing more than repeating a set of incoherent, unintelligible sounds. In the loss of self, in the escape
from self, consists the freedom and enjoyment of that
act. The worshipper has found that object to which
the eyes of himself and of all creatures were meant
to be directed, in beholding which they attain the
perfection of their being, while they lose all the feeling
of selfish appropriation which is incompatible with
perfection. They gaze upon Him who is the all-
embracing Love, with whom no selfishness can dwell,
the all-clear and distinguishing Truth, from which
darkness and falsehood flee away; and they are
changed into the same image, and their praises are
only the responses to the joy with which He looks

upon His redeemed creation and declares it very good.

Let this service seem foolish to whom it will, we know not only that it must be acceptable to God, because He is a spirit, and because He is truth, and because He seeketh them to worship who will worship Him in spirit and truth, but we know also that it meets all the deepest wants which men, in the student's garret, in the palace and the hut, have been all, by different methods, trying to express.

The man of earnest meditation, hating the world's turmoil, angry at its meanness, yet amidst many thoughts of pride and discontent retaining a desire for its good, learns that to seek *truth* is the proper end of his life,—to find it, his only felicity ; and he strives, and toils, and suffers, and if perchance the vision of some principle of living power dawns upon him, he shouts εὕρηκα through the universe. His joy is true joy ; yet when he thinks of the thousands of living creatures, men like himself, to whom his discovery will do no good, who must groan and die still, his labour seems all vanity, his truth a dream, and he curses himself for having dared to dwell so apart from human sympathies. The gentle and generous man, nursed amid kindly and family influences, his imagination early trained to converse with lovely objects, his heart and conscience not seared, sees a *beauty* living and moving through all things, and pursues it with an insatiable passion. He cannot doubt the reality of his faith, though men call it a delusion ; that which has so possessed his being and exalted it, cannot be a lie. But what mean pain, and confusion, and death ? Are they merely shadows to make the light shine brighter?

—No! they master it, they obscure it. He becomes saddened; the glory has fled from the earth, and he sees not how it can ever return again. Thus in their solitary hours have men, according to their different tendencies and education, been haunted by the vision of a truth for which it were worth while to die, and of a loveliness which must be the sole charm of life; and the one has seemed to dwell only in cold words and propositions, and the other to be ever changing its shapes, and vanishing at last altogether.

Meantime the business of the world has not been intermitted; kings have been reigning and dynasties changing; and men have felt that unless there were some awful *Law* which those kings acknowledged, and which lasts amidst all those changes of dynasty, society was a mere dream and impossibility. Philosophers have felt that such a Law must be; politicians that they must create the impression of it. But what is this Law? There are times when you cannot put aside this question—when it is asked, and must be answered; for men rise up and say, that it is but a cobweb imagination which has been cut through by swords in former days, and which they with their brushes can now sweep away entirely. Where is its birthplace and its home, the warrant of its authority, the guardian of its permanence?

Yet supposing this question too were answered, there is a universe of distinct living beings groaning for a daily subsistence. What shall we say of these? "Try and make them philosophers," cries one; "teach them to understand the truth of things; teach them to see the fair proportions of things." Well! this is plausible—let us begin. "But no," says another, who seems to be wise, "this will never avail. What will your people care about the sun and stars? They are men; they feel that other men have ruled them, and not for their benefit; they want to be rulers themselves. Give them some share in the State; then it will be time to think of making them natural philosophers." We are convinced by the wisdom of these remarks; we see that men cannot be satisfied with merely contemplating things at a distance; they must feel that they belong to a system; they must feel that it does not move without them. And though we do not like to give up the hope of seeing our brethren better acquainted even with the wonders of the world about them, we acknowledge that the world in which they are actually to live and move must be one of human feelings and hopes. But when we ask you where and how you are making the experiment for raising the poor man to a feeling of his position, for giving him citizenship and political power, we are bound to confess that we can see nothing but a scheme to rob the poor man of that which he has already, to take from him all sense of dignity and freedom and equality, and reduce him into a condition of hopeless slavery.

Now supposing it were possible that truth and goodness are not abstractions, are not formulas, but are realities; and, as the traces of them have been seen in the acts of persons, so that they dwell absolutely in a Person; supposing it were true that this Being is the King of kings and Lord of lords, from whom all law derives its life and potency; supposing this Being has established for Himself a witness in the heart of the poorest man in this world, and has decreed that there should be desires in that heart which anything short of

His own infinite perfection shall not satisfy; and has called this poor man to be a citizen of his kingdom, yea, a member incorporate thereof, and has said that he, as much as the richest man, is concerned in the order and organization of this kingdom, and may urge on the wheels in the midst of which the spirit of the living creature is moving: would it not then be true that the cravings of the philosopher, the necessities of the statesman, the hopes of the wayfarer, have all their highest interpretation in this worship which is said to be the idlest of all ceremonies? Are not the recorded deeds and desires of the world utterly unintelligible without it? If this ceremony were abolished, if the idea of a perfect Being united to man, inspiring him with prayer, and hearing his prayers, were lost out of the universe, would not the imperfect hope of the philosopher die too? would not the belief in Law become impossible? would not each man sink further and further into solitude and brutality, finding none able to raise him, none who was not assisting to deepen his degradation?

The Romish System.

But still these old Liturgies are in some sense Popish. The prayers in them have reached any modern nations which may have adopted them through Popish hands; they have received a Popish imprimatur. Nay, portions of them may be actually the composition of Bishops of Rome, or of persons who acknowledged their supremacy. What can be said to rebut this charge? Can it be pretended that there is an exact chronological line, at which what we please to call Catholicism ends and what we call Popery begins? Would we reject a prayer of Bernard's as passing the limit? If not, may there not by possibility be one by A Kempis or even by Pascal, which we would not utterly disown?

To these questions I answer precisely as I did in the former case; I want no chronological lines. I am quite ready to use a prayer of A Kempis or of Pascal or of many a person less commonly tolerated among us. Why I conceive the older prayers are in general likely to be better than those which have been composed in any part of Europe for several centuries I have explained; but that explanation has no direct connexion with the question before us. If there be no clearer and more palpable distinction between the forms of the Catholic Church and those to which the Romish system has given birth, than that which is arrived at by special pleadings about the date of the birth or the degree of the soundness of particular men, I at least would rather leave the question unresolved.

But if the main and characteristic glory of the Church be precisely this, that it is brought into the Holiest of the Holies, not into the figure of the true, but into the presence of God Himself; if this be the grand point of separation between older forms and the cold efforts of modern devotions, that with holy fear and confidence they claim this privilege; if ascriptions to the name of the Father, the Son, and the Holy Ghost are continually on the lips, always in the hearts, of those who wrote them, giving at once the essence and the body to their supplications; if each individual member of the Church be in these forms supposed to

join with the whole of it in every act of confession, of
petition, or of thanksgiving; if this union of each with
all be involved in the fact that these prayers are offered
up for the merits and mediation of the one Lord of the
whole body; if it is on the ground of these merits
and this mediation that the poorest member of the
flock may join with saints and angels about the throne
because the virtue and life of both are in Him; if to
these same causes is owing the freedom of the older
prayers from those fetters of time and locality which
mankind in the person of its King has shaken off; if
therefore in these qualities consists their Catholicity,
we have another, a more righteous and a more safe
measure, for determining the value of the system
which takes to itself the Catholic name. For that this
system does in its mildest form embody the doctrine
that men who are members of Christ's Church and
body *cannot* enter into the Holiest of the Holies, *cannot*
present themselves before God, *cannot* ascend up
where Christ has gone before them, unless they
approach through intervening mediators; that this
notion is practically and constantly embodied in
those forms which would be recognised by all as
truly and properly Romish; that the mediators are
not merely ideals of human excellence and beauty, but
also the helpers and heroes of particular towns, professions, individuals; thus much will not be denied
even by those who are most eager to disclaim the
charge of positive idolatry. Now, more than this I do
not want. I do not care to dwell upon those practical
results which seem to me to have followed quite inevitably, and by a far stronger necessity than a mere
logical one, though by that also, from these premises;

I do not care to establish the fact, which seems to me written with sunbeams on the history of Europe, that a continually downward progress from Divine worship to hero-worship, from hero-worship to natural, must be the consequence, when that first fatal step is taken of doubting or denying that the communion between God and His creatures is really established in the incarnate Son, that the union of men with their Lord has been completed and cemented in Him. I simply take my stand upon this ground. I say, " By these acts you Romanists have set aside so far as in you lies, the very meaning and end of the Church's exist-ence; have destroyed the very principle of its union and fellowship; you have reduced it into a set of inco-herent fragments held together by no Divine law, and therefore needing some wretched human law to give it consistency." I repeat it, *as far as in you lay*, for you have not done the work. A mightier power has been traversing your schemes and preparing the way for their ultimate confusion and discomfiture. Not with-out you but within you has there been a seed of life with which these seeds of corruption and death have been seeking to amalgamate, because they could not destroy it. These old, holy, reverent forms have been mocking your inventions as no vulgar Protestant scoffer was ever able to mock them, mocking them by witnessing that the blessings which those inventions offered were not too great for men to dream of, but too poor and pitiful for them not to trample under their feet when once they know out of what curse they have been delivered and to what height they have been raised.

These forms witness to us of holy men whom we

are to remember, and with whose special graces we may sympathize, just because we are united like them to Him of whose fulness all have received, and grace for grace. Let them be multiplied if you will, let each age contribute its quota to the goodly company, let all the blessings which through them Christ has bestowed upon His flock or upon any the least portion of it (for blessings to a part are blessings to the whole) be thankfully commemorated. The forms bear no protest against such recollections; rather teach how it is possible rightly to entertain them. But the moment any one of these holy men is so regarded, that his translation out of this world shall not be a sign to the poorest man who stays in it of his own fellowship with an unseen Lord, but shall rather be a restraint upon his spirit, a fleshly impediment to communion, an earthly dream to obscure the vision of a heavenly reality, that moment the principle of these forms is assaulted, and any new language which may be introduced into them sanctioning such an inversion or denial of the doctrine of the communion of saints stands out in the most broad and palpable contradiction to the living words in which they have embodied it.

These forms invite us on certain days to remember our Lord's acts, condescension, humiliation, triumph. They teach us that if we forget the days, we shall be in danger of forgetting that of which they speak, and therefore of sinking back into that dark, idolatrous, divided state, out of which by Christ's work we have been brought. For there is not and cannot be any return to the state of Jewish outlooking and hope; denying the fulfilment, we lose also the expectation; we lose everything but a confused dream of a possible blessing. But if through any degrading sensualization of this testimony men shall come to fancy that the Church is not really redeemed, justified, and glorified in Christ, but that by the keeping of these days, or by any observances whereby they preserve their own fellowship with the Church, these yet unobtained blessings are to be purchased, then the forms which commemorate these days, as the great signs and trophies of Christ's accomplished work, do far more by anticipation to refute such a shameful and ignominious delusion, than all the words which can be devised after it has become prevalent. These forms authorise certain days and seasons, during which the members of Christ's body may enter into his humiliation, and chasten themselves with his stripes, that so they may keep down the evil inclinations which separate them from their brethren, may sympathise in the sorrows of mankind, may realise the blessings which are given to the whole Church. But, if any selfish and lying spirit should go forth proclaiming that by these fasts and penances for subduing the flesh that blessing is to be obtained which is given without money and price, that by them the individual man who performs them is put into a higher individual condition, and has a right to claim something for himself on that score which as an ordinary Churchman is not his, then these forms of humiliation do pour such contempt upon that godless and uncatholic pride, as no one who thinks all restraints upon self-indulgence vain and childish has ever been able to express.

I might go on through a number of other cases, but these will suffice as hints. They prove, I think, that there lies hid in these ancient forms of worship, something of that power which I attributed to Baptism and the Creed; a power before which all human systems, and therefore the Romish, the most complete of them all, must at last shrink and quail.

SECTION IV.—THE EUCHARIST.

IN all those old forms of worship of which we have been speaking, there is one service which is supposed to be of a higher character than all the rest, and to give them their worth and their interpretation. This is the service which belongs to a feast, called sometimes the Lord's Supper, sometimes the Eucharist, sometimes the Communion.

This feast does exist at this day in every part of Europe, in various districts of Asia, of America, of Africa. It has existed for 1800 years. It has survived, therefore, all those changes of which we spoke when we were considering Baptism and the Creed; it has been the most holy symbol to nations, between which race, political institutions, acquired habits, had established the most seemingly impassable barriers. In each of these nations, during that course of years, there have been endless conflicts between rich and poor, nobles and plebeians. Nevertheless this feast, during the time when these conflicts were the greatest, was acknowledged as the highest gift to the great, and yet as one in which the lowest were intended to share. During the same period the boundary line between the untaught and the scholar was even stronger and more marked than that which was made by wealth or honours. The baron might need the help of the serf; the student seemed to dwell in a region altogether his own, yet he acknowledged that in this feast he found the deepest, most unfathomable subject for his thoughts and speculations, and that the most unlearned might possess its blessings as much as himself. When the Reformation came it may be supposed that one at least of these phenomena ceased; that this feast was no longer regarded as the centre round which religious and philosophical meditations naturally revolved. Unquestionably there was a change in this respect; it was the *effort* of the Reformation to detach itself from this centre; to a certain extent the different reformed bodies succeeded in discovering each a separate centre for itself. But it is equally true, that in spite of this effort the Reformers were compelled to make their views respecting this feast the characteristic and distinguishing feature of their systems. Because they could not agree respecting its character and validity, all the terrors of a common enemy, all the sympathies which attracted them to each other, were insufficient to bind them together.

Through the seventeenth century the strife continued; new religious and philosophical systems were completed or established; still the Eucharist, in Protestant no less than in Romish countries, was a strange remnant of the past, which could not be passed over, which it was most hard to compress into any of the systems, and yet which must be brought into them, seeing that it was continually asserting its power in defiance of them. The eighteenth century came, and the same processes which were used for shutting out the invisible in every other direction, were applied also in this. And yet tens of thousands of men and women in every part of Europe, would in that day have rather parted with their lives, or with anything more dear to them, than with this feast. And now in this nineteenth century there are not a few persons, who, meditating on these different experiments, have arrived at this deep and inward conviction, that the question whether Christianity shall be a practical principle and truth in the hearts of men, or shall be exchanged for a set of intellectual notions or generalizations, depends mainly on the question whether the Eucharist shall or shall not be acknowledged and received as the bond of a universal life, and the means whereby men become partakers of it.

Supposing this notion to be utterly extravagant and false, yet it must be interesting to know what the institution is which seems to have obtained so many willing and so many reluctant testimonies to its importance. Now to describe its nature may be difficult, without entering on some of the points upon which these parties are disagreed. But its origin is not a matter of dispute. Protestants, Romanists, Greeks, all who receive it, refer it to the same period of time, and practise it in obedience to the same authority. All would say, "The night before the crucifixion of Jesus Christ, when He was keeping the passover with His disciples, He took bread and wine, and blessed them, saying, 'This is my body, this is my blood; do this in remembrance of me.' This is the meaning of our custom; we continue it in subjection to this command."

Now these words were addressed to a little band

of disciples; to them, and only to them. There was no multitude present, as in the case of many of our Lord's discourses; no distant bystanders to whom the sentence might apply: "What I say unto you, I say unto all." Neither is there any express language affirming that the command given to these poor fishermen on that night was meant to extend to other ages. They might only signify that a person who had been deeply beloved was leaving with the friends from whom he was about to be separated a token and memorial of his intercourse with them. The words, indeed, "This is my body, this is my blood," might sound strange and hyperbolical, especially in a moment of what seemed final separation, for then the utterances of such a friend would be especially simple and awful, as we know that His other utterances were; but yet they might only signify, This will remind you of my person, and this of the blood which is about to be so unrighteously shed. Such an explanation, however embarrassing, would be the easiest, nay, it would be the only possible one, unless there were some circumstances connected with the whole character of Him who spake the words, with His other acts and purposes, with the time when they were spoken, which determined them to a different sense.

Suppose now that the person who spoke these words was the Son of man and the Son of God; suppose at the very time He spoke them He had been declaring Himself to be the way through which men must come to the unseen Father, to be the truth, to be the life, to be in that relation to his disciples in which the vine is to its branches, to be about to

bestow upon them a Spirit who should guide them
into the knowledge of the Father and of the Son;
suppose Him to have told His disciples that they were
the appointed messengers of these truths to men;
suppose Him to have prayed that not only they, but
all who should believe in Him through their word
might be one in Him as He and the Father were one;
suppose Him to have connected all these mysterious
words with the giving up of Himself to death; suppose
death to have been felt in all ages and in all countries
to be the great barrier between the visible and the
invisible world; suppose sacrifice, or the giving up of
certain animals to death, and the offering them to
some unseen Ruler, had been felt in all countries which
attained to anything like national fellowship and consistency to be the means whereby they could approach
that Ruler's presence, obtain His favour, remove His
wrath; suppose sacrifices to have been the most
essential part of the Jewish institutions, the most
important element in their worship, the only way
whereby they could draw nigh, as members of a
nation, to the God of their nation; suppose them
however, to have been taught, both by the law which
appointed those sacrifices and by the prophets who
expounded it, that they were not valuable for their
own sakes, but were accepted when they were performed by God's appointment, through His priests, as
a confession on the part of the offerer, that he had
violated his relation to the head of the commonwealth
and to its members as a submission of the will, as a
prayer to be restored to that position which through
self-will had been lost, or else as a means of expressing
that entire self-surrender, which was implied in the

fact of belonging to the Divine society; suppose that
the feast which the disciples were keeping with their
Master was the most purely national and strictly
sacrificial of all the feasts, that one which celebrated
the first deliverance and establishment of the nation,
and which recalled the fact that it was a nation based
upon sacrifices in which every Jew realised the blessings of his covenant, rejoiced that God was his King,
knew that he was indeed an Israelite !—suppose all this,
and then consider whether that which seemed the only
possible interpretation of Christ's words, though a
most difficult and perplexing one, do not become
actually irrational and monstrous!

Consider whether anyone who believed what we
know the Apostles did believe respecting their Master,
His Person, His kingdom, could attach any but the
very highest significance to language concerning His
body and blood. Consider whether any persons who
believed what we know they believed respecting their
own office and work, could imagine that this significance was limited and temporary. Consider whether
persons who connected, as we know they did connect,
the kingdom whereof they were ministers with the
earlier dispensations, could believe otherwise than that,
by the same simple, wonderful method which had been
used in all countries, and had been appointed, as they
believed, by the authority of God Himself in their
own, by the method which had enabled the Jews to
enter into the fruition of their covenant and its privileges, and the neglect of which had again and again
cheated them of it, He meant to put them in possession of all the substantial good things which He came
to bestow upon mankind. Could they doubt that

when they ate this bread and drank this wine, He
meant that they should have the fullest participation
of that sacrifice with which God had declared Himself
well pleased, that they should really enter into that
Presence, into which the Forerunner had for them
entered, that they should really receive in that communion all the spiritual blessings which, through the
union of the Godhead with human flesh, the heirs of
this flesh might inherit?   Could they doubt that the
state of individual death which they had claimed for
themselves in Baptism, was here to be practically
attained by fellowship with Christ's death; that the
new life which they had claimed for themselves, as
members of Christ's body, was here to be attained
through the communication of His life?   Could they
doubt that if their spirits were to be raised up to
behold the infinite and absolute glory, here they were
admitted into that blessedness; that if their hearts
and affections desired a manifested and embodied
king, here they became united to Him; that if spirit,
soul, and body were to be subjected to the government of God's Spirit, that each might be delivered
from its own corruption, receive its own quickening,
and exert its own living powers, here each received
that strength and renewal by which it was enabled
to do its appointed work, to overcome its peculiar
temptations, to be fitted for its future perfection?
Could they doubt that if they were baptized into the
name of the Father, the Son, and the Holy Ghost,
and if this deepest unity were the foundation of such
a union among men as no barrier of time, or space, or
death, could break, here they were actually received
into communion with that awful name, and into com-

munion with all the saints who live by beholding it and delighting in it? Could they doubt that here the partial views and one-sided words and opposing thoughts of men, found their meeting-point and complete reconciliation; that here lay the clear vital expression of those distinctions which in verbal theology become dry, hard, dogmatic oppositions; that here it is apprehended how faith alone justifies, and how faith without works is dead; how it is we that act, and yet not we, but Christ in us; how he that is born of God cannot commit sin, and yet if we say we have no sin we deceive ourselves; how we may be persuaded that neither life nor death, nor things present, nor things to come, shall separate us from the love of God which is in Christ, yet may tremble lest we should be castaways? Could they doubt that it was their office to present Christianity in its different aspects to the different wants and circumstances of their own age and of ages to come; that it was the office of this sacrament to exhibit it as a whole truth, at once transcendent and practical, surpassing men's thoughts, not dependent on men's faith and opinions, and yet essentially belonging to man, the governing law of his being, the actuating power of his life? Could they doubt that they were to lay the foundation of the Church on earth, and that this sacrament was to give it permanency, coherency, vitality throughout all generations? And if this were their faith, why, I ask, is it not to be ours? What has happened to rob this sacrament of its meaning, or to make that meaning less applicable to us of the nineteenth century than it was to those who lived in the first, less necessary for us than it was for them? The answers to these questions are various.

OBJECTIONS.—*The Quaker.*

In this case, as in that of Baptism, the Quaker believes that we have adhered dangerously to Jewish precedent, have preserved signs when they should have been abolished, have followed shadows when the spiritual substance was that which we should have apprehended. But here the sin is more flagrant. The essence of Christianity lies in the reality of the sacrifice which we, after the example and by the power of Christ, are able to offer up. For the surrender of ourselves, the true self-annihilation, this ceremony is substituted, a ceremony clothed with great names and fictitious attributes, in order that we may excuse ourselves from the necessity of any practical sacrifice.

I am not unwilling to incur the charge of tautology, for the sake of noticing again the first and more general of these complaints. For they receive a new and most valuable illustration from the special arguments which are connected with them. It will be remembered that the difference between us and the Quakers in the other instance seemed to be this. They suppose that the Christian Covenant, because it is spiritual, dispenses with that method which was sanctioned by divine authority in the earlier dispensation. We believe that the Christian Covenant, because it is more spiritual than the Jewish, requires another application of the same method in order that the difference may be perceived. Having the sign of the lower covenant to compare with the sign of the higher, I can understand wherein the one surpasses the other; the Quaker, being unable to make any such comparison, only talks of the distinction, cannot appre-

hend it in fact, cannot even express it in language:
while he rates the old far below its true value, he yet
continually in his thoughts reduces the new to a level
with it, in his practice makes the perfect spirituality
of the latter to consist merely in the absence of a
characteristic which the degree of spirituality possessed by the former made necessary. Thus much
with reference to the preliminary act or condition of
the covenant. Applying the same rule to the results,
privileges, and enjoyments of it, the Quaker asserts
that the Jew realized the blessings of his covenant in
a sacrificial feast; that the blessings of ours being
spiritual, such a method is, in our case, impossible.
We affirm, that the privileges which the Jews realized
in their festivals were spiritual privileges; that the
privilege of looking up to an invisible Guide and King
and Friend, and rejoicing in Him, was a spiritual
privilege; that the privilege of feeling themselves a
nation was a spiritual privilege; that these are
emphatically the privileges which the spirit of man
craves for; that God gave them to the Jews in a most
simple, reasonable method; and that when we understand what the things given were, it becomes difficult
to imagine how by any other method they could have
been received. We affirm again that our privileges
are higher than those of the Jews, but higher only as
being the perfection of what they had imperfectly.
They are the privileges still of fellowship with God, of
fellowship with our brethren; but of fellowship with
God as with a Being who has entered into a direct
union with our race in the Person of His Son; of
fellowship with a Race in its Head, not merely with a
particular Nation. Now we want to know what there

is in the character of these blessings which makes a united festival unsuitable for the realization of them? It was suitable, nay, actually necessary for the realization of the others; shew us in some other way than by merely repeating the words, carnal and spiritual, how the change has taken place?

We grant most freely that there must be a change in the nature of the institution appropriate to a change in the nature of that which it expresses. We grant that Christianity is nothing, if it be not the actualization and substantiation of a union which was before to a great extent prophetical and ideal. We grant that a mere shadow, a pictorial feast, would be more inconsistent with the nature of the Gospel, than even of the Law—though inconsistent with either, seeing that in each case the feast ought to put the receivers of it into actual possession of that which at the time they were capable of possessing. But admitting all this, the questions recur, " Can there be no feast, which is applicable to the position of Christians, as the feast of the Passover was to that of the Jews? Have those who deny the existence of such a feast, stigmatizing it as a mere ceremony and phantasm, shewn that they retain the substance of Christianity?"

To examine this last point, let us consider why it is that the Quaker protests against this particular institution. The Christian sacrifice, he says, ought to be real; the giving up of a man's own self to death according to the example of our Lord and Saviour. Our Lord's death in itself was most real, carried into every act which He performed and every word which He spoke; how can we think that we manifest that death in a service less actual, individual, continuous?

From this statement it will be seen at once, that the *end* of Christianity, according to the Quaker, is individual self-denial or self-sacrifice. Christ perfectly sacrificed Himself; by Christ's power in us we may do the like; this is their habitual language. Now that Christianity *involves* this, that there is no meaning in it if the principle of self-sacrifice be not at the root of it, I believe I acknowledge as strongly as he can. But as we both agree that our Lord's example is the one by which we are to shape ourselves, that the type of sacrifice is in Him, I must inquire whether He referred to sacrifice as the object of his life, or only as the indispensable condition of it. The answer which He gives on this point seems to me very express. He declares that He came to glorify His Father's Name, to do His Father's Will. He declares that He came to die for the sheep. Because He glorified his Father's Name and would not glorify His own; because He would not be an individual man but would identify Himself with the lowest condition of those whom He was not ashamed to call His brethren, therefore do we see in Him the perfect example of self-sacrifice. The whole idea of His life is lost the moment we forget this. Imagine Him coming into the world not to manifest God, but to exhibit a specimen of glorious heroic self-sacrifice; not to die for men, but to shew how He could die, and the example perishes. We have an object presented to us which no man who has been used to contemplate his Lord with anything of love or devotion, could bear to look at. And yet if we believe that the *end* we are to keep in view in our own lives is this of self-annihilation, we either must make this change in the image we profess to copy, or else forget it altogether and fix our eyes only upon ourselves.

Nor is this all, as the history of the Quakers has proved. This doctrine of self-sacrifice and self-annihilation, when it has not led them into conscious self-righteousness and self-glorification, has occasioned a miserable confusion respecting their own lives and duties. If the Spirit of Christ, they have said to themselves, be leading us to entire crucifixion, shall we not be resisting him if we keep alive any peculiar affection or faculty? And yet the same conscience which seemed to enjoin self-sacrifice, said also, How dare you crush those powers, energies, and affections which God has given you, and of which you are to render an account to Him? The difficulty is most practical, the contradiction most agonising. And the fruits of it to those who have witnessed it, have been as distressing as to those who have been exercised by it: one part of them, thinking that such feelings must be the consequence of a dark superstition, fly to infidelity or indifference; another, more earnest and sincere, seeing that the sacrifice of Christ has been lost sight of in these efforts after self-sacrifice, have violently denounced all such efforts as godless and vain, and adopting sound language respecting the all-sufficiency of the one sacrifice, have made it a foundation for Antinomian doctrine and practice.

But if we kept this thought steadily before us, that the hallowing of God's name is the end for which our Lord lived and for which we are to live; that to give Him thanks and praise for that which He is and for that which He has done, and so to enter into the perception and apprehension of that which He is and

that which He has done, is the highest felicity which
we can attain; that our Lord who was one with the
Father did in all the acts of His life exhibit this perfect
sympathy with Him and delight in Him, and submission
to Him; that the voluntary sacrifice of His body to death
was the final and consummate act of sympathy, delight,
submission; that as self-will and disobedience are the
obstacles to the communion of men with their Creator,
so are they obstacles to communion with each other; that
the same act therefore which removed the only obstacle
to the one communion removed also the obstacle to the
other; that the cross of Christ is the centre point of
all fellowship; that while we seek our fellowship there,
affirming ourselves to exist only as members of Christ's
body, and to derive our life from Him, we may find
strength habitually to deny ourselves according to his
example—we surely obtain an idea of Christianity
altogether different from the other, and yet one which
includes all the practical truth of it, and which must have
hovered as we know it did hover before the minds of
the early Quakers, in order that they might be able
to conceive their own narrow and fragmentary notion.
A person who lives in the light of this truth must look
upon the sacrifice of Christ as *distinct* from all other
sacrifices, because it is only by means of it that we are
brought into the presence of God or are made one
body. He cannot look upon the sacrifice of Christ as
separate from any other sacrifice, because he conceives
all sacrifices to derive their worth and meaning from
it. He must regard self-sacrifice as the necessary
element of a Christian life. He cannot permit it to
assume a self-conscious and therefore contradictory
character by regarding it as the means of procuring

a blessing, when it is in fact the fruit and the fruition
of a blessing already procured. He must consider
every Christian obliged to mortify his selfish nature,
in order that he may offer an acceptable sacrifice to
God. He cannot confound the mortification of the
evil nature with the destruction or weakening of a
single faculty which God has bestowed. For those
faculties are impaired and ruined by the dominion of
the evil nature; they are strongest when it is most
subdued. They must be kept strong because God
requires them as a sacrifice; and the more they are
sacrificed to Him the more strength do they acquire.

We have seen yet another instance in which the
Quaker, refusing to maintain what he calls a mere
form, has utterly perverted or lost a principle. I do
not charge it upon him as a special sin that he has
inverted the notion of sacrifice, has substituted means
for ends, has introduced self-righteousness under the
name of self-forgetfulness. These tendencies are
common to all ages, they are precisely the tendencies
of our individualizing natures. In this respect the
Quakers are not different from the rest of men. The
sin which I do charge them with is this: that when
Christ had, of his love and mercy to mankind, provided them with a simple and wonderful testimony
against these narrow notions and dividing tendencies;
when He had embodied in a living feast the complete
idea of His kingdom, which we, looking at things partially, from different sides, through the prejudices and
false colourings of particular times and places, are continually reducing under some name, notion, or formula
of ours; when He has made this feast effectual for
imparting to men a faith far above the level of their

ordinary theories and speculations; when He had given it as a bond to all peoples and languages and generations—they chose to fancy that His ordinance signified nothing, that they had a much better storehouse for His truths in their own fine thoughts and spiritual apprehensions. Of this sin I maintain that they are suffering the punishment in the almost entire loss of that Spirituality and that Universality which they hoped by these means to attain.

2. *The Zuinglian, the Calvinist, the Lutheran.*

1. There is one objection to my statements on this subject in which pure Protestants would in general agree. They would say that when I call the Eucharist a sacrificial feast I am using dangerous language, incompatible with the full recognition of Christ's finished sacrifice upon the cross. "If it be sacrificial it must be propitiatory; the words are convertible; then what becomes of the doctrine of the Atonement as it was held by the Reformers?"

Starting from this negative point of agreement our opponents soon divide themselves into several classes. To the first the Eucharist appears a mere memorial of a past transaction. When I treat it as a substantial feast, as in some strange way identified with the spiritual things of which it speaks, and as being a channel through which actual blessings are received, I am using phrases, they say, for which Scripture gives no warrant, and which are contrary to plain sense and experience.

The second class think differently. According to them the true believer does realize in the sacrament an actual mysterious blessing. He not only recollects a past good; he is conscious of a present good; Christ is with him in the feast. The mistake I have committed consists in supposing the good to exist in the Sacrament apart from the faith of the receiver. Such a doctrine unsettles the very foundation of Protestant Christianity.

The third party by no means agree in this opinion. They think that the Sacrament has a reality in it which it does not receive from the mind of the partaker. Christ is actually consubstantiated with the elements. The error of the principle I have maintained consists in this, that it supposes us to be brought into a holy and Divine Presence, and yet offers no explanation of the way in which so wonderful a transaction takes place.

Before I consider the first objection, in which Zuinglians, Lutherans, and Calvinists agree, let me remind my readers of the remarks which I made under the last head. I affirmed that Quaker history had proved the incredible danger which results from supposing that our Lord's sacrifice is merely a pattern or example of our sacrifices, or merely the power by which these sacrifices are effected. It must have an entirely distinct character; otherwise it is of no worth as an example or as a power. And I maintained further that this distinct character, in virtue of which it is an example and a power, is exhibited in this Sacrament, and that by losing this Sacrament the Quakers have lost the sense of it. I think these assertions hardly bear out the suspicion that I confound the sacramental act,—an act performed by men and therefore their act, by the hypothesis one of our sacrifices,—with the sacrifice of Christ; or suppose that the necessity of the one proves the other incomplete. Every word I have used leads to precisely the opposite conclusion. I have maintained that because the sacrifice had once for all accomplished the object of bringing our race, constituted and redeemed in Christ, into a state of acceptance and union with God, *therefore* it was most fitting that there should be an act whereby we are admitted into the blessings thus claimed and secured to us. And because those blessings were not given to the generation which lived in the days of our Lord's incarnation and death, but to all generations, therefore is it fitting that this act should be renewed through all generations; and because those blessings do not belong to one moment of our existence but to every moment, therefore is it fitting that the act by which we receive them should continually be renewed by us during our pilgrimage on earth. When we say then that our feast, like that of the Passover, is sacrificial, we do not mean that it does not commemorate a blessing which has been fully obtained and realized; if we did we should violate the analogy in the very moment of applying it; for the Passover did commemorate a complete deliverance and the establishment of a national state in consequence of that deliverance. But as that deliverance was accompanied with a sacrificial act, and by a sacrificial act accomplished, and yet in this Passover the act was perpetually renewed; because in this way the nation understood that by sacrifice it subsisted and consisted; and because by such a renewal its members realized the permanent and living character of the good that had been bestowed upon them, so it is here. The sacrifice of Christ is that with which alone God can be satisfied and in the sight of which alone He can contemplate our race; it is therefore the only meeting-point of communion with Him: but this communion being established, it must be by presenting the finished sacrifice before God that we both bear witness what our position is and realize the glory of it; otherwise we have a name without a reality, and with the words "finished and complete" are robbing ourselves of the very thing which makes it so important that we should prize them and preserve them.

Why these considerations have been overlooked by Protestants I think will be evident from the remarks which were made in the former part. The worth of Protestantism consisted in this, that it asserted the distinct position of each man, affirming that he was a person and not merely one of a mass. This truth had been working itself out into clearness for many centuries, but the process was a strange and painful one. The conscience is that which tells each man he is a person, making him feel that which he has done in past time to be his own, giving him an awful assurance of identity, responsibility, permanence. Overburdened with the sense of evil, it sought for a remedy; it was commanded to perform certain services in the hope of finding one; with each attempt the sense of moral evil increased. The Reformers found that the whole scheme was a delusion. The services presumed that freedom of conscience which men sought to acquire by them; without it they were not true godly services. The emancipation of the conscience was therefore that which they sought as the step to all good; they declared that by faith in Christ, grounded upon acts of complete redemption done on their behalf, they could alone obtain it.

How true this language was, what a curse had come upon the Church through the denial of it, how necessary it was that, at that time especially but also at all times, it should be proclaimed, I have contended again and again. But it is equally certain that as the Quakers believe self-sacrifice, so the Reformers believed the emancipation of the conscience, to be not a necessary condition of our moral being but the end of it. Whatever contributed to this end was necessary, whatever did not contribute to it was worthless. The belief of Christ's sacrifice upon the cross was that which had given peace to their consciences; that it had any purpose save that of giving peace to the conscience was more and more forgotten. And therefore it became necessary to explain how it accomplished this purpose. Then began all the theories about sacrifice, satisfaction, and imputation, which I spoke of as at once so fatal to the principles of the Reformation and to the practical life of Christianity, as affording no comfort to the humble heart, as leading to all disputes and separations, as preparing the way for the infidelity of the eighteenth century. These hungry notions of the understanding being substituted for the clear, simple belief of the Reformers that we are adopted into Christ by Baptism and are therefore children of God and may draw nigh to Him in all duties and services, confessing the sins which have polluted us and separated us from Him, turned everything into confusion. Men knew that they were not approaching God with pure consciences; the Reformers said that if they did not, the service was a mockery; they therefore sought hither and thither for some better kind of faith which could give them relief; not finding it, they deemed the whole Gospel to be a dream and fable.

2. But that which lay beneath all these dark imaginations and sad results was, I believe, the imperfect apprehension which the Reformers themselves had of the nature of the Communion. This feast, says the Zuinglian, is nothing but the memorial of a past transaction. That it is the memorial of a past transaction is of course assumed in every word I have said. If it were not it could have no pretence to the name of Eucharist; it would bear no analogy to the Passover. But the Passover had not merely reference to the past. The Jew had been brought out of Pharaoh's government and brought under God's government. In commemorating the past emancipation of his nation he claimed for himself a privilege which belonged to it then. It would, I think, be insulting the Zuinglian to suppose that he thought the Christian ordinance, in this respect, different from its predecessor. He is particularly practical and rational; he must therefore know well that no men ever did or ever could celebrate with the least heartiness and affectionateness an event which they did not suppose in some sense to be the cause or the commencement of an improved condition of things, that condition of things being one with which they were in some way connected. The Zuinglian then cannot mean by his words "Simple memorial" that there is nothing of present continuous interest in it; if he did he would suppose, contrary to all his professions, that our Lord's religion imposes, as a test of obedience, a most dry, dreary, unmeaning ceremony. But if he allows, as of course he will, that certain effects have followed from

our Lord's death, in which we are partakers, and that these effects, and not merely the cause which produced them, are recalled to us by this feast, then the question immediately occurs, What are these effects? The great effect which we believe to have proceeded from it, that in which every other is included, is that thereby we are made capable of entering into the presence of God; that a mercy-seat is revealed to mankind, where his Maker may meet with him. Supposing this were so, this must surely be one of the effects which is brought to our recollection by the Eucharist. I do not object to the word *recollection*; there is nothing in it which is not applicable to a Living Actual Presence. What I plead for is the duty of recollecting that presence in the Eucharist, *because it is there.*

But the Zuinglian will ask, Why there, and not elsewhere? The question may bear two constructions. It may mean, Why may we not feed upon the sacrifice of Christ at all times, and thus enter into the presence of Him who perfectly delights in that sacrifice? Or it may mean, God is omnipresent; why then are we not always in His presence? Evidently these two thoughts are of the most different kind, and originate in most different states of feeling. The first suggests to us the highest standard of perfection which a Christian can propose to himself, and yet a standard which, if what I have said be true, must be a most real and reasonable one: for that the Church *is* brought into the presence of God, is the first principle of the New Dispensation, the one which is especially involved in this sacrament; and if every one of us ought to consider himself a member of the Church, this wonderful privilege belongs to us, not in proportion as we raise ourselves to some individual excellence, but in proportion as we renounce all such distinctions, and yield ourselves to the Spirit who dwells in the whole body. What then I should say, in reference to this view of the case, is precisely what I have said in reference to the Quaker doctrine. If we acknowledge that the light is somewhere concentrated, that it reveals itself to us in some way which it has chosen; that the revelation is not for us only, but for all; if we make this acknowledgment practically, we are at least in the right road to the realization of that blessing which it is so truly affirmed that we ought to seek. Otherwise we shall fancy that we produce this presence by our acts of meditation or faith; we glorify ourselves for these acts, and for a reality we get a dream; then we gladly betake ourselves to the other doctrine, which comes forth with the boast that it asserts " the Omnipresence of the Deity."

So I believe it has happened with the Zuinglians. An early disciple of the school, attaching an almost superstitious veneration to the Bible, would at once have rejected this phrase as incompatible alike with its letter and its spirit. He would have asked how it could be reconciled with the words of the Book of Genesis, which speak of God as meeting Adam in the garden, as coming down to see the tower which men had builded, as appearing to Abraham at the tent-door? A Zuinglian of the next century would have learnt perhaps to use the phrases, "figures," "eastern allegories," and such like, in reference to these passages. Still he would have said to himself, " Honest men use allegories and figures for some purpose; they mean something by them; it is a *truth* which they wish to convey. But if I admit these phrases, 'ubiquity,' 'omnipresence,' in their ordinary sense, I must suppose the Word of God less honest and true than the words of men; for these stories, instead of implying or hinting a truth, involve the direct contradiction of one." But a Zuinglian of the third century will have mastered all these difficulties. He will at once dispose of these scriptural expressions, by calling them "anthropomorphic," or indications of a low state of civilization; or with less honesty he will pass them over altogether, only assuming that the phrase, "Omnipresence of the Deity," must be good and true, whatever else, either in the early thoughts and feelings of men, or in the revelations to which these have been leading, should happen to be false.

Let us consider then for a moment the philosophy of this phrase. It has been adopted to convey the impression that the limits of space are not applicable to a Divine and absolute Being. But does it convey this impression to any one who is capable of reflecting upon his own thoughts? Is "everywhere" less a word of space than "somewhere?" Did the ancients less imprison the Divine Essence in forms, when they spoke of it as inhabiting every tree and flower, than when they viewed it in the person of a Jupiter sitting on the Thessalian mount? No! in proportion as they attached personal qualities to their Jupiter, in proportion as they believed that He was capable of loving and hating, and that He had the feelings of a father, they were conceiving of Him infinitely *less* under the limits of space (and of time also) than when they were translating His name by "the air," and regarding

Him as a subtle fluid diffused through every portion of the universe. In the one case they were dreaming of a SPIRIT with whom men might converse; a Spirit indeed mixed of good and ill—their own image—but still to be apprehended by that which is spiritual in man: in the other case their thoughts were wholly physical; not the less so for being rarefied and subtilized; or if there was any thing else in them, it was what they derived from the older faith.

In strict conformity with this principle is that passage of our Lord's teaching which is so often quoted to prove a very different doctrine. He told the woman of Samaria that a time was coming when neither on Mount Gerizim nor at Jerusalem should men worship the Father. He does not give as the reason, "God is everywhere;" but He rises at once to the higher level; He says "God is a Spirit, and they that worship Him must worship Him in spirit and in truth." And He connects with these words what would seem to modern thinkers the most direct contradiction of them: "We know what we worship, for salvation is of the Jews." Unquestionably such language would have been utterly inconsistent with the Omnipresent doctrine; it was no wise inconsistent with the doctrine, "God is a Spirit." Every step in the Jewish revelation and history had presumed that truth, and had been preparing the way for the full manifestation of it. Every step of it had been more fully bringing out the idea of God as the Holy One, as the Moral Being, the object of trust and awe and reverence. And in nothing had this idea been more expressed, than in those arrangements which seemed to localize the Divine Presence. Because He was the

VOL. II.

Holy One, He must not be worshipped in all the forms of nature and visible things; He must be viewed as distinct, personal; He must be approached, in the temple, through the priest with the sacrifice. By all these means, now regarded as so sensual, men were taught that it was not with their senses that they were to apprehend God; that it was that in them which desires truth and holiness which must seek Him, which by a wonderful method He was drawing towards Himself. And therefore, though simple people who had sought God without the law, might be far better prepared to welcome Him who brought their sins to their mind, and told them all things that ever they did, than the proud idolater of the law could ever be; yet those who had profited by the law, those who were Israelites indeed, and without guile, those who had served God day and night in the temple, and waited for the consolation of Israel, were far better prepared than any others could be to see the glory of God in the man Christ Jesus; to feel that there was no contradiction in the perfectly Holy One inhabiting a body of human clay; that it was a low, carnal, sensual notion of the Godhead, one which really identified Him with physical things, and therefore subjected Him practically to the laws of space, which made it seem to be a contradiction.

I maintain, then, that the highest, clearest, most spiritual, most universal idea of God which any creature can attain to, is not that which he receives from a dream about the attribute of omnipresence, but that into which he enters when he contemplates the fulness of truth and holiness and love, the absolute and perfect Being pleasing to identify Himself with a human soul and body, to suffer with them, to raise them out of death, to raise them to glory. We have not here an attempt to merge complete spirituality and distinct locality—each of which is demanded by man's reason, each of which is necessary to the other—in a wretched abstraction called ubiquity, a notion vacant of all substance and reality, only serving to puff up the mind with the vague consciousness of possessing a great idea, which it really needs but has missed altogether. I should be scrupulous about the use of such language as this, in reference to a phrase which is so prevalent among religious people, and which may therefore have some sacred associations connected with it, if I did not see that it had been the means of perplexing the minds of little children, of making moral and Christian education almost impossible, of introducing infinite vagueness and weakness into our pulpit discourses, of preparing men's minds for a settled and hopeless pantheism. That it has also been the means of lowering and confounding our feelings about the Eucharistic feast, is implied in all its other effects. But here it has met with an enemy able to cope with it. The impression that this sacrament is a reality, in spite of all men's attempts to prove it and make it a fiction, has kept alive the belief that the presence of God is a truth and not a dream; and that we may enter into it in a better and truer way than by fancying ourselves in it, when we are only indulging pleasant sensations and high conceits.*

* Mr. Coleridge has expressed all that I have been saying on this momentous subject in these striking words : " All this comes from the young men of this day having been educated

G 2

But if I maintain so strongly that it is only with the spirit that we can hold communion with a spiritual Being, how do I differ from the Calvinists, who admit that there is a Presence in the sacrament to those who believe? I do not think that I differ from them except when they differ from themselves. I no more suppose that our spirits can perceive a spiritual object without faith, than that our eyes can perceive a natural object if they be blind. Faith is as much that exercise in which the spirit is and lives, as sight is the exercise in which the eye is and lives. What more does the Calvinist require? He requires that we should suppose there is no object present, unless there be something which perceives it; and having got into this contradiction, the next step is to suppose that faith is not a receptive, but a creative power; that it makes the thing which it believes. We have seen what a tendency to this belief there has been among all Protestants; but we have seen also that there were characteristics in the creed of the Calvinist which ought especially to have delivered him from it. His principle is to refer every thing to the will of God, to suppose that nothing originates with the creature. How then has he fallen into an hypothesis apparently so foreign from his deepest convictions? He has been driven into it by his habit of resolving his belief of the Divine Will into his doctrine of individual Election. He cannot suppose that God has any higher end in His manifestations than the redemption and sanctification

to understand the Divine Omnipresence in any sense rather than the alone safe and legitimate one, THE PRESENCE OF ALL THINGS TO GOD."—*Aids to Reflection*, p. 398; and consider the whole passage from p. 388 to p. 401.

of particular men; the idea, therefore, of the God-Manhood, of God manifesting Himself in the person of His Son, shrinks and dwindles into a mere expedient for accomplishing His objects of mercy towards the favoured members of the race, and by necessary consequence the belief that He has devised a means whereby men, as members of a body, may apprehend Him who is the head of the body, loses itself in this strange attempt to conceive a presence which is not a presence till we make it so. Still it is a curious and interesting fact, that the form and principle of Calvin's doctrine, as distinguished from his system, was mainly upheld by his faith in this sacrament; and that when his followers approximated, as of necessity they did, more and more nearly to the Zuinglian doctrine on this subject, the system became more and more prominent and exclusive.

It is a great transition to go from either of these views to the Lutheran, wherein the actual presence of Christ as the ground of faith, and not as grounded upon it, is so unequivocally asserted. It might seem that in doing so I must change the character of my statements; that whereas I have hitherto been endeavouring to assert this presence against those who deny it, I must now, if I discover any difference with this class of Protestants, point out the danger of carrying a true principle to its extreme. But I shall make no such change, and I see no such danger. I complain of the Lutheran, as I do of the Zuinglian and the Calvinist, for seeking the deliverance of the individual conscience as an ultimate end; and therefore for failing to acknowledge the completeness and integrity of the blessing which Christ has bestowed upon his Church. Whatever logical perplexity the Lutheran has fallen into; whatever violence he has done to the understanding by his theory; whatever of confusion he has introduced between the sensible and the spiritual world, is, as I conceive, the consequence of his not taking the language of our Lord and of his Apostles in a sufficiently plain and literal sense. Our Lord says: "This is my body." St. Paul addresses the Ephesian converts as sitting in the heavenly places with Christ. He tells the Philippians that their bodies shall be made like unto Christ's glorious body. Surely this is Christianity. It is the Gospel of the deliverance of the spirit and soul and body from all the fetters by which they are held down, and prevented from fulfilling each its own proper function—from maintaining their right relations to each other. And this emancipation is connected with and consequent upon, our union, as members of one body, with Christ, the crucified, the risen, the glorified Lord of our race. Now, if these be the privileges of Christian men, and if these privileges, whatever they be, are in this sacrament asserted and realized, what a low notion it is, that we are invited to hold communion, not with Christ as He is, not with His body exalted at the right hand of God, but with a body consubstantiated in the elements.

Think only of the freedom, the fellowship of hope —not only compatible with, but inseparable from, humiliation and fear—implied in intercourse with the Prince and Forerunner who has actually broken through the barriers of space and time, whose body has been subjected to the events and sufferings of mortality, and who is now glorified with the glory which He had with the Father before the worlds were, and hereafter to be manifested in the sight of quick and dead. Bring these thoughts before you in connexion with the words: "This is my body," and with the command that we should show forth his death till He come; and then reflect, if you can, upon the logical dogma of Consubstantiation, the notion that all these blessings do in some way dwell in the bread and wine. Surely what we need is, that *they* should be made a perfectly transparent medium through which His glory may be manifested, that nothing should be really beheld by the spirit of the worshippers but He into whose presence they are brought. For this end the elements require a solemn consecration from the priest, through whom Christ distributes them to His flock; not that they may be clothed with some new and peculiar attributes; not that they may acquire some essential and miraculous virtue, but that they may be diverted from their ordinary uses, that they may become purely sacramental. No doubt the world is full of sacraments. Morning and evening, the kind looks and parting words of friends, the laugh of childhood, daily bread, sickness and death; all have a holy sacramental meaning, and should as such be viewed by us. But then they have another meaning, which keeps this out of sight. If we would have them translated to us, we need some pure untroubled element, which has no significancy, except as the organ through which the voice of God speaks to man, and through which he may answer: "Thy servant heareth." Such we believe are this bread and wine when redeemed to his service: let us not deprive them of their ethereal whiteness and clearness by the colours of our fancy or the clouds of our intellect.

Rationalistic Objections.

The philosophical objections to the Eucharist in our day will generally take some such form as this. "The Christian mysteries are evidently a continuation and adaptation to new circumstances of those which formed such an important element in Pagan worship. It would be wrong to say of either, that no meaning is involved in them, that they are merely the inventions of priest-craft. Unquestionably the Samothracian worship did express, not only to those who took part in it, but to the Greeks generally, something deep and awful, something which lay beyond the region of their sense and ordinary experience. The priests availed themselves of the feelings respecting the invisible, which are so curiously wrought into our being, sometimes for a good purpose, sometimes for an evil one. As long as their own faith lasted, they did much to keep alive what was good in the minds of their countrymen; the mischief was, that they continued to practise the rites long after it was possible to attach any value to them; hence insincerity in themselves and growing superstition and debasement in those who looked up to them. Then the old forms of religion passed away, and after an interval of mere scepticism, some new one, suitable to the stage of progress which the world has reached, was of necessity introduced; this, of course, must have its mysteries. They were destined to pass through the same process as the others; first honestly received as the symbols of that which men's hearts and consciences dreamed of, then sinking into mere impostures. The effort to speak of them now as if they had any reality or significance is a deceitful effort; in persons of any intelligence, a consciously deceitful one; in others, an instance of the mad fanaticism which seeks to galvanize that which has been long dead."

That there is much plausibility in this statement, and that there are some undoubted truths in it, few will question. The danger is, that one set of persons, being shocked at the conclusion, should not dare to ask themselves what the truths concealed in it are, and should therefore go away with an uncomfortable sense of being only half honest in a service which they nevertheless feel that they cannot part with; and that another class, taking as little pains to sift assertions which come to them with such an air of evidence and wisdom, should adopt them as the satisfactory explanation of difficulties which seem half historical, half personal, and which, if they can but be cleared out of the history, may, it is hoped, cease to perplex us in our own lives. Let it then be conceded at once, 1st. That there is a point of connexion between the Christian mysteries and those of the old world. 2ndly, That the priests in the old world did, as it has been said they did, partly keep alive in the worshippers a sense of what is true and unchangeable, partly sanctify and perpetuate the transitory notions and degrees of knowledge which belonged to their own or a previous stage of civilization. 3rdly, That the priests in the old world did, as it is reported of them, gradually become deceivers both of others and themselves. 4thly, That neither of these evil tendencies has been confined to the heathen world, but has been manifested just as strongly in Christian Europe, and has connected itself especially with the

sacrament of which we are speaking. 5thly, That
we are not, any of us, free from either of these
tendencies now; that we are as liable to them, and
as likely to fall into them, as our forefathers in any
age. 6thly, That the temptation to practise those
galvanic experiments upon obsolete customs, which
have been alluded to, has been strong at all times,
and may, on some accounts, be particularly strong
at this time. All these concessions I make without
a moment's hesitation, and I will now proceed to
examine them in detail.

1st, It is not pretended that the resemblance
between the old mysteries and the Christian mysteries
consists in any similarity of actual rights or practices.
It lies, according to the statement of these philosophers, in the deep acknowledgment which there
has been in all ages of a something which the senses
cannot grapple with, and which is most awful and
necessary for men. That this feeling belongs to
the most permanent part of our being; that it cannot satisfy itself; that of every faith, and every
society, the deepest principle must be mysterious:
this is admitted by both parties. Thus much is
involved, and so far as I can see, no more is involved,
in the assertion, that the mysteries of Eleusis have
that which corresponds to them in the Christian
Church.

2ndly, The confusion in the minds of the ancient
priest, as well as of the ancient worshippers, was of
this kind. He believed in an awful Being above
man, and not cognizable by the senses; he believed in
an outward universe speaking to the senses. Whether
that Being, and this world, were distinct or the same;

whether he stood apart in his own awfulness, or was
to be seen in the outward forms, or was to be recognized in the hidden powers and life of the universe;
whether he was nearer to man, according to the faith
of the heroic ages, or to the world in which man
dwelt, were the puzzles which nothing could solve,
and which the confused indefinite character of the
mysteries well expressed. Hence that mixture of a
permanent faith with transitory notions, which is so
often referred to. The physical world was an unknown unexplored world. Sensible observations,
which were, of course, various in every region, were
the groundwork of all the study respecting it; these
observations were generalized into theories; these
theories became parts of the sacerdotal theology. Its
nature was necessarily therefore determined by
localities, and alterable with the increase of experience. But being grafted upon that which was not
changeable, it was treated as if it possessed the same
sacredness; and both flourished and suffered together.
Hence—

3rdly, We are able to explain the causes of that
insincerity which distinguished the later from the
earlier priests. The moral aspects of the worship;
the reverence for that which the inner man desires;
the affections and sympathies which can be rendered to
that which is personal, and strictly speaking only to
that—these were most strong in the infancy of nations :
the sense of the absolute and the unapproachable lay
beneath these feelings, but was not brought out into
distinct consciousness. The physical notions which
were attached to these acknowledgments of moral
relations were of a simple kind, directly deduced

from simple sensible observations. In process of time, the one set of feelings became weaker and baser; the facts of the other kind, and the inferences from them, were multiplied. The remnants of ancient faith, and still more of ancient fear, became inextricably combined with these; human desires and sympathies inseparably attached themselves to, and embodied themselves in, visible things; these became the real objects of worship, in spite of an ever struggling conviction, that they were not meant to be so, and that the ceremonies and mysteries which had been handed down were not strictly appropriate to them. Meantime the philosopher having enlarged his sphere of outward observation, having felt an impenetrable depth, as well as an undefinable extent, in the world around him, having detected inconsistencies in the anthropomorphic notions of his countrymen, having crushed his own human longings, and lost his sympathies with individual men, begins to speak of the world as the one great mystery. That which he expresses in abstract language, is really the habit of thought in the age generally. The priest secretly confesses that it is his own; but, either from fear, from affection and reverence, from an honest conviction that he has something which the philosopher has not, from mere ignorance, from all these motives combined, or from lower motives than any of these, he cleaves to the old forms and language, cleaves to them so much the more tenaciously, because he doubts whether one part of them may not be as insecure as another, and therefore dreads lest the loss of any part should involve the loss of the whole. The people, meanwhile, are conscious of wants of which the philosopher takes no account, conscious that they are despised by him. They have no longer any guides to that which is higher and nobler than their own conceits; these must at all hazards be gratified; the priest seeks to gratify them, and sinks lower himself, while he drags them down in the attempt.

4thly, It is not difficult for any student of modern history, in both these cases, to perceive the parallel between heathendom and Christendom. If we look at the first ages, we see those deep thoughts concerning God, His being, His unity, His relations to men, which I spoke of in a former section, mixing themselves with, and sometimes almost losing themselves in, speculations about the outward world and the creatures which inhabit it—speculations derived from no revealed authority, ascertained by no careful study and experiment, founded on no satisfactory data; for the most part, the result of mythological or philosophical traditions. These speculations, however, could not be separated by men whose souls and spirits were wholly occupied with Divine contemplations from that which is Divine. They felt that God must be the author of the outward world, that it must be made for His glory, that there are in it marvellous types of that which is spiritual. They believed, moreover, that the visible and invisible had been brought into close and inseparable union, by the incarnation of the Son of God; that every part of their own lives, and of creation, was to be informed by the New Life which had been manifested; and they could not understand how they might maintain these principles, and yet not invest with a certain sanctity their own conceptions of the universe. Then came the downfall of that world under which the

Fathers lived, and the growth of the new forms of society in Western Europe. By the merciful providence of God, a great part of the treasures of past times was hidden from the Latin and Teutonic nations, that they might not be hindered from following their own peculiar and appointed course of discipline. This discipline led them into a class of investigations, upon which the Fathers had only in part entered, or which had been entirely subordinate in their minds to the higher theology—investigations respecting the nature of man, the laws and conditions under which he is and acts. Such inquiries, pursued with earnest and holy feelings, and as I think, with the most positively beneficial results, as far as their own peculiar sphere of labour was concerned, by the schoolmen, led, however, to increased confusion in the provinces both of theology and physics. For both alike were viewed through the forms and colours of the human intellect; the invisible relations which the heart and reason acknowledge, the visible things which the eye perceives, were alike subjected to our conceptions and theories, and treated as inseparable from them. In the sacrament of which we are speaking, the results were so striking as to be a clue to those which meet us in every other direction. In the age of the Fathers there might have been a frequent blending of physical with spiritual language; not in general arising from any unbelief in the distinct reality and substantiality of that which is unseen, but rather from a desire to invest the outward universe with a portion of its glory. But in the middle age all these expressions must be stiffened into a theory; logic must inseparably incorporate theological idea with the physical notion, and must itself claim dominion over both. And then it signified not how much the understanding recoiled at its own invention; the dogma was established, the sacrament meant transubstantiation, and those who admitted the institution to be sacred, must at all hazards receive the opinion.

5thly, Such being the state of things, it is not wonderful that for a time faith in the sacrament, as a witness of a real communion between man and his Maker, should be able to uphold the notion which was appended to it; that in a later time the extravagance of the notion should have served to destroy a faith already from other causes waxing weak; that the priests should have made desperate efforts to keep both alive together; that in doing so they should have resorted to arguments which made the evil part of their scheme yet stronger, and obscured still more its purer element; that the effect upon their own minds, and the minds of their flocks, should have been a still increasing insincerity. Nor must we suppose that these sad effects were stopped by the Reformation, or that after the Reformation they were confined to those who remained in communion with Rome. Every great shaking must bring out that which is true and sound in men's hearts, and make the untruth in those who have willingly yielded to it more palpable as well as more actually dominant. The first effect, I make no doubt, took place in the hearts of many Romanists. They were thrown back upon their higher moral principles; these they thought were invaded by the new doctrines; these could not be sacrificed on account of any intellectual puzzles and contradictions. On the other hand, a more

conscious and direct identification of the formula with
the principle must have been the consequence of the
decrees of the Council of Trent upon those who
yielded to them, and a disposition to invent some
antagonist formula would have been excited by the
same cause in the reformed bodies. While the controversies which these attempts awakened were proceeding in the religious circles, men in general became
occupied with that new class of thoughts to which I
alluded in my first part. The principle upon which
the outward world had been hitherto investigated was
shown to be impracticable; men were taught how
they might study it in itself, without imputing to it
their own conceptions; the new method was rewarded
with the most signal discoveries; gradually, as I
observed, a pursuit which had produced and which
promised such grand results, took the place of every
other. This alone was supposed to be founded upon
any sure data; if there were any other region, it could
only be examined according to these data. Of course
all the physical mixtures which had intruded themselves into theology, were scornfully rejected; this
was the first step. The next was a disbelief in those
forms and conceptions of the mind itself, which had so
much darkened the face of nature. And since the
Romanist theology was inseparably interwoven with
both physics and logic; the Reformation theology
not much with physics but even more with the forms
of the understanding; there grew up an almost un-
avoidable suspicion of both. And this suspicion
might only have been profitable, as in the end I
trust it will prove, if along with it there had not
arisen that entire disbelief in spiritual realities, of

which moral corruption was the primary, the pride
of physical speculation only the secondary, cause.
This incredulity found its way into the hearts of the
priests of both communions. In some it had the effect
of inducing a general latitudinarianism, a willingness
to abandon all ancient forms, a tolerance of all kinds
of language, because there seemed to be no truth to
which any of them was pointing. In others it
occasioned a pertinacious clinging to everything
which had been, through old tradition or modern
innovation, identified with theological principles. The
root of these evils was the same in the third age
as in the first. *God and the world were confounded.*
That which the spirit of man demands for its satisfaction, that which humanity seeks after as its object,
was identified with the visible things over which the
spirit is meant to rule, in which humanity is meant to
see the image of those realities that surpass it. Hence
the mysteries of Christianity, which the first age had
sought to connect with misunderstood terrestrial
things for the sake of glorifying them, which the
second age had connected with those forms and conceptions of our own minds wherein physical things
had been hitherto contemplated, were in the third age
described as utterly unmeaning by the wise and
prudent, who had learnt the right method of studying nature and the impositions which the mind
practises upon itself—were held fast with a loving but
trembling faith by the poor and the childlike, who,
amidst all perplexities will not forsake that which
their hearts tell them that they need.

6thly, I have traced then the causes and the progress
of the confusion which is common to the history of the

Pagan and the Christian world. And now the question occurs, who are likely to fall into this confusion in our day, and by what means is it to be avoided? I by no means deny that we, the priests of the Christian covenant, are in danger of falling into it. We hear many denials all around us; we are told that things are obsolete, which we feel were never so much needed as now; we are informed that what is objective is nothing worth, and we find from the history of the world that the subjective notions and fancies of men have brought all kinds of perplexities into it. We observe a continual inclination to reject that which seems to us solid and precious, and we are threatened that this inclination is to increase indefinitely. What so natural as that we should throw ourselves back upon the past, that we should pledge ourselves to what we think a determined resistance to the spirit of the age—not only seeking to retain what we have, but to recover what we have lost; that we should number among our losses the apprehensions respecting the physical world, which belong to the infancy of society, the logical systems which grew up in its boyhood; and that we should think the effort to regain these a proof of our reverence for God's sacraments, an acknowledgment of their permanent and real character? Such feelings, I say, are most natural, and just so far as we yield to them we shall unquestionably try to galvanize the habits and notions of a foregone period.

But why should we not yield to them? I answer: Because in doing so we shew that we are *not* free from the spirit of the age, but are infected by it; because in doing so, we shew that we are *not* impressed with the permanence and reality of God's sacraments, but have

yielded to the prevailing scepticism respecting them.
For what is the spirit of the age, as it exhibits itself in
those philosophers whose objections we are now considering ? I have endeavoured, in a former part of this
work, to shew that no persons are so disposed as they
are to confound God with the world—to look at this
visible universe, with its mysterious powers and properties, as the real Being, or at least as the greatest
manifestation of the real Being. This pantheistic
tendency is especially our tendency at this time; and
this has been in all past times the source of that confusion between the permanent and the transitory, the
essential and the accidental, which we are told, and
rightly told, to beware of. And therefore Christian
priests will not be the only galvanizers. It is to the
philosophers of the age following the promulgation of
Christianity, to Plotinus and Porphyry and Jamblichus,
that we are indebted for the most remarkable galvanic
experiments on record. They tried to reproduce the
old Pagan forms, expressly as a means of giving a
body to their philosophy, which otherwise they felt
that it had not, and as a means of resisting the
progress of the new kingdom. There are symp-
toms of the same inclination among us now. We
shall see more and more of them. Pantheism
never has existed, and never will . exist, in that
naked essential character which it affects. It will
beget idolatries, and since the imagination of man has
well-nigh exhausted itself in that kind of production,
these idolatries will not be new, but old. How may
they be withstood ? I believe in no way so effectually
as by the simple putting forth of this sacrament, not
clothed with a number of fantastic rites and emblems,

but in its own dreadful grandeur, as the bond of a communion between heaven and earth,—as a witness that man is not a creature of this world, but has his home, his citizenship in another,—as a witness that his spirit is not the function or creature of his body, and has not therefore need to make out its enjoyments from the things which the eye sees, and the ear hears; but that his body is the attendant and minister of his spirit, is to be exalted by it, is to bring all visible things under it,—as a witness that the Son of man is set down at the right hand of the Throne of God, and that those who believe in Him, and suffer with Him, are meant to live and reign with Him there. The forms of nature, the forms of the understanding, have striven to reduce this sacrament to their own level; it remains as a mighty power in God's hands, to raise man above these forms, into communion with himself.

The Romish System.

After the remarks under the last head, it may seem scarcely needful that I should vindicate my statements respecting this sacrament from the charge of Romanism; but since I have maintained that the character of the Eucharistic feast is sacrificial, that Christ is really present in it, and that the words of institution are to be taken literally; since it is very evidently implied in what I have said, that a certain order of persons first received the sacramental elements, and that a certain order ought to administer them now: it may be advisable to shew, even at the risk of some repetition, wherein I am opposed to the Romish theory upon each of these points.

1. I need only ask the reader to compare the observations which were made respecting the difference between the Catholic and the Romish idea of Baptism, and the Catholic and Romish forms of worship, with those which have been made in this section respecting the question of sacrifice; in order that he may perceive the principle which governs all three cases. I complained that the baptized man, according to the Romish theory, only receives a momentary gift, and is not admitted into a permanent state; and that the worshipper, according to the Romish notion, is purchasing some future benefit by his acts of devotion, not claiming a blessing which has been already purchased for him. It is impossible that he should not act in strict conformity to these maxims when he is dealing with the sacrifice which is the foundation of the Christian's state, and the consummation of the Christian's worship. The Eucharistic sacrifice is of course regarded by him as the means of obtaining those advantages and blessings which Christ's sacrifice has not fully procured for us, or which we through our sins and negligence have lost. Such, I need hardly say, is the view commonly presented of it by Romish writers, and such is the view against which all the attacks of the Reformers were directed; consequently the doctrine which I have put forward, that this feast derives its peculiarity, derives its sacrificial character, from the fact that a complete sacrifice has been offered up for man, is far more formally and practically opposed to Romanism than that which is prevalent in our day. There is no formal opposition between the doctrine which denies the very existence of a Eucharistic sacrifice, and that which affirms it to

be the carrying out of an incomplete sacrifice made for us by Christ. The two opinions contradict each other, but they cannot be brought into comparison; each is continually gaining strength from the denial which is contained in the other: but what each asserts, or to what test they can be brought, the supporters of them are constantly puzzled to discover. Neither is there a practical opposition, for the Protestants are constantly losing sight of the finished sacrifice of Christ, in their anxiety to assert the importance of human faith; and the Romanists are constantly trying, through a violent effort of recollection, assisted by visible images and presentations, to bring back the very event of our Lord's crucifixion, and all the circumstances attending it: so that there is an unconscious confession on the part of the one, that there must be acts of ours in which the blessing of the sacrifice is realized; on the part of the other, that it is that one sacrifice, and not any repetition of it by us, in which all virtue dwells. I maintain that the sacrament being acknowledged as the sacrificial feast of the new dispensation, realizes and harmonizes these two truths, satisfies the meaning which the Romanist feels that he cannot part with, and so enables him to cast aside, as degrading, dangerous, and antichristian, that doctrine which has been one of the greatest barriers between him and his Protestant brethren.

2. To the same habit of mind which introduced this view of the Eucharistic sacrifice, we must attribute the entertainment which was given by the Church, after some hard struggles, to the doctrine respecting the transubstantiation of the elements. I have discovered the intellectual origin of this dogma

in the scholastic philosophy ; but that philosophy
could never have given it currency, if there had not
been a moral predisposition in men's minds to receive
it.   The cry for some signal proof of condescension to
our low estate, the sense of a weakness which could
only be met by a mighty act of Divine humiliation,—
these feelings characterised the Middle Ages, and constituted their strength.   The belief that by these acts
the spirit of man was to be raised out of its grave of
sense, was to be made capable of actual communion
with the invisible and the absolute ; this belief
hovered about many minds, was conveyed in many
emblems and enigmas, was actually grasped by some
earnest and thoughtful men, but never really entered
into the practical life of the period.   To shew forth
acts of bravery, condescension, sacrifice, and so to
glorify God, was the desire of a number ; to inspire
others with the same ambition, the aim of a few.   But
everywhere one may trace the wish to see the likeness
of God in visible things, and under earthly conditions,
rather than the craving to see Him as He is.   I have
no need to inquire how far good or evil preponderated
in this temper of mind.   That it was a very imperfect
one, most will be ready to acknowledge ; and that its
imperfection laid it open to invasions of gross sensuality, is only questioned by resolutely one-sided or one-
eyed inquirers.   In such a state of mind it was impossible that the thought of communion with Christ
where He is, should be as distinctly presented to the
best men in their best moments, as it may now be
presented to indifferent men who may very little
realize their own vision.   The discovery, therefore, of
a substitute for this faith, of a way in which Christ

might be believed to be present by a fresh act of descent and condescension into the circumstances of human nature, was naturally and eagerly welcomed— the obstacles which the understanding opposed to the opinion readily swept away. What sensuality and death grew out of this notion, were fostered by it, and helped to keep it alive; what profaneness mingled in the speculations to which it gave rise, how it connected itself with every other shape of idolatry, I think all ecclesiastical history demonstrates. But I have no belief that the demonstration will be heeded, that facts will not be perverted and explained away, that the natural results of a system will not be treated as if they might be condemned without any reference to the system itself, unless men be led to perceive that there is a spiritual truth which this doctrine has been counterfeiting and keeping out of sight, and to which it is in far more direct antipathy than it ever can be to the different Protestant and infidel notions which have been set up against it.

3. It is evident from these remarks, and from all which I have said in this section, that I do not seek to get rid of the papal notion respecting a real Presence, *merely* by saying that what is spiritual is also most real. I do indeed look upon that proposition as nearly the most important one which a theological student can think of or remember, and also as the one which Romanism is most habitually denying. But I have maintained, that in order to the full acknowledgment of Christ's spiritual presence, we must distinctly acknowledge that He is clothed with a body; that if we lose this belief, we adopt a vague pantheistic notion of a presence hovering about us

somewhere in the air, in place of a clear spiritual apprehension of a Person in whom all truth and love dwell; that the spiritual organ therefore does demand an actual body for its nourishment; that through that spiritual organ our bodies themselves are meant to be purified and glorified; that this sacrament meets and satisfies the needs both of the human spirit which is redeemed, and of the body which is waiting for its redemption. But all these admissions only bring out the difference with the Romanist into stronger relief. To enter into fellowship with Christ as He is, ascended at the right hand of God, in a body of glory and not of humiliation, this must be the desire of a Christian man, if he seek the presence of a real, not an imaginary object, if he desire his body as well as his spirit to be raised and exalted. On this ground then he must reject all theories which involve the imagination of a descent into the elements; on this ground, also, he must feel that the intellectual contradiction which such theories contain, and even boast of, is the counterpart of a spiritual contradiction still more gross and dangerous.

4. I must say a few words before I conclude upon the difference between my views and those of the Romanists, respecting those who administer this sacrament. The pure Protestant expresses his differences in such words as these. The Romanist, he says, unhappily connecting the idea of sacrifice with the Eucharist, necessarily supposes that the Christian Church must have its priests as well as the Jewish; we rejecting the first idea, of course reject the second. Now as I have so carefully connected the idea of sacrifice with the Eucharist, it follows from this state-

ment, that if I suppose it to be administered by human hands at all, I must suppose those hands to be, in some sense of the word, sacerdotal. Nay, it would seem to follow by almost necessary inference, that if I suppose the Jewish sacrifice to have passed into something higher, I must suppose the Jewish priesthood to have passed into something higher. And this in fact is my belief. I do think that a Melchisedec priesthood has succeeded to an Aaronical priesthood, even as the power of an endless life has succeeded to the law of a carnal commandment. I do think that he who presents the perfect sacrifice before God, and himself and his people as redeemed by that sacrifice, has a higher function than he had who presented the daily offering, or made the yearly atonement before God. I do think that he who is permitted to feed the people with this bread and wine has a higher work to do than he who came out of the holy place to bless the people in God's name. And I complain of the Romanists for lowering this office, for depriving it of its spiritual and Catholic character, for reducing it to the level or below the level of that which existed before the incarnation. No honour which is put upon the person of the priest can make amends to him for the degradation which he suffers by being treated as if he were without the veil, pleading for admission into the presence of God, not claiming the privilege for himself and his people of being admitted into it. No emblems which exhibit his own mysterious glory and beauty can be any compensation for the loss of the belief that he is permitted with open face to behold the glory of his Lord. Above all, the differences which are made between him and his flock, especially that most gross and offensive one, by whatever arguments it may be palliated, of permitting him alone to receive the sacramental wine, do but show that he is not like his Lord, that he is not one of many brethren, but has only the melancholy delight of fancying that there are blessings reserved for him in which other men are not sharers. Herein he is far below the Jew. The high-priest believed that he was one of a kingdom of priests; that he received his garments of beauty and his holy mitre because he was their representative. A Jew would have answered to the complaint of Korah, "Ye take too much upon you, seeing that all the congregation are holy, everyone of them,"—'We take this upon us which has been put upon us, *because* the congregation is holy, and because it would not be holy if we were not consecrated to be witnesses and preservers of its holiness.' A Jew could see that the oil upon Aaron's head went down to the skirts of his garments. It is not surely for Christians and Catholics to set up an office in the Church against the Church itself, to set at nought the ascription which they are appointed to offer up in the name of the whole body: "Unto Him that loved us and washed us from our sins in His own blood, and hath made us kings and priests unto God and His Father; to Him be glory and dominion for ever and for ever." But I am intruding upon the subject of the next section.

SECTION V.—THE MINISTRY.

It is commonly observed, that a sacerdotal caste has three invariable characteristics. It assumes a lofty dominion over the minds as well as the bodies of men, it imposes a very heavy yoke upon both, it is opposed to every thing humane and expansive.

How much warrant there is for these accusations, every one who reads history must perceive. And assuredly these evil tendencies have not been confined to one set of circumstances or one form of religion; they have manifested themselves in Judea and Christendom as well as in Hindostan. They may therefore be fairly considered as belonging to human nature, and as being especially likely to assail anyone who anywhere and under any conditions, assumes the office of a religious guide and authority.

That this institution has not been *merely* fruitful of evil, the impartial enquirer, especially in the most modern times, is ready to acknowledge. But he rightly observes, that we must not restrict the advantages it has produced to any particular system. Much has been done for civilization by Memphis, and Delphi, and by the Brahmins of the East. And it remains, he says, to be proved, that the idea of the priesthood does not involve tyranny and narrowness, though at certain periods the tyranny may have been useful, the narrowness common to all classes.

Undoubtedly this is the real question. If we should find upon inquiry that the fundamental principles of a sacerdotal caste, amidst all its outward varieties, are those we have just set down, it ought to be got rid of as soon as possible; and it will disappear as soon as truth and honesty have gained the victory, which we at least are bound to believe they will ultimately gain, over fraud and falsehood. If on the other hand it should be found that an idea of the priesthood, curiously and exactly opposite to that which presumes dominion, restraint upon the human spirit, confinement of men within certain districts and habits of thought, to be its objects, is embodied in the forms and language of the Christian Church, we may perhaps ask ourselves whether this may not be the idea after which men in all ages and in all religions have been feeling; whether the good which is attributed to them have not been the consequence of their attaining to some apprehension of it, the evil they have done, the consequence of their losing sight of it or contradicting it; whether therefore the triumph of truth over falsehood may not be exhibited in the full accomplishment of this idea, not in the destruction of the institution which has witnessed for it and preserved it.

Now these facts are indisputable, 1. The whole sacerdotal caste in Christendom has the name of *ministers* or *servants*. From the Bishop of Rome down to the founder of the last new sect in the United States of America, every one who deals with the Gospel at all, or pretends in any sense to have a Divine commission, assumes this name as the description of his office. 2. The most remarkable power which these ministers have claimed, and that on account of which the greatest homage has been paid to them, is the power of *absolving* or *setting free*. This claim has in a manner been universal. Luther believed that he was to absolve as much as Tetzel. Every person who says that the sole office of a minister is to preach the Gospel, says so because he believes this is the way to absolve. There are most serious differences about the nature of the power and the mode in which it is to be exercised, none at all about the existence of it, and about its connection in some way or other with the Christian ministry. 3. The third fact is this. In Christian Europe, ever since it became Christian, the most conspicuous order of ministers has been one which assumed to itself an universal character. The overseers or Bishops of the Christian Church have felt themselves to be emphatically the bonds of communication between different parts of the earth. The jurisdiction of each has been confined within a certain district; but, by the very nature of their office, they have held fellowship, and been obliged to hold fellowship, with those who lived in other districts, who spoke different languages, who were bound together by different notions and customs. Now though such an order may be very far more dangerous, and may have been felt by the rulers of particular countries to be far more dangerous than that kind of priesthood which confines itself within a particular region, yet it is evidently of an entirely different kind. Whatever this institution may have effected, it seems to aim at establishing a more extended commerce and fellowship among men. Looking at it superficially, one would say that this ecclesiastical order imported something more comprehensive, more diffusive, than any civil order which one can think of, unless it should be some one which attempts universal conquest, and destroys its character as an order by the attempt. And yet

this episcopacy has not been merely an accidental
addition to, or overgrowth upon other forms of priesthood. In those countries where it is recognised,
it has been the root of all other forms, and has been
supposed to contain them within it. It has been
believed, as a necessary consequence of the importance attached to the Eucharist, that an order of
men must exist in the Christian Church corresponding
to the priests of the old dispensation, with the difference that the sacrifice in the one case was antici-
patory, in the other commemorative. This office has
been associated with that absolving power of which I
spoke just now. Yet it has been always supposed to
be included in that of the Bishop; and where it is
assigned to a distinct class of persons, that class
receives its authority from him. In like manner there
has been acknowledged in the Church an order whose
functions are evidently distinct from either of these;
whose main object is to provide for the bodily wants
of men, or only to announce to them spiritual truths.
Yet even this office has been understood to be only a
delegation of certain powers inhering in the Bishop,
which he has not leisure to discharge, and no person
can undertake it, in the countries which recognize
episcopacy, without such a delegation. So that an
office implying an intention so very remote from that
which the word priest ordinarily suggests to us, would
seem to have been the characteristic one in the Christian Church, that which includes all others, and out of
which they arise.

But I have used the phrase, "the countries in which
episcopacy is recognized." It is important, that we
should consider what these countries are, lest we should

be drawing an inference respecting the nature of this institution which facts do not warrant. Let, then, the reader call to mind, first of all, the circumstances of the Eastern Church for the last fifteen or sixteen hundred years. Let him think of it at the time when Constantinople was in its glory, of the different sects which broke from it, of the horrible contentions which took place between those sects and their common mother. Let him remember the degradation which every part of this Church, and every one of these sects, has suffered from the Ottoman power, and let him then reflect that in whatever countries they may have dwelt, to whatever circumstances of good or evil fortune they may have been exposed, whatever strifes may have gone on amongst them, this institution has been preserved by them all. Let him next consider the different circumstances under which Christianity was preached and adopted in the different nations of the West, the different influences to which it has been subjected, the different characters of the different races which compose it ; and let him then remember that all these nations, under all these influences, amidst all their conflicts with the eastern part of Christendom, did, without one clearly established exception, preserve this institution till the sixteenth century. Let him consider the circumstances of the Reformation leading to the separation of the nations, to a violent conflict with the old system of Europe, to an excessive magnifying of individual faith, and then reflect that this universal institution was preserved in all the Latin nations—among the Teutonic nations, in England, in Denmark, and in Sweden; that it was rejected, and that not without great reluctance, in certain parts of

Germany, in Holland, in Switzerland, and in Scotland; that in each of these countries some witness of its existence has been preserved; that in at least one of them there are those who think that it is more necessary now than in any past time. Let it be remembered, further, that this institution has passed over to the continent of America; that it has established itself in a set of colonies founded by Puritans and Quakers; that it grew up after the influence of England had ceased in those colonies; that without the least state patronage it is making itself an instrument for diffusing the Gospel from those colonies to many parts of the world. These are the pretensions which Episcopacy makes to the character of a Catholic institution.

It is implied in what I have said, that this institution has a character of permanence as well as of universality. It is implied also that this permanence is something different from the permanence of a custom which has first derived its significance from some local accident, and then has perpetuated itself by the care of some body especially created for its conservation. For we have seen this institution maintaining itself amidst the oppositions and contradictions of bodies differing most vehemently with each other; we have seen it reappearing when all local habits and customs were adverse to it. How then has it been preserved or seemed to be preserved? It has been preserved by an act of consecration performed through the agency of three existing Bishops; signifying, according to the faith of all the nations and ages which have retained it, that the person newly entering upon the function receives the same kind of authority and the same kind of gifts as those who were first endowed with it.

It must be quite evident to the reader, that the facts which we have now been considering touch the very heart of the questions which I have been discussing in this work. These questions have been, Is there any meaning in the words Kingdom of Christ? Do the words mean what they seem to mean? Are there any facts in the history of the world which seem to shew that they denote that which is really and actually existing? Now we have found a series of facts, all, it seemed to us, bearing to the same point, all proving the existence of a universal and spiritual society; a society maintaining its existence amidst the greatest perplexities and contradictions; a society of which all the conditions are inexplicable unless we suppose it to be connected with, and upheld by, an unseen power. But as all these signs which we have considered hitherto exist for the sake of men, so also they imply the agency of men. And upon the character of this agency must depend the whole character of the kingdom itself. It may be something else, but it is not a commonwealth, not a kingdom according to any admitted sense of the word, if it have not certain magistrates or officers. Practically these exist even in those societies which boast most of their self-government; they have officers, whatever be the tenure of their office. And, therefore, we must either give up all that we have previously maintained as untenable, or we must steadily consider this question—What kind of officers would be consistent with the character of such a kingdom as those other signs speak of? It

would seem clear that as all these signs pointed
to an invisible presence, and were intended to admit
men into it, these officers must be constituted with
a view to the same end. They must be intended
to bring before men the fact that they are subject
to an invisible and universal Ruler.

And if so, it would seem also necessary that they
should exhibit Him to men in that character and
in those offices which He actually came to perform.
If He came not to be ministered unto but to minister,
if His exercise of power was a ministry, theirs must
be so too. They can look upon themselves in no
other light than as ministers; they cannot suppose
their power diminished by this acknowledgment;
they cannot suppose that their power will be real,
if not exercised with a continual recollection of it.
If one chief part of His work in the world was to
absolve men from past evil, from the power of present
evil, from the danger of future evil; and if there be a
continual necessity for all men who come into the
world, that they should have this absolution, and if
He exercise His powers or make Himself manifest in
any way through men, one must suppose that they
would be called especially to represent Him in this
office of Absolver. If His greatest purpose was to
bind men together in one family, if the office on which
He entered when He ascended on high, was that of
Head and overseer of this family; if all His other acts
and services to men are implied and presupposed in
this, one must conceive the highest office of His servants
would be to exhibit Him in this character, and so to
make it known that His kingdom was a real kingdom,
and one that ruleth over all. If, finally, Jesus himself

when upon earth received a formal and outward designation to the office which He had undertaken, that it might be signified to men on what terms He held it—not as a separate independent Being, but as one with the Father, and honouring Him in all His words and acts—it would seem reasonable to expect that an equally formal and visible designation would bear witness to men, that those offices which are fulfilled for their sakes, by creatures of their own flesh and blood, are not held in virtue of any qualities or merits in those creatures, but are held from Christ and under Christ by persons who can exhibit His character truly only just so far as they perform their work faithfully.

But is there anything in the language of the New Testament which accords with these anticipations and explains these facts? One would think that this language, like that which refers to the institution of Baptism, must lie on the very surface of the record, and yet must connect itself with all its deepest announcements; otherwise it can be no authority for institutions which pretend to embody the whole character of the new dispensation. A few casual hints could never suffice as the warrant for fallible men to suppose that they were meant to be the ministers of Christ and to present Him before men. Still less could such hints be an excuse for sinful men who should take upon them, in God's name, to absolve their brethren. Least of all could they justify the existence of an order, which assumes such a singular position, and claims such high functions as the Episcopal. The mere appearance of such an office, even in the time immediately following our Lord's departure from the world, ought not, I think, to be looked upon as a sufficient reason for its claiming to be an estate of His kingdom, if He did not expressly and formally institute it Himself.

We turn, then, to the Gospels for the purpose of inquiring whether they offer any guidance upon the subject; and we are immediately encountered by the history of the selection and appointment of a set of men who were emphatically distinct from all classes which had existed in the Jewish polity. They are, indeed, carefully connected with that polity; their number shows that they were meant to remind the Jews of the tribes into which their nation had been distributed. They were all Jews, and their first commission was strictly confined to the house of Israel. But these circumstances only make the peculiarity of their office more remarkable. The most evident indications were given to them, even from the first, even at the time when they were least capable of understanding the nature of their service, that it was meant to transcend national limitations. At the same time, even while they were falling into the greatest confusions respecting the place which they were to occupy in the world, even while they had need to be reminded continually that the kings of the Gentiles exercised dominion over *them*, but that it was not so to be in the Church; they were still assured, in the strongest language, that they were to perform a wonderful work, and to be endued with wonderful powers; that he who received them would receive their Master; that they were sent forth by Him, even as He was sent forth by the Father.

Everyone must perceive that these intimations are not scattered carelessly through the Gospels, that they form a part of their very substance and tissue. It was in teaching the disciples that those who became as little children were greatest in the kingdom of heaven, that their rule was to be a service, it was in the acts which accompanied these teachings, that our Lord's own life and image are most distinctly brought before us. Evidently He never separates the thought of training them in their office from that of performing His own. As evidently He is training them to an *office*; He is not teaching them to be great saints, to keep up a high tone of personal holiness as if that were the end of their lives. But He is teaching them that they have a work to do even as He has; that He is straitened till He can accomplish His; that they must be straitened till they can accomplish theirs; and that in trying to accomplish it, they will most find that they are lights of the world, and that they must derive their light continually from Him. So that if we called the four Gospels 'The Institution of a Christian Ministry,' we might not go very far wrong, or lose sight of many of their essential qualities. Above all, one would not lose sight of the different crises in our Lord's life, and of their connexion with different discoveries of grace and truth to man. Before the resurrection there was merely the general commission, "Go and preach the Kingdom of God. Heal the sick. Cast out devils. Freely ye have received, freely give." Far deeper views of their office were brought out in those conversations which our Lord had with them the night before His Passion; views all connecting themselves with the awful facts of which they were to be witnesses, and with the mysterious service which they had been performing.

But it was not till our Lord came back from the grave, with the witness and the power of a new life for man, that He breathed upon His disciples and said, "Receive ye the Holy Ghost. Whosesoever sins ye remit, they are remitted; whosesoever sins ye retain, they are retained." It was not till He was just leaving them that the commission was given, "Go ye into all nations," and the promise, "Lo I am with you always, even unto the end of the world." And it was not till He had ascended on high that the powers for fulfilling this commission were confirmed, that a sign was given of the existence of a union which the distinctions of nations and language could not break, that they were declared to be the pillars of a universal Church.

Now these poor fishermen could not doubt for a moment that these powers belonged to them officially, and not personally; and therefore the chief question to be considered is this : Did they suppose this kingdom was to die with them, or that they were to perpetuate its existence ? Were they to perpetuate it in the manner in which our Lord Himself had established it, or in some other manner ? Was the change which the new circumstances of the Church necessarily occasioned in the position of those who were to be its ministers, to be a change in the nature of their office and institution, or only a change in their numbers and in the circumstances of their jurisdiction? Supposing the latter to be the case, were those who succeeded to the Apostolic office to reckon that they derived their powers less immediately from Christ, that they were less witnesses of His permanent government, than those who received their first commission from Him while He was dwelling upon earth? If these questions be answered in one way, those nations which have preserved the episcopal institution have a right to believe that they have preserved one of the appointed and indispensable signs of a spiritual and universal society. If they are answered in the other way, it seems difficult to understand how such a universal society can exist at all.

The Quaker.

But we must consider the arguments of those who think otherwise. The Quaker tells us at once that we have described a formal and not a spiritual ministry; a ministry of the Old Testament, not of the New. 'A true minister is consecrated such by an inward call. The voice of the Spirit, not of men, invites him into God's vineyard. Older and more experienced men may judge whether his vocation be a real one; but they do not give him his appointment; still less can they confer one upon persons not chosen by God. Under the old dispensation there was a succession to the office of priest in a certain family. Such an arrangement belonged to the time; it is done away in Christ. And even under the first covenant there was a race of prophets who simply obeyed the Divine voice, simply spoke and acted as they were moved by the Holy Ghost. The (so called) Church of Christ has adopted the obsolete part of the whole system, has rejected the living and spiritual part of it. Lastly, the Christian teacher is fitted for his work by the teaching of the Spirit, not by the preparation of human culture.' Each of these points deserves a careful consideration.

1. It follows from that doctrine of Baptism, which lies at the threshold of our Churchmanship, that we suppose every Christian infant to be taken under the guardianship and education of God's Holy Spirit. In the faith of this truth, the well-instructed parent brings up his child. Whatever of stern discipline he uses to curb its self-will, whatever of tender affections he manifests to call forth in it corresponding affections, hath this end, that the subject of his visible and temporary government may be brought to feel that it is under the government of an unseen Teacher; that the object of his imperfect and wavering love may perceive that it is unceasingly tended and brooded over by a love which is unchangeable and imperishable. Which life-giving truth, when it has dawned upon the mind of the child, will create some blossoms and buds there, upon which the parent will gaze with an anxious but confiding eye. Strange thoughts and impulses before unknown; wonder respecting his own condition; hopes stretching into infinity; a deepening sense of ever-present evil; a brightening view of an ever-present Deliverer: such mingled emotions, as he watches them arising, the foster-father knows assuredly to be indications that his care has not been in vain, and that the boy is learning the secret of his other— his royal—parentage. And, gradually he imparts to him the conviction, that not merely his adoption and expected inheritance appertain to another region than this, but that all the dim desires and longings which have pointed to them, have been heavenly inspirations. Joyful and consolatory tidings indeed—yet not precious only for their own sake, but as interpreting other feelings and impulses which are to arise within him here-

after. For now the questions, What is he? or, Whither he is going? are not all that occupy him; but, What relations exist between him and his fellow-men? How is he to act upon them? What is his destined vocation? In pursuing this inquiry, he will remember, first of all, that which he has often been told by his earliest instructors, that just so far as he nourishes all gentle affections within him, and keeps himself from sensual defilement, and seeks the temper of a little child, and thinks on things which are lovely and pure, and maintains a cheerful heart, and does good according to his opportunity, and strives to avoid noisy excitements of the flesh or the spirit, and is not impatient of present perplexity, or greedy of distinctions—so far he will be able, in quiet meditation and prayer, to learn the mind of the Spirit, and to know in what part of his vineyard God has destined him to labour. And then, if the circumstances of his outward position shew him that he is intended to be one of those who minister to the carnal necessities of men, and the apparent end of whose vocation is mercenary, he will be sure that in this station, whether esteemed among men or not, he is to glorify God, and vindicate his calling from every deserved reproach, maintaining a free and noble and heavenly spirit, amidst all temptations to be sordid and secular. Or if a secret impulse of his spirit, not the less to be heeded because outward influences and early education may have co-operated with it, or have created it, should lead him to those pursuits which have their basis in science, and require in him a scientific insight, as well as all diligence in the study of experiments and facts—then, whether it be man's physical structure, and the secret powers of his life, and the circumstances of his diseases and decay, which most engage his thoughts—or whether it be the civil ordinances, by which our social position is upheld, and our wrongs redressed—or whether he is drawn to look still more comprehensively at our different relations, and to meditate on those mysterious powers of sympathy, or fear, or awe, which are the real bonds of human policy, he will feel that it is a Divine Instructor who is marking him out for a physician, a lawyer, or a statesman; and to the same watchful guidance he must look to direct his intellect while he is preparing for the work, and while he is actually engaged in it to preserve him in the fear of God and in honourable, affectionate thoughts of his fellow-men, that he may not dare to follow any low or selfish impulses, or be ever tempted to think of his brethren as the legitimate victims of quackery, chicanery, or party-spirit.   Nor can I so far yield to prejudices and feelings which I respect, and which I would not wish to remove from the mind of any Quaker till I can shew him what I conceive is the truth which they pervert, as not to carry this principle a step farther, and to maintain, that every soldier of really brave and gentle heart has been led to reflect on the preciousness of national life and the duty of upholding it even at the cost of individual life, awful as that is, and has been taught to dedicate his energies to the preservation of this higher life, not by an evil spirit, but by that same Spirit of truth and love, who, when He would lay the foundation of His new kingdom on earth, chose for the first subject and witness of it a Centurion of the Italian band.   But, when a young man, studying in all things to approve himself to his great Taskmaster, finds not in himself any of these particular promptings, but rather a large and general desire to be the servant of his race—when a certain stronger sense is given to him than to others of man's highest destiny, mixed, perhaps, with a less keen perception than in other men would be desirable of those necessities which, though they may be baptized with a heavenly life and adopted into religion, are themselves of the earth, earthy—when spiritual forms, which the majority have need to see reflected in sensible mirrors, rise up before him in their naked substance and majesty—when good and evil present themselves to him, not as means to some result, but as themselves the great ends and results to which all is tending—when the conflict which is going on within himself, leads him to feel his connection with his kind—when there is imparted to him a lively sense of temptation, and of its being most perilous to those whose objects and vocation are the highest—when he has been endued with a certain habit of measuring acts and events, not by their outward magnitude, but according to their spiritual proportions and effects—when he has been taught to reverence poverty and helplessness—when he has understood that that truth is the highest, not which is the most exclusive, but which is the most universal—when the immediate vision of God, and entire subjection of heart and spirit to his loving will, seem to him the great gifts intended for man, after which everyone for himself and his fellows may aspire: then, surely, if a strong combination of outward circumstances do not oblige him to what perhaps is a still more glorious, though more painful, task of yielding to a wisdom which he adores without understanding, he may conclude that it is to no partial or specific service, but to that one which we emphatically call THE *Ministry*, that the Divine Voice is inviting and commanding him.

Thus far, then, our opinion respecting inward calls seems to accord with that of the Quaker, only that we carry it farther. He considers that there is one inward call, which is needful for a Christian, and another which is needful for the Christian preacher. We contend that every Christian should believe himself called to every work in which he engages; and that except he believe this, the work will be unholy and cheerless, pursued without confidence in God or any expectation of high and worthy fruit. Not that in this I mean to explain away the express call of the minister, as if it meant nothing more than what everyone pleases it to mean; my wish is rather to maintain, that the language, which we use in reference to the highest pursuit, determines the tone which we should adopt in speaking, or at least in thinking, concerning all our pursuits. Other men may have honourable thoughts and inspirations, and may honestly obey them, and silently and implicitly attribute them to their true source. But the minister of God, with fear and trembling indeed, but still without cowardly diffidence, is to declare to himself and to others, the real fountain of that which is within him. He cannot teach others to believe themselves the temples of the living God, if he dare not acknowledge the plain consequences of this doctrine in relation to himself.

But then this question remains,—If, in every rightly ordered community, the tradesman, the lawyer, the physician, the soldier, the statesman, believes that the secret influences which determined him to embrace his own vocation in preference to any other were not themselves his title to enter upon that vocation, but only the predisposing motives to seek for such a title,—is the analogy in this instance violated, is the immediate minister of God in a different predicament? Does the secret call in his spirit make him a minister, or does it only set him upon inquiring what is the lawful way of becoming one? I confess I do not understand what should make the difference. I can see, indeed, that the call is to a higher work. I can see that it has need to be more distinctly apprehended as to its principle and origin, by him whose very outward duty is a spiritual one than by others. But I cannot see that the difference is one of kind, and that while the Spirit of God in all other cases moves a man to adapt himself to some rule or order, here it teaches him that he has no need of such an order, but that the "motion" is a substitute for it. I should have expected, certainly, that the minister of God,—if his very name be not a mere invention; if there be any communication between heaven and earth; if any men be intended or called to teach their brethren in matters directly pertaining to God,—should receive his commission in some very different way from that in which the member of any other profession receives his. I should have expected that some scheme would have been devised, to shew that he did not derive his authority from the king of his land, or from any learned incorporation, or from any limited power whatever. But I should never have expected that, whereas in other cases the witness of a man's own mind, and its inward impulses, though

most needful for his own satisfaction, though most
needful to convince him that he is walking in the
road appointed for him, are yet considered wholly
inadequate to confer authority, and affirm his position
to others, here, in an office especially instituted for the
sake of mankind, for the poor and ignorant,—an
office in which the individual performing it is to be
especially hidden and forgotten, and the majesty of
God asserted,—these motions should be all in all, and
no token given which all men alike can apprehend, as
to the extent and derivation of the influence which
they are intended to obey.

2. Next comes the question, so often discussed in
previous sections, of the relation between the Old and
New Testament. In the Jewish Commonwealth, as
the Quaker confesses, we discover at first a strict,
definite organization; a priesthood limited to a certain
tribe, a place and time appointed for sacrifices, the
sacrifices themselves appointed. Here is a rigid
system, the author of which now and then, as in the
case of Eli, asserts as well his own prerogative, as the
fact, that this, like every system, exists for an end and
is not itself an end, by infringing some of its maxims.
Yet we know that this Divine precaution was not
adequate to prevent a dead sense of routine, injurious
to the working of the system itself, from creeping
over the hearts of the people who were subject
to it. Wherefore, the next contrivance which we
notice in this celestial machinery, seems intended
to counteract this tendency, without any violation
of uniformity. When the ecclesiastical constitution
had been well established, and its principle explained by its operation, a new order of men is

raised up, for the express purpose, it seems, of proving that forms and institutions are indications of our relation to God, and means of attaining to intercourse with Him, but neither create the one, nor are substitutes for the other. This being the very intent of the Prophet's vocation, several consequences follow inevitably. His functions cannot be defined in a ritual. It cannot be ascertained by a formal law, as in the case of the priest, to what portion of the community he shall belong. Either of these limitations would defeat the end of his existence, he would cease to fill his proper place in the great order. The prophet lives as the witness of a continual presence and power dwelling in the nation, which it may forget, but of which it cannot rid itself. He must rise up, as the emblem of the conscience which he awakens, of the law concerning which he testifies; he must come as a thief in the night upon the guilty soul; he must not allow it to forget itself in the dizzy whirl of events, or the monotony of observances; he must make it feel that both alike speak of a living person, who is coming out of his place to judge, whose day is at hand. To fasten this fact upon the mind and heart of the people, he must oftentimes do strange acts; he and his children are for signs and wonders; he must walk barefoot; he must carry on a mimic siege; he must see his wife die and not weep; he must marry an adulteress; by all means he must break the yoke of familiarity and custom. And yet he is most orderly. From first to last he is a witness for order. The neglect of institutions, the indifference to Divine precepts, the recklessness of the everlasting covenant,—these are his charges against kings, and priests, and people. If he reveals the inward law of God, it is in the outward law that he learns its nature and mystery; if he desires communion with God, it is in the temple he expects to enjoy it, and to behold His glory; if he is stricken with a sense of his own iniquity, and of his people's, it is a coal from the altar touching his lips, which purges it away; the desolation of the beautiful city calls forth all his human feelings; the loss of the Shechinah is the key-note to his most melancholy and awful religious musings.

Such are the most obvious characteristics of the Jewish prophet, the appointed witness for a spiritual faculty and life in man. According to the doctrine, then, that an outward appointment is the great cause of corruption and hypocrisy in the Church, it ought to appear that the race of prophets was far more uniformly pure and exemplary than the race of priests; that the abominations which we know are charged upon the one, had no counterparts among the other. But if we are to believe Scripture, this was not the case at all. There were just as many false prophets as there were scandalous priests; just as many who pretended to be uttering the word of the Lord, when they were but speaking a vision of their own hearts, as there were who could not distinguish between the clean and the unclean, or who made the offering of the Lord to be abhorred. There were as many who abused the spiritual call as the outward ordination. But this remark is by the way. My main object is to fix the reader's attention upon this point, that the best prophets were still Old Testament ministers; that they were not ministers of the Spirit.

The Quakers will not deny this. But wherein did the prophet come short of the dignity of a New Testament minister? He exactly answers to their definition of one. Take away the law, the priesthood, the sacrifices, and leave simply the prophet, and we have the Quaker idea of the Christian ministry in its most noble and complete manifestation: for the Jew is a witness to spiritual life; he obeys a spiritual impulse; he speaks of the Living Word dwelling in the heart; he speaks by the Spirit. Surely, if they are right, the prophet stands on a much higher level than Peter and Paul, the witnesses for outward acts, the preachers of Christ's death and resurrection. And so the early Friends evidently thought; for all the precedents of their proceedings are drawn from the records of his. Their sudden appearances, and utterances, and witnessings at the gates of cities, were copied (not accurately, I conceive, since the reverence for order and institutions, for sacred places and national worship, which were so conspicuous in the original, were wholly omitted in the imitation—but still copied) from the acts of the Old Testament seer, and had no sort of type or warrant in apostolical practice. For, strange to say, the apostles of our Lord, appointed to introduce a new dispensation, addressing a sense-hardened people, and foretelling the most awful crisis of their history as at hand, did nevertheless, in their outward conduct and bearing, entirely depart from that prophetical model which was constantly before their eyes, and which, for other purposes, they studied most diligently. All the sensible and startling peculiarities of the prophetical character were abandoned by men who proclaimed that they were sent by

Heaven to announce the fulfilment of the promises made to the fathers, the accomplishment of law and prophecy. Far, indeed, were they from saying, that the function was obsolete; its essential characteristics were represented in themselves. They had no authority to declare that even its accidental features were lost, any more than they had authority to abolish sacrifices or circumcision. Agabus might still bind the girdle on his hands and feet; the daughters of Philip the deacon might prophesy; but the especial ministers of the New Covenant were throughout asserting for themselves a different function from this. They would not even submit to the voices of brethren or sisters whom they acknowledged to be rightfully inspired. Paul went up to Jerusalem in defiance of their expostulations and warnings.

But whence this difference? What is the explanation of it? We say, that the difference arose from this, that in the days of the prophets the Spirit was not yet given, for that Christ was not yet glorified. The priests and sacrifices in the Jewish Commonwealth testified of a Divine constitution established in the Word. The order of prophets testified of a Divine Spirit actuating and energizing in man; but as the person of the Word was not yet manifested, so neither was the person of the Spirit. The mystery was hid for ages and generations. Each new step in the Divine plan is a preparation for the discovery of it; and faithful men are enabled to apprehend it before it is yet fully made known; first, by the undeviating regularity of the priesthood, like the settled succession of day and night; then, by the gusts of prophetical inspiration, like the wind blowing where it lists; lastly, by the inseparable connection of one with the other. The one, when alone, a mere collection of chords, from which no sound of music could proceed; the other, at best, a mere Æolian harp, from which a sweet note might now and then come forth, but utterly incapable of satisfying the soul with any sustained or continuous harmony. But when the Son of God came in human flesh, to proclaim Himself the source of all the order of the universe, it was inevitable that the outward organization which had been foretelling His advent should be converted into one which assumed it for its ground; and for the same reason it was to be expected, that when the Spirit of Truth, who proceeded from the Father and the Son, was given by the ascended Lord, to testify of the Father and of Him, the prophetical dispensation, which had been opening the way for this great manifestation, should undergo a corresponding change. The occasional glimpses of a Divine Lord of man, the beautiful vision in the plain of Mamre, the angel in the bush, and he who did wondrously before Manoah, — these preludings of the incarnation, as Bishop Bull calls them, had been lost in the full swell of the words, "Lo, I am with you always." The crucified man had been declared, by the resurrection, to be the Son of God with power, — the ever-present King of man. But the foretastes of *this* revelation in the Old Testament, did not fall farther short of the revelation itself, than the sudden inspirations under the Old Testament fell short of the meaning expressed in the words, "When he ascended up on high, he received gifts for men, that the Lord God might *dwell* among them." The Apostles, therefore, could not, without sinking their dignity as New Testament ministers, have given the same form to the prophetical office which it had assumed under the old dispensation. They believed themselves to be continually, not momentarily, inspired; they felt that it was their sin to doubt of this continued inspiration; a sin not to act upon the principle of it; a sin to do anything which would weaken the perception of it in the minds of those to whom they preached. They therefore delivered their appointed message with perfect calmness and coherency. They had their commission, and this was a surer token that they had the Spirit with them to govern them, than any impulses and emotions could possibly have been. They were therefore always ready to preach, and always able to be silent. This was their notion of a New Testament ministry, and we say it ought to be ours. As ministers of the New Covenant, we must draw our rule of conduct from Apostles and not from Prophets. It is nothing to us that the holy men of old were sometimes called from the sheepfolds to be the witnesses of a spiritual presence to the people, and that this inward call sufficed, without any other designation. We know that the Apostles of our Lord received from Him a formal and express designation, before He gave them powers to go and preach in the villages whither He Himself would come; that after His resurrection, He gave those Apostles a new and more awful commission, accompanying it with the words, " Receive ye the Holy Ghost;" that after His ascension they completed their numbers by an external arrangement before the Holy Ghost endued them with powers to testify of the risen King. It is nothing to us if these

Prophets, in exact conformity with the nature of their office, and the end for which it was instituted, waited for a conscious afflatus before they could utter their Divine oracles. We know that St. Paul said,—" If I do this willingly, I have a reward; but if *against my will*, a dispensation of the Gospel is committed to me. . . . A necessity is laid upon me, yea, wo' is me, if I preach not the Gospel." We know that he set it forth as the peculiarity of a New Testament preacher, that he put no veil over his face, that he used great plainness of speech. We know that now his preaching consists of a plain statement of actual facts, now of a long historical deduction, now turns upon some point connected with the habits, national character, and circumstances of the people to whom he speaks,— is not merely eloquent, but at times most skilfully rhetorical,—but never exhibits a man over-mastered by a power which prohibits him from expressing him-self in that way which is most suitable to the spiritual wants of his hearers. Was this because he wanted zeal? Or was it because he possessed an intensity of zeal which would never permit him for a moment to lose sight of the end of his apostleship; to sacrifice it for the sake of any pleasant feelings or emotions; to think about his own mind, when his business was to go forward; or to overlook any instruments which God had placed within his reach? Was it because he had not the Spirit? Or was it because he was under the habitual government of that Spirit who hindered him from surrendering himself to his own tastes or emotions, to his own projects or fears, and which con-verted every object in nature or art, all history, all passing events, to the service of the sanctuary? Once more, it is nothing to us that, under the old economy, there were prophetesses as well as prophets, and that during the interval between the establishment of the Christian Church and the destruction of the Jewish Commonwealth, this part of the system may, like all its other mere accidents, have been gradually disappearing indeed, but not have actually ceased. If there had been any restriction whatever, any, I mean, but what is reserved in the depths of Divine Wisdom, as to the subjects of the prophetical call, it would not seem to have answered its purpose as a balance to the rigid formality of the priestly institution. But when the Apostle of the Gentiles announced, that he would have women keep silence in the churches, we perceive at once that the principle which had been all along asserted in the regular organization of the Jewish Church, now that the formal constitution had been brought into union with the spiritual power, was to become a universal law. If St. Paul had merely suggested this rule as one which was expedient, in order to meet Jewish and heathen prejudices, we easily admit that the Omnipotent Spirit might be expected at different periods practically to annul it. But if he was actually restraining a practice common among both Jews and heathens, and if he was doing this professedly upon principles connected with the divinely appointed relation of the sexes to each other, we can have no doubt that the Spirit of Order, by the mouth of his chosen witness, was announcing the law of his own commonwealth. And that the Holy Spirit does not break down eternal laws and ordinances, for the mere sake of bearing witness to his power, is one of the fundamental maxims of Christian morality; because power is the handmaid of love and order, and when it forsakes their fellowship, and claims a separate existence, is devilish, not godlike.

In this case, as in all the others we have as yet considered, it seems that the Quaker is guilty of the very sin which he imputes to his brethren ; that he is the reviver of the old economy while he is professing to assert the glory of the Gospel. And it will be seen how remarkably his complaints against a succession of ministers illustrate this tendency. Just as he will not allow that in a universal and spiritual dispensation Baptism can take the place of Circumcision, the Eucharist of the Passover, so he cannot understand how in such a dispensation the succession by merely laying on of hands can take place of the Levitical and Aaronic succession. And just as I maintained, that the difference between a national dispensation and one which is spiritual and universal is realized in the difference between these two sets of institutions, and is lost when the old institutions are merely abolished ; so I maintain, that the same difference is set in the clearest light by the change from a ministry which is permanent in a particular tribe and family, to one which is perpetuated by ecclesiastical tradition, and that those who, upon Quaker grounds, reject this last method as carnal and secular, have no escape but that of slavishly imitating the most superficial and transitory peculiarities of a bygone period.

3. The last point to be considered is that of ministerial gifts. There were, as everyone knows, under the old dispensation, schools of the Prophets. But we must not lay such stress upon this fact as to deny, that in many cases the Prophet's call was itself

that which endowed him with the functions necessary for his task.   At any rate there was, it should seem, no outward act by which he became invested with the powers that he afterwards exercised.*   If what I have said respecting the nature of his office be true, it could not have been otherwise.   There was no great difficulty in understanding, that the Priest might be attired with his solemn robes, and invested with his awful authority, by a rite of consecration; his endowments were matter of formal, legal explanation.   But no idea which had yet been presented to the mind of the Jew, could have enabled him to understand how gifts of so subtle and inexplicable a character as those which the Prophets exercised, could have been transmitted by any similar method.   The man of holy meditation, whose life is a witness to his own continual sense of an unseen presence, comes forth, and awakens in kings, or priests, or people, the feeling of their own subjection to an eternal law, which they have forgotten or resisted.   By eloquence and song he rouses the spell-bound, death-stricken conscience of the nation; compels it to remember that it is within the bonds of an everlasting covenant; and shews what judgments must startle it out of its long sensual dream.   The acknowledgment of an operation from above, inspiring the understanding of the Prophet, comes at the same moment to the mind of the hearer with the consciousness of a secret wonderful operation upon himself.   He does not distinguish with any accuracy between the power which has raised the teacher into a

* The case of Elisha may be considered an exception.   But was not a prophet in Samaria in some sense a substitute for the priest, or, at all events, a witness for the institution?

poet, and himself into a man ; still less does he know from whom either impulse proceeds. He perceives only that there is some deep influence at work, invisible, indefinite, incomprehensible.

But, happily for that age, and for all ages to come, the duties of the Prophet were not limited to this task. Beneath this consciousness of a living judge spying out his ways, with the awful thoughts which it generates, other desires discover themselves in the mind of the holy Israelite, which the teacher is to educate by certain promises and glorious hopes. Through him man is to be taught, not only of that within him which fears and trembles before God, but of that which nothing but the vision of God can satisfy. The same event which is to set free the conscience, so far as its fears spring from the dread of sin, not the love of it, is also that which is to present these longings with their perfect object. The coming of the Lamb of God, who is to take away the sin of the world,—of Him who is to shew men the Father—this, consequently, is that glorious consummation of all past history, to which the prophetic eye is always turned, and in the glories of which every true Israelite, whether still sojourning on earth or departed from it, understands assuredly that he shall be a partaker. But on this hope is entailed another, equally exhilarating and still more mysterious. The spirit in man, striving after this perfect Object, hereafter to be revealed, feels that when it is admitted to behold him, it will need to be sustained by a life proceeding from Himself—feels that, if it is admitted to converse with Him, it will need the assurance that He also is conversing with it. An unspeakable communion, a Spirit

witnessing with our spirit, nothing less than this can
be the boundary of the aspirations which have been
thus wonderfully called out. The Prophet meets this
deepest cry of the inner man ; and the promise of the
Spirit being poured from above, and the desert blos-
soming with the rose, is indissolubly linked to the
promise of a King who shall reign in righteousness,
and in whom the glory of the Most High shall shine
forth.

As the mind of the Prophet himself rose to the level
of these anticipations, it is impossible but that he must
have perceived a distinction between that spirit in him
which longed for intercourse with the Everlasting
Spirit, and those faculties of thought and expression,
by which he was able to impart the desires and hopes
with which he had been inspired, to other men. Both,
he will have felt, are subject to a Divine impulse, a
Divine government, but one is in some sense a Divine
faculty, meant for fellowship with that which is Divine,
not realizing its own properties but in that fellowship;
the other is meant to obey a motion with which,
strictly speaking, it cannot sympathise. But the
deeper, the diviner faculty, is the more universal; this
belongs to me as a man ; this is the privilege of my
race ; the other is specially imparted to me for wise
and gracious purposes ; distinguishing me from my
fellows ; to be received as an awful trust ; to be used
for their benefit. Hence, in that great period of
manifestation to which he looked forward, he will, at
times, have anticipated, — first, that in close connection with the revelation of Him who is the
object of desire to all nations, there would also be a
revelation of Him who had been moving secretly

the hearts and understandings of men; next, that this revelation would in some striking manner be at once the assertion of Him as holding fellowship with men universally, and as bestowing those special gifts by which some men are qualified to be the guides and teachers of their brethren.

Whether this anticipation did take a definite form in the minds of the Prophets or not, we can tell how it was realized. The Son of God selects His chosen servants, the heralds of His kingdom, from the fishermen of Galilee. With them He converses for three years, teaching them to apprehend mysteries which had been kept hid from generations; telling them that they were permitted to see that which Kings and Prophets had not seen; in all His intercourse with them, still treating them as men destined for a work — not merely imparting to them a knowledge of truth, but a method of communicating it. But, after the call which these disciples had received; after the wonderful discipline by which He had so long prepared them; after He had reappeared to them in His risen form, and breathed on them, saying, " Receive ye the Holy Ghost;" still He told them that they were to tarry in Jerusalem to receive the promise of the Father; and that then, and then only, should they have power from on high to perform their work. As I have remarked before, they were met, not as individuals, but as a college; they had formally completed their number when this promise was fulfilled. And what was the fulfilment? The deep mystery of it, I have contended before (herein following the Church, which has fixed Trinity Sunday to follow next upon Whitsunday), consisted in the formal declaration of the Holy Spirit as a Person, the assertion of the Divine Unity of the Father and the Son in Him, and in the establishment of a Universal Church. But this is inseparably connected in Scripture with the conferring of powers on a set of men previously marked out to be Ministers of Christ. The call of Christ was not sufficient; here was a formal endowment with the gifts which Christ had designed for them when He bade them leave their nets, and which He had now received for them on high.

Signs, we know, accompanied the first great declaration of this Divine Presence in the Church. Those signs were like the twig or clod of earth which in ancient feoffments attested the delivery of a portion of land to a certain person and his heirs for ever. We should as little expect them to be continually repeated, as that the twig or clod should be solemnly presented to the new possessor, whenever he performed a fresh act of ownership. But the principle asserted by these signs, we affirm to be perpetual. The Spirit of God, by a wonderful demonstration, declares that He is dwelling among men; that an organized body of men has been provided for His habitation; that through this body His blessings are to be transmitted to the world; that through a portion of this body, His blessings are to be transmitted to the rest. Everything on this great day of spiritual inspiration speaks of preparation, order, distinction, unity. No chance or casual moment is selected, but the period of an ancient festival; no secret place, but an upper chamber in the temple; no chance individual, but men who have been for years openly preparing for the work. Whatever system, then, teaches that a minister is not publicly, and openly, and once for all endowed with certain powers and faculties for his work, these powers being sustained within him by the constant presence of Him who bestows them; whatever system conveys the notion, that the minister, being such by virtue of his inward call, is either then invested with the requisite gifts, or receives them afterwards, from time to time, by sudden movements and inspirations, we affirm is essentially an Old Testament system. And the consequences of such a system must infallibly be these:—The mere spiritual faculty, which is awakened in him by the voice of the Spirit of God, will be confounded with that Spirit himself; his personality will be forgotten in his operations; there will be a fearful confusion between the human speaker and the invisible power which speaks in him, alternating with a continual attempt to separate them; the intellectual faculties and endowments will first be despised, because they are supposed to have no connexion with the Spirit; and then will be confounded with the faculty which is truly Divine and spiritual in man, when both are found to proceed from the same source, and the former to be the means of evoking the latter. I say, if we considered wherein the Old Testament system was defective, and how the blanks are filled up in the New; and then heard of a scheme in which these blanks were restored, without, however, a restoration of those other portions of the old system, which prevented that which was necessarily imperfect from being evil, we should look for all these mischiefs as the fruits of it. And the actual history of the Quakers fulfils every one of these predictions. The belief in the Personality of the Spirit, in his difference from the spiritual life which He originates, has been that truth which they have found it most difficult to realize, and which has been continually slipping away from them. Their ministers, even in the best age of their society, were almost idolized. They have veered continually between contempt for the intellectual powers generally, and a vast over-appreciation of them, when they seemed to be under spiritual guidance. And all these contradictions are now reaching a head, and threatening the extinction of their body.

The Presbyterian.

We pass to those whose objections are principally and expressly against Episcopacy. Some of these turn upon the idea of the Church, some are derived from the letter of Scripture, and some are founded upon experience. The first take this form—' Christ is the only Bishop of his Church. All attempts to substitute another overseership, for His, are founded upon a misconception of our relation to Him. The words, " Call no man your father upon earth, for one is your Father which is in heaven," though they do not interfere with the acknowledgment of spiritual fathers in some sense, for St. Paul constantly calls himself one, do assuredly confound all such pretensions to fatherhood as the Bishops by the very nature of their office put forth. Assumption and domination, the very opposite qualities to those which should appear in a ministry, are implied in the conception of this function. And secondly, it is not borne out by the least warrant of revelation. That the word

ἐπίσκοπος is to be found in the Acts of the Apostles,
no one will dispute. But it is found in such connex-
ions as shew that the officer whom it denotes was not
distinguished from the Presbyter—that the Apostles,
at all events, did not look upon the distinction as in
any wise connected with the being of the Church.
If, then, we would have a Church upon a scriptural
platform, framed according to Apostolical precedent,
there seems little doubt that Bishops would find no
place, or a very unimportant place in it. But, thirdly,
it may be said that we cannot return strictly to those
precedents, that the Church has a principle of life
and authority in itself, and that we are to consider
the way in which institutions have actually developed
themselves. Very well; then look at all the cruelty,
usurpation, pride, secularity, which have been manifested by these spiritual fathers. And then say,
whether the history of the Church be not as conclusive a witness against them as the words of
inspiration.'

It is evident that the objection which is founded
upon the constitution of the Church, does not merely
affect the principle of Episcopacy. Its application is
very wide indeed. Presbyterians in general have
perceived that it strikes at the notion of any human
priesthood. If the fact that Christ is the universal
Bishop, interfere with the existence of earthly Bishops,
the fact that He is the Priest of his Church, of course
makes it impossible that any inferior person should
usurp that name. Probably the last case will be felt
to be stronger than the first; at all events, many
persons are found to denounce the use of the words
ἱερεύς and *Sacerdos* in the Divine economy, who will

contend stoutly for the importance of Bishops. Now I wish it might be considered, that if these phrases be on this ground denied to the ministers of the Church, they must on the same ground be denied to the members of it. The words, "We are made Kings and Priests unto God," which are so often quoted to confute the pretensions of a particular caste or ministry, are themselves profane and dangerous words. They are appropriating to the servants the acts and offices which, according to this doctrine, exclusively appertain to the Lord. Nor can the argument stop here. There must be a careful weeding out in theological books, and above all, in the Book of Revelation, of every phrase which, being first used to describe the head of the body, is afterwards applied to the body itself, or to any of its members. I beseech any one calmly and seriously to reflect upon the effect which such a change must produce—I do not say in the dialect of Christianity, but—in its deepest and most essential principles. For surely, if it have one principle which more essentially belongs to it than another, this is the one, that the language which makes Christ known to us, is the only language which can fitly make the Church known to us. Not merely Catholic divinity, but Puritan divinity, recognises the identification of offices in Christ and in his faithful members, as involved in the very idea of the Gospel. Where, I ask, is the line to be drawn?

Whence arises the propriety of the doctrine, that the state of the whole Church, and of each member of the Church, is the image of his state who has redeemed it; and the impropriety of the doctrine, that every

office in the Church is the image of some office performed by Christ in his own person—is the means by
which that office is presented to men, and made
effectual for them through all time?

I have no more earnest desire than that the
proposition which I have put forward: '*If the
Incarnation mean anything, if the Church be not a
dream, all offices exercised by her on behalf of humanity
must be offices first exercised by Christ*,' should be set
side by side with the Presbyterian proposition, '*It is
profane and wicked to apply to ordinary human
creatures, the names which designate the works and
offices of Christ*,' that each should be pushed to its
furthest consequences, and that each should be submitted to the judgment of the holiest men among
those whose educational prejudices would lead them
to reject Episcopacy. I have no fear as to the result;
and I am quite sure that a great collateral advantage
would follow from this method of considering the
subject. We are constantly asked how we dare to
lay so much stress upon an outward ordinance, as if it
had anything to do with the great essential truths of
the Gospel. Is it not at best a mere outwork of
Christianity? Our answer is derived from this great
Presbyterian argument. That cannot be a trifle which
involves the most opposite conception of the whole
order of the Church and of human society. If the
objection we have been considering be a true one, the
language which the most earnestly religious men have
been using, at the times when they were most religious,
when they were striving to express the most spiritual
and fundamental truths, is inconsistent language, and
must be abandoned. If, on the other hand, our

principle be a true one, it must be a question of the highest practical moment, whether the idea of Christ's Episcopacy or of his Priesthood can be preserved among men, when that, which upon this hypothesis is the Divine method for preserving them, has been rejected.

2. 'But this view, however it may be defended by theories, receives no justification from Scripture.' I admit at once, that if the Acts of the Apostles were set before me, and I were desired to make out from them alone what the office of the Overseer was, as distinguished from that of the Presbyter, I should decline the task as hopeless. Nor do I think, that if I were allowed to add to the hints which this book supplies, all that I could gather with respect to these particular names from the Epistles, I should be much nearer to satisfaction. My difficulty, I confess, is to understand how, from these scattered notices, the Presbyterian has been able to arrive at the clear and satisfying conclusion, that the whole Church for thirteen centuries, and the greater part of the Church for sixteen centuries, has been utterly wrong in believing that such an officer as the one who is understood by the word Bishop is meant to exist in it. I should be sorry upon such evidence to condemn the very paltriest ceremony which could allege a similar prescription in its favour. Of course, therefore, I should be equally sorry to put in such evidence as supplying the original title-deed of the institution. For, were there no other, I should scarcely know how to state the question which is to be settled. The Presbyterian would not allow me to word it thus: 'Did there exist in the time of the Apostles an order of priests distinct

from that of Bishops?' for he does not admit that there is an order of priests any more than one of Bishops, nor should I be at all anxious to ascertain how soon the functions which I attribute to the priest became separated from those which I suppose belong to the Bishop. The only point, therefore, which could be brought into debate, would be whether the word ἐπίσκοπος always means, in the language of the New Testament, the pastor of a number of congregations, and the word πρεσβύτερος always means, in the same language, the pastor of one; a question which I should be inclined to answer in the negative. But when I turn again to these Acts and these Epistles, I find a name which puzzles me much more than either of these; one which meets me at every turn, one which is implied in every sentence of them, one of which I must get a solution somewhere if I can. What manner of people are these *Apostles* whose acts are recorded in the work of St. Luke, whose letters are preserved for the perpetual instruction of the Church? It may be answered, 'They were the persons selected by our Lord to be with Him in His temptations while He was upon earth, and to bear witness of His resurrection after He had left the world.' No doubt these were the functions of the first twelve disciples. The Incarnation of Christ was to be the ground of the new kingdom; it was needful that there should be persons who had seen and handled the Word of life. About this matter there is no dispute. The question is, first, whether the fruits of the Incarnation ceased with the time when our Lord left the world, or whether they only then began to shew themselves; next, whether the form which Christ Himself gave to the infant kingdom, was the form which it was to retain through all the future circumstances of its development; and therefore, 3rdly, whether the office of the Apostles was to be defunct when the particular circumstances which made the name appropriate had ceased to exist. If the apostleship were inseparably connected with its first accidents, it would seem strange that St. Paul, whose calling was of an altogether different kind from that of the twelve, who had not been with our Lord during his stay upon earth, who was expressly a witness of that state of glory in which we believe that Christ is now, as much as when He stopped the persecutor on the way to Damascus, should have so eagerly asserted for himself the position and the powers of an Apostle. It would seem strange, too, that those powers, in virtue of which the other Apostles were able to go forth witnessing of their Master's resurrection, were not those which they derived from Him while He was upon earth, not those even which they received from Him immediately after His resurrection, but were those which came upon them after He had gone out of the sight of men, and was ascended on high that He might fill all things. The question, therefore, to be decided when this evidence is brought before us, is simply whether there was or was not to be continued in the Church, any office corresponding in its essential characteristics to that one which we judge from the New Testament to be the distinguishing one of the Church at its foundation. The common opinion is, that by the perpetuation of this office the Church has been perpetuated; the connexion of different ages with each other realized; the wholeness and unity of the body declared. The changes which have taken place in the condition of this office we suppose to be changes as to name, as to the number of the persons filling it, as to the limits of their government; changes, some of them presupposed in the very existence of a body which was to have an unlimited expansion; none of them affecting its nature or its object. The Presbyterian says that no institution of the kind does exist in the Church; that is to say, that the platform of the Church in the present day is not the apostolic platform. Yet he says this in the same breath with which he protests against our departure from the simplicity of the New Testament practice, and calls upon us to abandon all ecclesiastical precedents for the sake of conforming to it.

3. One of the main reasons which he gives for this exhortation, is the gross corruption and secularity which have been the result of the Episcopal system wherever it has been established. I neither meet this charge by saying that there is no foundation for it, nor by explaining away the instances which are brought forward in support of it; nor by resorting to the seldom satisfactory common-place, that the abuse of an institution is no argument against its use. I might with far more reason and success produce the facts, which prove that in nearly every case in which the Church has enlarged her borders, in which the commission, " Go ye into all nations," has been really acted out, Bishops have been the instruments of fulfilling the command and obtaining the promise. But I would rather place the argument on another ground: I would undertake to shew, and I would go through all ecclesiastical history in support of the position,

that the secularity of Bishops has been in all cases the
effect of their *not* believing in the dignity and divinity
of their own ordination ; that the assumption of any
particular Bishop has always been the effect of his
denying the dignity and effect of his brethren's ordination.   You shew me a Bishop who is in all respects
a splendid feudal lord, with his hounds and his falcons,
his sumptuous table, his armed retainers.   Well !
I see a man who feels about his office, just as you do,
that it carries with it no Divine authority; that he is
under no responsibility for the exercise of it except to
the class in which he moves, and to the civil power
which has added certain honours to it.   My wish is to
cure him of the habit of feeling which you would rivet
in him.   But you will say, perhaps, ' Were he a
Christian minister he would not be tempted to this
secularity.'—What do you mean by such words ?
Do you mean that he would not be tempted to *any*
secularity—that the parochial clergyman, comfortably
settled in his manse, has not the temptation to sink
into the habits of an ordinary member of the middle
class ; that the mendicant friar, or the itinerant Protestant preacher, is not liable to be infected by the set
to whom he ministers, and by whom he obtains his
livelihood ?   You cannot say this without outraging
the authority of Scripture and the witness of experience.   Secularity of some kind (of what kind the
character of the age, of the man, of his company,
determines) has assailed, and must always assail every
man in this world ; and I believe there is no deliverance from it for any man, but in the belief that he has
a vocation.   Whether it is in accordance or not with
the order of Providence, that the ministers of Christ's

flock should be also ministers of the nation, and that each class of the nation should feel the influence of some one of its classes, I shall consider in a future section. On the subject of Episcopal assumption, I need only refer to the history of popes and patriarchs for a proof, that the occasion of it is ever an exaltation of some advantage of place or circumstance connected with the order above the order itself.

Objections to an absolving power in ministers.

I have said that the main principle of the Presbyterian argument is as directly opposed to the idea of a priesthood as it is to the idea of Episcopacy. In dealing with the one question, then, I have implicitly discussed the other. Moreover, the doctrine of a priesthood is so much involved with the doctrine of sacrifice, that my last section may be looked upon as a sufficient statement of my views respecting it. Still there is so much horror in many minds of that absolving power which I have attributed to the Christian Bishop and to those whom he endows with it, and their complaints involve consequences of so practical a character, that I think I should be wrong not to give them a separate consideration. I do not class them under the head of Presbyterian objections, because there are many Episcopalians who appear to share in them. They may be expressed thus:

'According to St. Paul, those who believe in Christ are justified from all things from which they could not be justified by the Law of Moses. Ambassadors are sent forth to declare Christ's Gospel to men, in order that they may not be prevented from believing by the want of hearing; in order that if they believe they may receive this justification and freedom of the conscience. This is the true office of the minister; all others are accidental and subordinate to it. He may own orders and governments in the Church, Presbyterian, Episcopal, Apostolical, what you will; but the preaching of Christ is his true and essential function: his commission is to do this, this first, this above all things. When he pretends that he has some other way of relieving the conscience than this; when he says that he has the power of pardoning and absolving,—that he may pronounce men free from their sins,—he is not only committing a fearful usurpation upon the rights of Christ, he is actually misunderstanding and denying the true character of his own office. He deprives himself of his true power, in his eagerness to grasp a power which has never been given him by God, and can never be of the least use to man.'

There is one point which is very important to take notice of in reference to this subject. According to the idea which has always existed in the Christian Church, the same person to whom the function of absolving is committed has also the function of administering the Eucharist. These two duties never have been separated, and it is most needful that they should be contemplated in their relation to each other; for if the Eucharist be that act in which the worshipper is especially brought into direct communion with his Lord, that act in which the mere human and visible agent is most entirely lost and forgotten, or only contemplated as one who bears witness that He whom he serves is a living and actual person, we must suppose that this is a key to the whole character of the office, in whatever way it may be exercised. If, again, the Eucharist involve at once a confession of sins on the part of the receivers, a thankful acknowledgment of a state of fellowship and blessedness with their Lord, into which they have been brought, though they may have walked most unworthily of it, the acceptance of a pledge of forgiveness for the past, strength for the present, a strength only to be realised by union with the invisible Lord, a promise of future blessings, to be attained in the same way and in no other, this would seem to determine the nature of that particular function which the minister presumes to exercise when he pronounces absolution. His whole object is to present Christ to men and men to Christ really and practically. Suppose him in the congregation, he is there to represent its unity, to offer it before God as a whole body, to confess the sins which its members have committed by separating themselves from the body. Then he is a witness of Christ's continual intercession for the entire Church. Suppose him alone, with any particular member of the congregation, he is with him to preserve him in the unity of the Church, to present before God his tears and contrition for having lived unworthy of his position in it. Then he is a witness of Christ's distinct intercession for every member of his flock. But still this can be but half his duty. The incarnation means very little, the kingdom of God is a mere delusion, if there be not a voice speaking from heaven as well as one crying from earth : if the one be not an answer to the other, if the minister may not say to the congregation, 'God has heard your petitions, rise up as pardoned men, with strength to offer up praises and prayers, with strength to do your work,' the confession is but half real, the Gospel is not real at all. And if he may not say in like manner to the sick and solitary penitent, God accepts thy tears and pardons thy sin, I do not see what he means by saying that he has authority to *preach* forgiveness of sins. He preaches forgiveness to those who will accept it, understanding its nature and purpose; receiving it not as a licence to the conscience, but as a deliverance of it. He delivers forgiveness under precisely the same conditions. How many of the congregation are in a state of mind to claim their fellowship with Christ and each other, and so to take the mercy which is freely given them, whether the individual man can do this, God only knows. The absolver at all events has spoken the truth; he has acted out his commission; the rest he must leave. His public preaching, his private exhortations, are all intended to remove some stumbling-block out of the way of those to whom he has been sent; to explain to them the meaning of their confession and of his absolution; to prevent their offering the one or receiving the other in vain; to hinder them from turning either to an evil account.

Supposing this to be the case, it would seem that there is no greater peril in this doctrine, than in the one which makes preaching the main work and office of a minister. As to misconstruction, there is, at all events, no greater likelihood of it in the case of words which are not our own, which are spoken in the name of God, and on the most solemn occasion, than in the case of words, which, under whatever teaching from above, we have composed, which must be mixed with our own peculiar modes of expression and habits of thought. So much I think most be admitted by every one who considers the subject without prejudice. And the question which such a person might be inclined to ask, would perhaps be this: ' Where is the great difference? You mean by your absolving power just what others mean by preaching the Gospel. Let this be clearly understood, and then no Christian would object to your statements any longer.' My answer is, I cannot make this explanation, because it would not be a true one. I do conceive, there is very great difference between the notion that the act of absolution which the minister pronounces in the name of the Church is that act which interprets the object of his preaching, and the notion that he is sent to preach, and that because he preaches, he may, in a certain sense, absolve. The difference seems to me to be this: in the former case the minister presents Christ actually and personally to his congregation. His office is a witness of Christ's presence among them, of Christ's relation to them. It is grounded on the acknowledgment of an actual union between the body and its Head. In the other case there is much speech—it may be eloquent, it may be true speech— about Christ, his work, and his offices. But it is

> a painted ship
> Upon a painted ocean;

a description of what is very good and beautiful, and what man wants, but not the thing itself, not the reality. I appeal to the history of modern preaching whether this be not the case, and to the complaints of men in all directions, whether it is not felt to be the case. And if so, it must be a serious question in what way those ends may be best accomplished, which I fully believe that the objectors I am now addressing sincerely desire, the end of bringing men more directly in contact with the true and unseen Absolver; the end of making His ministers understand that they are nothing except as representatives of Him, that they do nothing, except as they lead men to the knowledge of Him. Let it be considered patiently and calmly, whether a priest, who habitually believes, that as he may confess in the people's name, so he may absolve in Christ's name, must not have a humbler sense of his own insignificance, a greater confidence in an invisible kingdom, a more serious conviction that all men are meant to be members of it, than one who believes that he has ever so many gifts, merely bestowed for the purpose of enabling him to announce the message of salvation. And do we not find, in fact, that the best of those men, whose education and theories would induce them to adopt the latter opinion, have been led in practical life, in the conduct and discipline of their flocks, in their intercourse with them as well as in their discourses to them, to act upon the former?

The followers of Mr. Irving.

Out of the heart of Presbyterianism have arisen a class of persons, whose objections to our Episcopacy assume the most opposite form possible to that which we were just now considering. A few words respecting this modern development of ecclesiastical feeling will throw great light upon the whole subject.

In answering the Quaker argument respecting the

relation of the Old to the New Testament ministry, I have maintained the idea of ministerial Succession to be one which is justified by the analogy of God's dealings, and which has not been made obsolete by any of the new conditions which the Gospel dispensation has introduced. The difference in the mode of presenting or manifesting the idea seems to be clearly determined by the difference between a national and a universal kingdom : the hereditary tradition, accompanied with a solemn consecration, expresses the character of the one ; make consecration the substance of the tradition, and abolish the family limitation, we have the true nature of the other. This conclusion is so obvious, and has been so much assumed in the history of Christendom, that there would seem to be no occasion for disputing about it, except with those who, like the Quakers, reject outward ordination altogether. Admit ordination, and you admit the principle of succession ; you admit the improbability of that succession having been, in any important instance, infringed by those who habitually recognized it ; at all events, you admit that the *onus probandi* lies upon those who allege such an infringement, to shew when it took place and wherein it consisted.

This, I say, would be the natural state of the argument, supposing no other consideration to intervene. But the sons of those who had abandoned Episcopacy came to feel that a great link—if my view of Episcopacy as the great bond of a Christendom life be the correct one, *the* great link—between them and the older Church had been cut off. They were therefore much more concerned than their fathers, who were not equally conscious of this severance, could be, to prove :

first, that there was some flaw in the idea of succession as it obtained among Episcopalians generally; secondly, that they possessed some adequate substitute for this idea. The flaw was easily found. The whole Church, to say the least from the time of Hildebrand, but most likely from a much earlier time, down to the Reformation, had been, with the exception of a few witnesses in the valleys of Piedmont, a popish and corrupt Church; through the Bishops of this Church and no other the transmission of powers and gifts must have come to those who claimed them in later days. But secondly, it was said that the reformed bodies had lost nothing by the breach of formal ministerial connexion with the first ages, seeing that they had preserved the really important succession; they had inherited the pure apostolical doctrine.

Now just so long as men could calmly acquiesce in the notion that Christians form a sect professing certain sound opinions, more probable and more useful than those of Mahomet or of Confucius—just so long as this notion was felt to correspond with the descriptions which our Lord and the Apostles give of the purposes for which they came into the world—these two statements seemed reasonable and satisfactory. It was nothing strange that the sect should almost cease for a time, or be only preserved in a few men, about whose very names there is great confusion, about whose opinions and practices a much greater; nothing strange that identity of opinions (though it might be somewhat hard to establish in a court of law the identity of the dogmas of the New Testament with those which prevailed in Scotland and Germany during the eighteenth century), should be received as the one sign that the sect had reappeared. But the moment any one was awakened to the fact that the Gospel spoke of a kingdom—a kingdom actually to be set up among men—they became exceedingly perplexed. At first it was easy to treat these words as belonging to the future, as pointing to that which shall be after a second appearing of our Lord, not to that which was the effect of his Incarnation and Ascension. But there was much which could not bear this construction; and supposing there was to be a Church in the world at all between the first and second advent, it must be something answering to these words, it could not be something wholly different in kind from that which they set forth. But a sect professing certain dogmas, would be something wholly different in kind from the Church therein spoken of. There was still an escape to the idea of a purely spiritual body, but that escape was fairly open only to the Quakers, and with them the Presbyterians had no sympathy. They had admitted an organization; they had said the spiritual life of the Church ought to express itself through this organization; they had looked upon the ministry as forming an indispensable part of it; they had constantly referred to the Scriptures as exhibiting the model and idea of the Church's constitution.

Pressed by these difficulties, the late Mr. Irving, in his commentary on the Book of Revelation, betook himself to the belief that the Kirk of Scotland had preserved a succession of ministers in its Presbytery; at the same time maintaining, as stoutly as any one of his countrymen could, that a human Episcopacy is incompatible with the idea of Christ's universal lordship. But it could not escape a person of so much reflection and honesty as Mr. Irving, first, that whatever succession of a ministerial kind had been foretold in the Scriptures, or believed in any age of the Church, was an Apostolical succession; that is to say, a succession of persons possessing the essential part of the Apostolical functions. And it was equally clear, that by his own argument he denied the descent of any *such* function upon the Scotch ministers. His position, therefore, could not be long tenable, and either Mr. Irving himself, or certainly his followers, soon abandoned it for another. They admitted, to a certain extent, the truth and validity of the Episcopal succession which had been in the Church hitherto; they admitted, at any rate, the importance of the idea of such a succession; but they said that something was yet wanting, and had been wanting ever since the first ages, to give the Church its true completeness: *viz.* a distinct order of Apostles, who should either supersede the present order of Bishops, or, at least, to whom they should do homage, and from whom they should derive their authority.

Now setting aside all questions which are merely collateral to this doctrine, as to the way in which the persons of these Apostles are to be ascertained, &c., the reader will see at once how much plausibility there must be in it, to men in the state of mind I have described. They have been taught that the Church for many centuries was in a kind of abeyance; they know from experience that no part of it is in a right condition now; they think that the faults they see are faults arising from disorganization; if they can discover a defect of organization which has existed from the very first ages, how easily are these facts explained, how evident the origin of them ! In like manner, the habit which they have received from their instructors, of looking to the Scriptures as the true guides to all notions respecting the nature of the Church ; and the conviction which they have acquired in their maturer years, that the Scriptures derive their explanation from the history of the Church, are by this hypothesis reconciled. They do homage to the plain letter of Scripture, and yet it is a letter which means nothing except in reference to the progress of Christ's kingdom. Thus, too, they are able to connect the idea of a restoration of spiritual life and spiritual gifts to the Church, with the strongest recognition of its organic and visible character. When there are such inward reasons for acquiescence in this faith, there is little use in making assaults upon its outworks. Men are not likely to be laughed out of an opinion which seems to bring all their other thoughts into harmony, merely by being told that they are paying a superstitious homage to the number twelve, or that the sudden recovery of an apostolic order after an intermission of eighteen centuries is most improbable. They will say, in answer to the first objection, that even if there be no meaning and mystery in numbers, they have the warrant of Scripture for attaching this number to this particular case. And in answer to the second, they will say that if it be the purpose of God to uphold His Church in the world, and to heal the breaches in it, they think it reasonable to believe that He will, by any means or by any interference, renew that which seems indispensable to it.

Nor can I help perceiving that the arguments by

which Episcopacy and Episcopal succession are some-times defended, have a tendency to strengthen these convictions. As Presbyterians have been the persons with whom writers on this subject have chiefly held controversy, they have in a manner assumed the existence of two orders in the Church, and tried, by such means as they had, to prove that a third was also necessary. Now this method of resolving the Church ministry into deacons and presbyters *plus* an episcopate must certainly leave an impression on the mind of any careful student of the New Testament, that this episcopate can have no close connexion with that apostolic order which is evidently the root of all others, and in which they all originally dwelt. Again, from certain ways of speaking respecting the Episcopal succession which have been prevalent among us, the feeling has certainly been communicated to many minds that it is necessary, because the *first* Apostles had an ordination from Christ Himself, and because the effect, or a certain portion of the effect, of that ordi-nation has communicated itself through a series of hands to those who represent them in later ages. I do not say that any defender of the succession would state the reason for it in this form, but certainly the contemners of it must suppose that it is intended; otherwise they would not resort to their jokes about a virus which must have lost its power by repeated inoculations, or about gifts which must have been spoiled through the unclean hands that have trans-mitted them. And supposing such a feeling in any degree to prevail, we can conceive how utterly shocking it must be to men whose belief is that Christ is still present in the Church, and that He would still

M 2

communicate actual powers to His ministers if their
faithlessness did not interfere.

But supposing it were calmly represented to those
who have adopted this theory, that, according to the
doctrine which has always prevailed in the Church, the
episcopate does contain in it the administration of the
sacraments, the delivery of absolution, the preaching
of the Gospel, the ministering to the sick and poor—
all the *functions*, in short, which were at any time
committed by our Lord to His immediate disciples;
and that the Bishops have, and ought to believe
they have, all needful *powers* for performing these
function: 2ndly, that their connection with previous
ages and with the first Apostles is maintained expressly
as a witness of the permanent constitution of the
Church, and therefore of the continued abiding of
Christ in it, and of each Bishop in each age being His
servant and the receiver of gifts and powers directly
from Him—they may begin perhaps to view the whole
subject somewhat differently. They may examine
somewhat more carefully into the grounds upon which
they have rested their belief of a super-episcopal
order, and if they should be convinced that any charm
which there may have been in the number of the
Apostles had reference to their Jewish position, and
was broken by the act of Christ Himself when He
called Paul to the same dignity, and through him
destroyed the middle wall between Jews and Gentiles;
that it was, at least, more likely, *à priori*, that an
office which had been established with so much
solemnity would be upheld by Divine power, than that
it would be destroyed by human unbelief; that in all
other cases unbelief displays itself in doubting and

denying the existence of powers, and mistaking the
character of a function actually possessed ; that such
unbelief will account for all the painful phenomena
which the history of the episcopate presents; they
may ask themselves with some anxiety, whether there
be any reason to expect that an order will be introduced
by signs and wonders which seems to be already in
being, whether there be anything to justify them in
standing aloof from the body of Christ's universal
Church, and in not submitting to those whom He
has Himself placed over it.

The Philosophical Objector.

Between this class of reasoners and the one with
whom I am next to engage, there seems to be not
one point of mutual understanding. The modern
rationalistic philosopher admits that the word 'priest'
is one which contains much historical significance ;
nay, which even yet is not obsolete, and may have a
good meaning. 'The error which men generally commit in this, as in all other cases, is that they do not
distinguish between the essential truth and the fleeting
applications of the word, that they do not see wherein
the real and valuable power of the priest consisted, and
who inherit that power in our day. Churchmen boast,
it is said, that priests were the conservators of letters,
and that they led men into the belief of a government
which is not outward but inward, not over the body
but over the mind. True, they did so; and for this
we are to remember them with gratitude. But they
who possess their name, and pretend to a formal succession from them, have no such influence; they do

not preserve science or letters, they are afraid of
both; they are anxious only to keep up their religious
system.   The real men of letters and of science, those
who make us feel what are the bonds of spiritual
intercourse between persons of different nations and
kindreds, those who lead us to the apprehension of
fixed laws—these are the true priests, these possess
the faculty, the true insight, to which men involuntarily pay homage; the more they have been recognized, the less has the outward ordination and the
nominal priesthood been regarded; ultimately they
alone will be honoured; the counterfeit thing will be
cast out as withered and worthless.'

There are indications in this language of a desire,
which I, at least, cannot regard without the greatest
sympathy—a desire to discover that which is real, and
to separate it from whatever is artificial, temporary,
and insincere.   I shall not inquire whether this desire
dwell deeply in the hearts of all who adopt the phrases
which express it; whether these phrases may not be
as easily learnt by rote, and as glibly repeated as any
others; whether they may not offer to some the
promise of an easy and comfortable substitute for any
zealous efforts to disengage their own minds from
the frivolity and falsehood which they so eloquently
denounce.   Such questions each person may fitly
propose to himself: I would much rather deal with
these words as they came forth from the person who
utters them with the least self-deception, with the
most inward longing to be honest himself and to make
his neighbours honest.   To such a person I would at
once concede that this main proposition is right.   The
man of letters and the man of science, I believe, are

called of God to the work in which they are engaged; they are his ministers—I would earnesly wish that they might feel themselves to be so. I will go further; I will admit that their function, especially that of any one who has a real poetical gift, does answer in several most important respects to that of the ancient prophet; that they may, without any impropriety, be said to perform a similar office, and to be endowed with powers which correspond to the circumstances of their different periods. In what sense they do not correspond, in what respect the words of the Jewish prophet have become a *Scripture* and are taken out of the circle of ordinary words, I hope to consider in the next section. Now I am speaking of them as living, acting, speaking men, and, looking at them in this light, I think it far more important to mark the grounds of their essential resemblance, than the occasions of their difference. So far from wishing the modern poet or philosopher not to consider himself as possessing a high vocation and a real inspiration, it is the feeling which I should most wish to awaken and cultivate in him. What I dread is that he should *not* feel this, that he should think his words are his own; that he should glorify himself on his powers, and so inevitably deprave them and abuse them. The misery of the last age, of its poets especially, was that they utterly cast away this belief. When they talked about a Muse speaking to them and teaching them, they did not mean what they said; it was a phrase merely which they adopted because Homer had used it and Virgil had copied it. There was not even the least sense of the words having been once spoken honestly; the poor old singer to the maidens of the Greek isles had, forsooth, invented a very clever and cunning 'machinery.' And those who could write edifying critiques on "Paradise Lost," could suppose that Milton had solemnly invoked that Spirit, who prefers before all temples the upright heart and pure, with the same profaneness, to assist him in a task of the same kind. What could an age which cherished such thoughts have produced, but ingenious satires upon the follies of the day, and elaborate efforts to clothe the ancients in its laces and ruffles?

By all means, then, let those who feel their gifts strong in them, train themselves to an awful and humble acknowledgment of them, and of the source from which they proceed. It is not the inclination which the students and artists of our land show to put forth these claims on their own behalf, which should make any religious man tremble. Just so far as they do this, they have taken a great step out of the infidelity of the last generation. What is alarming is the pretension which accompanies these claims; the loud talk about powers and faculties not derived but inherent; the practical evidence which our men of talent furnish by their scorn and contempt of others that they do rest upon these inherent powers, and do not recognize any sustaining, quickening inspiration. Now I cannot think that men who indulge in this language are likely to be prophets themselves, or to recognize the prophetic gift in their brethren. It seems to me, therefore, most needful for the sake of our men of letters and of the world, that both they and it should be reminded, by some clear and visible tokens, what they are, whence

their power comes, under what conditions it must be
exercised, who renders it effectual for the good of
men.   But no one desires that they, in their own
persons, should receive a visible designation.   Such a
designation would be incompatible with the character
of their office, and it would convey little instruction to
other men respecting their own position, seeing that
they regard the poet or man of letters as a person of
a peculiar order, following an impulse different from
that which they obey, and pursuing a different class of
objects.   But supposing there existed any set of men
who were occupied about the most obvious and interesting circumstances of humanity, those which are
common to the tradesman and mechanic with the man
of genius, those which are most strange but yet are
continually recurring, about marriage and sickness,
life and death; and supposing that while thus dealing
with that which belongs to all men, they were yet
dealing with it as related to those awful and inward
feelings which carry us out of the visible into the
unseen world; supposing they even connected these
earthly accidents with certain fixed and eternal laws
of that region, this class would seem to be one, which
from the general, continuous, and practical nature of
their duties, might well be selected as signs and instances to all men of the meaning and derivation of
all power; to the sage, of the meaning and derivation
of those powers with which he is especially entrusted.
Such a class would be the natural link between those
who are continually liable to lose their sense of a
Divine government in the monotony of daily occurrences, and those who are liable to lose it in the consciousness of their own energies.   And if it should

come to pass that the selected class should itself lose sight of its position by falling into either of these temptations, if it should merely court an outward distinction, and occupy itself in a round of outward services, forgetting its mysterious meaning; or if, in the desire to assert its difference from other vocations, it should become proud and self-exalting: then I know not what better or more terrible witness can be borne against these sins, what more terrible prophecy of the effects which must flow from them, than that ordination which has marked it out for the highest and lowest ministries; which has declared, that we exist for the sake of men, that all our authority is from God, that our only safety is in forgetting ourselves, our highest privilege to be instruments in connecting the members of our race with each other and with their Lord. Abolish our ordination, and you lose the strongest testimony which you have against our sins. You lose, too, I am well persuaded, one of the greatest securities against the degradation of our poets and men of learning, through sensual contamination or through spiritual pride.

The Romish System.

It remains that I should explain wherein the views I have expressed on the subject of the Christian ministry differ from those of the Romanists. It will be obvious at once, that on some most important points, I must be in agreement with them. For I have spoken of ministers as representing Christ to men; I have maintained that the absolving power is not a nominal but a real one; I have maintained that the

Apostolic functions and authority still exist in the Church; I have admitted that the Judaical institutions have their counterparts in the new dispensation. Let us inquire under each of these four heads, what points of similarity there are between that which I have asserted to be the Catholic principle, and that which is acknowledged to be the Romish one.

First, I have spoken of ministers as representing Christ to men. Long before there was the assertion of a supreme vicar of Christ upon earth, there was a feeling in men's minds, that the office of the priest is *vicarial*, that ministers are deputed by our Lord to do that work now which He did Himself while He was upon earth. This notion has gone into the heart of the Romish system. I believe it has created the system. Now those who laugh at the notion of a man like Athanasius contending to the death about an iota, will, of course, be much amused by my affecting to discover an important difference of signification in the words *representative* and *vicarial*. And, certainly, if the difference between the Nicene Fathers and the Arians was a difference about a word and not about a reality, those who contended upon either side were very weak and vain men. And if I suppose any charm to reside in these two words, so that the one which I reject might not be used in a good sense, and the one which I adopt in an evil one, I shall be exhibiting a less pardonable instance of folly. But I will endeavour to shew that the difference to which I allude, whether it be rightly or improperly expressed by these particular phrases, is as essential and practical a one as it is possible to conceive of. In the word *vicarial*, the Romanist means to embody his notion that the priest is doing the work of one who is absent, and who, only at certain times and under certain conditions, presents himself to men. By the word representative, I mean to express the truth that the minister sets forth Christ to men as present in his Church at all times, as exercising those functions himself upon which He entered when He ascended on high. Now it must be felt, I think, that this is a radical difference, not about a word, but about the most solemn question upon which the mind of man can be occupied. And it will be seen that it is no isolated difference. It stands in the closest connexion with all those which we have been taking notice of in former sections. The principle of the Catholic Church which I have endeavoured to develop in reference to Baptism, the Eucharist, the Creed, the Forms of Worship, is the principle of a direct, real, and practical union between men and their Lord. The doctrine of the Romish system, which we have discovered in each and all of these cases, is that the veil between us and the invisible world is not yet withdrawn; that offices and ordinances are not the organs through which men converse with their Lord and He with them, but are mere outward things, which He has stamped with a certain authority and virtue, or mere pictures which exhibit Him to the imagination. Happily, this system has never fully realized itself; there seems an impossibility in the nature of things that it should. The moment it becomes or nearly becomes that which it is always striving to be, it so entirely loses its meaning, it becomes such a merely oppressive phantom, that the judgments of God, and the faith as well as the infidelity of man, appear together to confound it.

2. It follows from what I have said, that the absolving power which I claim for the Catholic priest is altogether a different one from that which is claimed by the Romish priest. I do not say that it is a less power, it seems to me a much greater one. He who can, in Christ's name, declare to a man that the state of union with Christ, which was assured to him in baptism, is his state still; that he has committed evil by living inconsistently with it; that this evil shall not be imputed to him, though it may perchance be sorely punished for his good, if he turn to God and claim the better life which is his, in his Lord; that he shall have strength from Him to be His servant and do His will; that he shall know Him, and that this knowledge shall make him free: he who can pronounce these words confidently, because they are true and because he has received a commission to declare them to such and such men—neither their truth nor his commission being in the slightest degree affected by the unbelief and the consequent unrepentance of those to whom they are addressed—has a power of absolution affecting the past, the present, and the future, which he would be sorry indeed to exchange for any which have ever been exercised by those who claimed it vicarially as their own, not representatively as their Lord's. For he must perceive, if he know anything of history, that this vicarial power has been one which did not absolve the human spirit, but bound it with heavy chains, giving it no sense of the glorious liberty which Christ has purchased for it; not only leaving it but teaching it to grovel when God has provided wings wherewith it may soar. How could penances ever

have been translated from their proper and legitimate
use, as means whereby those evil habits may be subdued which make the spirit proud, and hinder it from
being free, into heavy shackles and torments of the
conscience, into checks upon all holy and thankful
devotion, into instruments of pride and self-exaltation,
if those who enjoined them had really felt that they
were acting on behalf of the great Redeemer and
Absolver; if they had not said within their hearts,
"The Lord delayeth His coming," and therefore had
thought themselves privileged to beat the men-
servants and the maid-servants, while they themselves
ate and drank and were drunken?   How could the
monstrous thought of indulgences ever have crept into
the minds of men who had not lost the sense of their
direct subjection to an invisible Lord, and therefore of
necessity had become the slaves of those whom they
professed to rule, obliged to cater to their fleshly and
worldly appetites, in order that they might keep them
in bondage?   These may be very old stories, but they
are written legibly upon the history of the world, not
to be exaggerated, doubtless, for the sake of establishing Protestant conclusions, but also not to be
erased by any chicanery of another kind; not to be
overlooked, because we may choose to fancy that other
facts of an opposite kind concern us more nearly.
Facts cannot contradict each other.   The records of
the miseries which the Romish system has produced,
cannot contradict those which prove even to the satisfaction of the most thoughtful Liberals of our day,
that the Catholic Church has conferred innumerable
blessings upon mankind. If we only understand
both they must confirm and illustrate each other.

What we want to discover is the point of their connexion.

3. This point, I believe, is found in that Romanist application of the vicarial doctrine which has reference to the episcopal or apostolic authority. According to the representative doctrine all ministers exhibit Christ in that office to which they are called. The whole body of bishops—each bishop in his own sphere—present him to men as the bishop or overseer of the Church. Once make ministers vicarial, and it is evident that we have the seed of an entirely new scheme. The oneness and universality of Christ's office of course distinguishes Him from each one of His representatives, and from the whole body of His representatives. But this oneness and this universality are utterly lost to the world, they are merely dreams—if Christ be absent from His Church. They must, therefore, be imaged somewhere, since they have lost their virtue as realities. Ministers must not only be vicars of Christ, but there must be a vicar of Christ; one who absorbs into himself, and exhibits in himself, his one and universal episcopacy. Here is the POPEDOM, an idea which may have been most gradual in its development, which could not come forth into actual manifestation as a Church idea, while one so very like it was openly realized as *the* idea of the World in the persons of the Roman emperors : but which, nevertheless, was latent in the minds of all ministers who assumed to themselves a vicarial character, in the minds of all laymen who acknowledged them in that character. The conception of an apostolical primacy in St. Peter, upon which it appears to rest, is evidently a mere creature

of this idea, a harmless, it may be a legitimate, historical theory when considered in itself; but when it has received the vicarial virus, capable of supporting one of the greatest denials and contradictions recorded in the annals of the universe. For this view of the Popedom is not merely that which came under our notice, when we were considering how men had been led to look for a great *dogmatist* to give them right and safe opinions; this is that other aspect of the office, its *kingly* aspect, that in which it presents itself either as the true law of Christ's kingdom, or as the flagrant transgression and violation of it. If Christ be really in His Church, if all the offices of the Church be declaring Him to men, *then* is the existence of a Pope the most frightful of all anomalies, then is his existence a key to all the other anomalies in the history of Christianity. If Christ be not really in His Church, if there be no real connexion between Him and those who speak in His name, or if that connexion be merely an individual one, and there be no spiritual constitution among men, then I own I do not see how the popish system can fail to commend itself to us as the most comprehensive, the most effective, the most practical, religious organization ever conceived of. Nor will this conviction be materially weakened by any display of the evils which the system may have produced. All these will be described as excesses. We shall be asked, what is so good or so Divine, that it is not exposed to corruption from the corruption of the human will? We shall be asked, how we can account for the good that flowed in the Middle Ages, not from a certain idea of Christianity merely, but from that idea as expressed in the organization of the Church?

I think we are able to answer, as we have answered before, 'This papal system is itself, in its simplest, best form, that result of the corrupt human will which you speak of. It is itself not the excess but the counterfeit of the Church constitution, the violation indeed of an idea, but also of the organization in which that idea is embodied. Because it could not destroy that idea or that organization the Church Catholic was able to diffuse some of those blessings which God meant it to diffuse. Just so far as the system prevailed, just so far as it did not contradict itself by asserting the principles it sets at nought, it has hindered God's mercies from reaching the world, it has turned them into curses.' Such language as this craves to be tried by Scripture, by history, by the conscience of papists themselves, by the truths which they profess, and which some of them, I am convinced, hold most dear. The other language which supposes that there is no spiritual constitution of Christ's ministry, has, I believe, done more, and is, at this present time, doing more to promote and establish Popery than all its own most diligent efforts.

4. I must still allude briefly to the connexion which I suppose, and which the Romanist supposes, to exist between the Jewish and the Christian economy. We are agreed so far as this—we both believe the connexion to be a real one, we both believe that it has to do with an ecclesiastical economy, we both believe that the forms of the Jewish Commonwealth, so far as they were not merely national or oriental, were translated into corresponding forms, and not merely into spiritual notions. Wherein then do we differ? In this all-important point, that we look upon the Incarnation,

the Resurrection, and the Ascension of our Lord, as declaring Him to be really and actually, not nominally or fantastically, head of the universal kingdom as the mortal High Priest had been of the peculiar kingdom, all the Jewish history being a preparation for the substitution of the one for the other. *They* believe that this High Priest has been succeeded in the new dispensation by one mortal and sinful as himself; that he is to preserve the doctrines of the Creed to the Church, while he practically and in his own person declares that those doctrines do not mean what they seem to mean; that a real connexion has not been established between man and God in the person of the Mediator; that the Church is not what her Creed affirms her to be, united to Him in His victory as well as in His humiliation. Again, then, we contend, and with so much more conviction and earnestness, as we approach nearer to the heart of the subject, that the Romish system and the Catholic Church, instead of being identical, instead of having any natural affinity for each other, are deadly opposites, one of which must perish if the other is to survive.

SECTION VI.—THE SCRIPTURES.

In a preceding chapter I inquired into the meaning of certain indications of a spiritual and universal constitution which offered themselves to us while we were studying the actual phenomena of the world and its past history. We wanted some help to explain these to us, and to tell us how they should exist, and yet the acknowledgment of this constitution by men should seem to be the exception rather than the rule. We found this help in the documents which compose our Bible. These documents profess to reveal a constitution, which is declared to be the Divine constitution for man. It is revealed first to a particular family, then to a particular nation, then, through that family and nation, to mankind. But this revelation is a history. The acts of this family and this nation, and the acts by which their possession becomes a universal one, embody the discovery. The oppositions which arise without and within this family and nation to the principle upon which they are founded, explain to us the contradiction between the will of man and the order in which he is placed. They make us conscious of the existence of two societies, one formed in accordance with the order of God, the other based upon self-will.

Now, as the Bible declares that the constitution which it affirms to be the true one should last for ever, and as it speaks of a society grounded upon that constitution which is to last for ever, we wished to inquire what signs there are of such a society in the world at this present moment. We have discovered some, which seem to import the existence of it; we have inquired whether they correspond with the signs of it which we found set down in Scripture. Thus we have referred to the Bible, not only to clear up our difficulties respecting the meaning of God in his universe, but also to tell us how far that meaning is effectual for us at this day, not only to make known the nature of the order in which we are placed, but also the outward shape of the body in which that order is expressed.

It may seem, then, that the purpose and character of the Scriptures have been already investigated as much at large as the limits of a book like this can permit, especially as the subject has already come before us in another shape, while we were discussing the opinions of different religious bodies. But it can hardly escape the observation of any reader, that if there be such a book as the Bible has seemed to us to be, it must not only interpret to us the signs of a spiritual and universal kingdom, but must be itself one of the most remarkable of those signs. And if so, we may, perhaps, by considering its relation to the other signs of which we have spoken, obtain a solution of some difficulties which much embarrass the modern student.

I. (1.) This view of the general intent of the Scriptures seems to shew how particular books may have been ascertained to form a part of them, or to have no claims of admission to them. To conceive the possibility of a canon of Scripture is the same thing as to conceive the possibility of Scripture itself. If one be necessary, the other is necessary. If one be supposed to be formed by human agency, there is no difficulty in supposing that human agency should have been most proper for the other. Regard the Bible merely as an isolated thing, and it is no doubt hard to understand how such an authority as that of fixing what it is, should have been exercised by any persons who were not employed in the writing of it. Look upon it as the witness of a permanent kingdom, believe that it is a part of the plan of God for the establishment and building up of that kingdom, and there is surely no difficulty in supposing that wisdom adequate to the work of determining, with all necessary practical exactness, what books did and what did not contain the authentic history of this kingdom, should have been imparted to men, whose offices proclaimed that they could not fulfil their most ordinary tasks by any wisdom of their own.

(2.) By looking at the Scriptures as the sign of a spiritual and universal kingdom, we seem able to reconcile several methods or schemes for interpreting them, which often present themselves to us as contradictory and exclusive. For instance, it has been one well known tendency of men to look for a mystical character in them, to suppose that beneath the letter some secret cabbala must be lurking. It has been the tendency of another class to maintain the strictness and sufficiency of the letter, and indignantly to repudiate every recondite meaning as inconsistent with the simplicity of a revelation. Now every sign of this kingdom which we have considered hitherto has partaken of this double character; it has pointed to a relation which is invisible, mystical, transcendent; it has been in itself plain, definite, visible. The relation which it expressed was real and permanent; here lay the necessity of a sign which had nothing in it of a fluctuating character, which did not derive its strength from the notions and apprehensions of men, which spoke to all. One would certainly expect to find the same principle holding good in the case of this other sign; one would think that the more simple, accurate, and historical the outward clothing was, the more it would be felt to embody some higher principle.

Again; it has been a great controversy whether

each part of these records should be taken to have a distinct definite meaning, applicable to some particular event and crisis, or whether it may have a remote application to some other crisis, or even to a series of yet undeveloped events. Now supposing the Bible to be the history of the gradual development and manifestation of a kingdom fixed upon certain permanent principles, it seems the most natural supposition, that it would always exhibit these principles in reference to some present or approaching contingency, yet that it would explain similar contingencies and circumstances to the end of time. Refusing to acknowledge the first event, we lose the principle; determined to restrict it to some other event of our own selection, we compel ourselves to depart from the letter without gaining anything for the spirit. We may be right in our feeling that the particular event we have fixed upon does fall under the law which this part of Scripture makes known to us; we are almost sure to be wrong when we restrain the application of the law to that given event. These conclusions proceeded naturally from the belief that the Scriptures are not to be looked upon apart from the spiritual kingdom.

(3.) Hence also we seem to obtain the solution of another, and what strikes many as a more difficult problem, Where are the interpreters of this book to be found? How is it at once to be a lawgiver, and yet to be subject to the maxims and rules of interpretation of those who are its subjects? The difficulty is the same as in all previous cases. Take the Bible as a solitary fact, speak of it simply as the Word of God addressing itself to man, without inquiring what this Word of God affirms man to be, what kind of order it

says that he is placed in; and there must be endless puzzles to ascertain in what position of simple
acquiescence of earnest inquiry such utterances are
to be received, whether each man is to grasp them for
himself, or whether his fellows are in any wise helping
him to grasp them.

But let it be supposed that the words speak as
they seem to speak, of men being placed in a certain
Divine order—of God, as addressing them in that
order—it would seem plain enough that the words
will be realized just so far as we avail ourselves of
our position, missed just so far as we reject it. The
difficulty of understanding how, through the help
of Christ's ministers, we may attain to a practical
insight into the facts and principles which this book
makes known, how, choosing to dispense with that
help, we shall be most likely to go astray, is precisely
the difficulty which is supposed in all education; or,
would it not be more correct to say, that here we
find the key to the puzzles of ordinary education,
because we arrive at a point, where we find God
proclaiming Himself as the Educator, and marking
out those through whom He will educate? The
difficulty which arises from the discovery that these
ministers may forget their task, and instead of calling
out the personal life and apprehension of their disciples, stifle them with mere words and notions, is
still the same problem of daily life repeated, only
that we perceive more clearly against whom the
sin is committed, and what the responsibility for it
is. The difficulty of comprehending how men should
teach out of a book, which they acknowledge to overreach themselves, and to be above them, is but the

difficulty of every magistrate and judge who is set for the purpose of bringing out into light and clearness the meaning of the Law which he both administers and obeys, who may, doubtless, put himself in the place of it, may read himself into it, may choose to keep it from men instead of guiding them into an intelligent submission to it, but who acts in this way at his peril, bringing himself under the sentence, if of no earthly superior, of One who yet, in this spiritual kingdom, holds his constant and acknowledged court of appeal.

II. These questions are debated between those who are agreed in acknowledging the Sciptures as possessing Divine authority. Let us now consider the objections of those who either reject the notion of a Bible altogether, or who see no special reason why the books which we hold sacred should usurp the name.

These objections may be stated in this way. 'Ever since the critical spirit and knowledge of modern Europe have been brought to bear upon these documents, it has been found more and more difficult to maintain the claims which are put forth on their behalf by the elder Church as well as by the Reformers. Supposing the doctrine of their inspiration, of their paramount authority to all other books, of their fixed and peculiar character, to be true, the detection of any unauthentic record amongst them, of any report which will not bear sifting, even of any considerable error in the reading of a text which had been used to support some opinion, must be sufficient to shake the credit of the whole scheme. It was, therefore, unquestionably honest in those early critics

who wished to assert the general authority of the
book, that they ventured to commence these fatal
inroads.   But if they were not stopped at first, they
certainly cannot be stopped now.   The principle of
criticism, which has been admitted as to a part, must
be applied to the whole.   Whatever maxim has been
thought just, and has stood the test of inquiry in
reference to other books, must be brought to bear
upon these.   And little help will be derived in our
day from those evidences, which in the last century
were thought so conclusive.   The credit of the book
was supposed to be sustained by the miracles which
are recorded in it, by the consistency of the facts with
the general testimony of antiquity, by the admirable
character of the four narratives which form the centre
of it, by its ideal truth and consistency.   Now those
miracles are the very stories which we require should
be accounted for.   The testimony of antiquity has
been proved only to establish the existence of certain
habits of thought and feeling in different nations,
which will themselves account for what has been supposed to be peculiar in these records.   The four
narratives have been subjected to a severe analysis,
and it has been found most difficult to understand
either their internal history or their relation to outward events.   Finally, the supposed ideal consistency
has been examined of the whole record, and has
been shewn, indeed, to be an explanation of the
phenomena of Christianity, but in a way most unsatisfactory to those who regard it as embodied in a
series of facts.'

This is a statement, I hope it is a fair statement,
of the objections which are now current in all parts of

society, and which, when they do not appear as a
complete system of arguments, are only the more
effectual, because they suggest the thought that much
has been left unsaid which would be quite conclusive
if it might safely be uttered.

I begin, then, with admitting that I do not see
how it is possible for those who look upon the Scriptures merely as a set of documents contrived for the
instruction of individual men, merely as a witness to
them of what has been done for them, of what the
plans and purposes of God respecting them are, to
encounter some of these arguments. I do not mean
that they may not encounter them practically, in what
seems to me a most honest and effectual method. If
they will resolutely hold fast that which they have
felt and ascertained in their own lives to be true; if
they will say, 'This we have learnt and received; the
Bible taught it us, and we cannot give it up for any
arguments;' I believe their position is a safe and
impregnable one. It is not a position of prejudice, it
is a reasonable and sound position; it is founded upon
the first and wisest maxim of ethical philosophy, Keep
what thou hast; add to it if thou canst; but if thou
wishest to realize more, never let anything which thou
hast realized be snatched away from thee. My fear
is that few people in our day are likely to be content
with this position. They will be going out of it with
their arguments and their evidences, with their attempts to prove how and why a book having the
character which they impute to the Bible, must be
Divine and perfect. Here I think they will be dis-
comfited. This logic is not a part of their realized
truths, it is something altogether extraneous to them.

And what is worse, they do not yet know what it is they are arguing about; for they may have derived these individual facts from the Bible; but the Bible itself evidently assumes to be something else; it assumes to be a collection of historical documents, and the question is, how this assumption is connected with that quality of it which they have discovered and recognized.

Are we, then, to hope that those who are willing to consider it principally as a collection of historical documents, and as such to defend it, will be able to maintain their position? I think writers of this class will bring forward much that is very valuable, much that their opponents cannot without great difficulty and without some dishonesty reply to; I think they will do more than this; they will be enabled to leave an impression upon thoughtful and sincere minds, that there are facts existing in the world now, and that there has been a series of such facts, of which these books may offer the explanation. But here again, the difficulty is to find how these facts cohere, how it is that they are related to the doctrines and principles which these books embody; why it is necessary to suppose any Divine oversight in the arrangement and preservation of them.

Are we then to say, as the objector affirms we must say, that criticism is wholly inapplicable to this particular set of records; that they must be taken for granted upon some authority or other, be it that of primitive antiquity, or of the Church in the present day; and that, being so taken for granted, all further inquiry respecting them is to be discarded? Every one will see that there is a plausibility in this opinion;

nay, there is more than plausibility, there is a truth
hidden in it which we must not deny. As long as we
receive the Scriptures at all, as long as we do not
determine absolutely to reject them, we must in the
education of our own minds, in the education of our
children's minds, take them for granted. We cannot
begin with being critics, or with making them critics.
If we do, we and they will assuredly be most miserable
critics, and as certainly we and they shall be nothing
else. But do we not in this respect deal with the
Scriptures as we deal with other books? We take
them for granted too; we do not in merely reading or
in teaching them, enter into a criticism of the sources
whence they are derived or of the conditions of their
authority. There comes a time, however, when other
books are subjected to this trial; it has been the will
of God that the book which we consider pre-eminently
His should be subjected to the same. It is a solemn
inquiry for us, whether we shall dare to pretend that
we will take better care of his book than He has taken
of it; whether we shall affirm that it cannot bear the
application of tests, which we believe that ordinary
literature will bear.

And this brings us to the main question which I
wish to place before the reader, What has been the
character of that criticism to which the Scriptures
have been for the most part subjected during the last
century and a half? I do not ask whether it has been
sound criticism, learned criticism, devout criticism. It
may have had any or all of these characters. But
what has been its object? The safest answer with
respect to the last century may be obtained from a
consideration of what was the object of *all* criticism,

whether it referred to the human body or the human soul, to the universe or to the creatures who lived in it. Nearly every philosopher of that day thought it was the business of his life to *analyze*; he was to analyze the operations of the mind, to analyze himself, to analyze his fellow creatures, to analyze the being of his Maker. Do I say that all this labour was wasted, that nothing came out of the inquiries and dissections of that period? I say no such thing; I believe much was learnt from them; that many false notions and phantoms, which men had transferred from themselves to the objects of their study, were got rid of; many idols thrown down, broken in pieces, and trampled upon, which had beset the caves of thoughtful men or the market-places of busy men. But the great lesson of all which this method of study bequeathed to us, was the lesson of its own utter incapacity to lead into the apprehension of any truth, though it might avail for the discomfiture of some error. Hence every step that has been taken in our day towards real profitable inquiry, whether in physics or metaphysics, has been a step out of this method, a step towards the investigation of the powers and principles of things as they exist; not an attempt, except for certain subordinate purposes, to reduce them into their elements. Above all, this change has been effected in reference to literature. Here the analytical spirit of the last age displayed itself in its full power; every book was to be cut up into its elements, and whatever elements did not please the critic to be cast out as worthless; nothing whatever was done in the study of a book as a whole, nothing towards the discovery of the purpose which actuated and informed it. The Scriptures were treated in the same manner. The fact of their constituting a whole, which had been felt as a whole by innumerable minds for many centuries, was more and more overlooked as utterly unimportant to the critic and the philosopher. He could not deny that they had a common name, but his business was to shew what separate items went to the composition of this name, and then to pursue his inquiries with as little reference as possible to it. Of course it was part of the ordinary philosophy at the period, that everything in this book, which spoke of invisible powers, should be explained away. The object was to discover how many of its elements might be preserved, without infringing upon the ordinary maxims of the time in reference to physics, metaphysics, and ethics.

Now I would say, in reference to these inquiries, just as I said in reference to all others undertaken at the same period, that I do not believe they were useless, or will ultimately be mischievous. If the student of the physics of the seventeenth century perceives that there were a multitude of strange theories and superstitions then accumulated and accumulating, which had need by some whirlwind to be swept away; the student of theology must equally confess that a number of hard, dogmatical abstractions respecting spiritual objects, and, not least, respecting the books which treat of these objects, were darkening the face of the heavens, and making men's path along their common earth less clear. That some fiery process would be necessary for the destruction of these, we might conjecture. Of what kind it should be, we could not be judges. God ordained that it should be this destructive analysis.

We cannot doubt that what He appointed was best. Many obstructions to the perception of that which is real and substantial have been removed out of the path of the young theologian; it is his own fault if he seeks for them again. He may, if he will, be less entangled with the abstractions and conceits of the intellect than his forefathers were. And in this case, as in the others I have mentioned, the analysts have conferred this great blessing on us—they have proved the inadequacy and feebleness of their method to explain any one living fact, or to lead us onward to any one important discovery.

When, therefore, the objectors of whom we are speaking, say that the Bible ought to be tried by the same rules as other books, we can perhaps go a great way with them, provided we understand what they mean. It always, I believe, *will* be tried by the same standard as other books; that is to say, the habits of mind which we cultivate in regard to one, we shall cultivate in regard to the other. When all books are merely cut up into their elements, the Bible will be dealt with in like manner. When other books, and the whole series of books which constitute the literature of a nation, are contemplated in reference to their principle or idea, it is utterly impossible but that these should be studied upon the same principle. And the question arises, what is this principle or idea? We have had occasion to consider that view of it, so prevalent in our day, which tries to separate the idea from the event, to exhibit the one as common to all ages, the other as its mere accidental temporary clothing. I have endeavoured to show how inadequate this doctrine is to account for the phenomena which present themselves to us in the history of the world; how it turns living ideas into mere notions and apprehensions of our minds, and so legalizes and stamps with authority the very superstitions from which it seeks to deliver us; how it confounds the permanent and the transitory in the very attempt to distinguish them; how it destroys human progress in the very attempt to assert it. If, indeed, it were possible entirely to separate this modern idealism from the old analytical method which it professes to supersede and to despise, we might easily prove the insufficiency of either. The chief strength of each lies in a vague notion of the one being the expansion and full development of the other; in a loose impression that the belief of inspiration, of miracles, of a Gospel history, which had been partially subverted by the one, has been completely subverted by the other.

The facts, in recent German history especially, which prove that the ideal system could not have been produced at all, if it had not been preceded by a vehement *religious* protest against the analysts, are not known or not heeded; and we are asked what hope there can be of maintaining our obsolete notions respecting a Divine order and a Divine book, when each age has furnished its own peculiar and appropriate refutation of them. Our answer is, 'No hope at all, if what you call our notions be not something more than notions, if they be not founded on eternal principles and truths. But, on the other hand, the belief that they have this foundation is strengthened not weakened, by the history of these different attempts to confute them; strengthened not weakened by the fact, that no adequate answer has been offered to the particular charges against the Bible, except by those who are willing to speak of the Bible in the way it seems to speak of itself, as the revelation of a Divine kingdom.'

1. Looking at it in this light, I would inquire, first, what difficulties there are in the old notion that the writers of the book were inspired men? According to the principle of a spiritual kingdom, as we have considered it, inspiration is not a strange anomalous fact; it is the proper law and order of the world; no man ought to write, or speak, or think, except under the acknowledgment of an inspiration; no man can speak, or write, or think if he have not really an inspiration. Is, then, the constant habitual confession of Divine teaching, the reference of everything to God by the writers of this Bible, something which stamps them with the character of impostors? Would not this seem to be the characteristic of true men? But still you say 'it *is* the characteristic of fanatics, of those who are not true men; where do you draw the line?' I draw it in this way :—I say, according to the principle of a spiritual kingdom, every man who is doing the work he is set to do, may believe that he is inspired with a power to do that work; every man who is doing some other work which he is not set to do may, indeed, say that he is using powers which he has received from above; but he is violating the purposes for which those powers have been given him; his will is obeying an impulse contrary to the will of the Being who bestowed the power. Here is fanaticism, here is confusion. The question, therefore, is not really, Were these men who wrote the Scriptures inspired by God? but, Were they in a certain position

and appointed to a certain work? So that we are
driven by this argument, as we are driven by the book
itself, from that which we read to that which we read
of. Was there such a society as that which this book
speaks of? was there such a nation as the Jews?
had they a history? was there a meaning in that
history? does this book explain to us their history
and its meaning? The question of inspiration belongs
to these questions—cannot be viewed apart from them.
If there be no spiritual kingdom in the world, no
kings, priests, prophets appointed by God, then
assuredly I cannot make out that the Scriptures
had a right to describe such kings, and priests, and
prophets. If there were such men, I have as great
difficulty in understanding how we can dispense with
such a record, or how any Being, except Him who
formed the society for the sake of His own glory
and for the good of His creatures, can have caused
that book to be written.

But it will be answered: 'This is evading the
difficulty. It is not merely the men, but the *words*,
which, according to the common theory, are inspired.
And though less extravagant theories may have been
invented and received among Christians, yet none
which denies a verbal inspiration or dictation is consistent with itself, is anything but a subterfuge.' Two
words are used here as synonymous, which seem to
involve the most different significations. When you
speak to me of verbal *inspiration*, though I do not
like the phrase, though it seems to me to involve
a violent—a scarcely grammatical—ellipsis, yet I
subscribe most unequivocally to the meaning which
I suppose is latent in it. I have no notion of inspired

thoughts which do not find for themselves a suitable clothing of words. I can scarcely, even in my mind, separate the language of a writer from his meaning. And I certainly find this difficulty greater in studying a book of the Bible than in studying any other book. The peculiarities of its language seem to me strangely significant. And yet its greatest peculiarity of all, if I may be pardoned the solecism, is its universality, its capacity of translation into any dialect which has a living and human quality, which is not merely the echo of passing impressions and the utterance of animal necessities. But just because I see this link between the inbreathed thought and the spoken word, I must reject as monstrous and heretical the notion of a *dictation*. I call it monstrous and heretical, for I know none more directly at variance with the letter and spirit of Scripture. If the hint of it is to be found anywhere, it is certainly in the history of the giving of the divine Code. *That* was, of course, a formal literal document, and therefore is signified to proceed formally and literally from its Author. Yet mark how carefully we are warned against the notion, so natural to the sensual and idolatrous heart of man, that Moses was a mere mechanical utterer or transcriber. Why are we told that he went into the thick darkness? why do we hear of his awful communion for forty days? why have we the records of his deep sympathy with his people, of his prayers, his meditations, his murmurings, if not that we may be exalted to understand something of the human privilege of spiritual intercourse, and that we may consider *this* the great privilege of the most honoured seer? And this surely is the object of all

Scripture, if it have any object at all, to withdraw us from outward sensual impressions of the Divine Majesty, to make us feel the reality of the relation between Him and His creatures, to make us understand that it is a spiritual relation, and that, *therefore*, it can manifest itself in outward words and acts. It is, then, no concession to the Rationalist, but a necessity of our own faith, that we should utterly reject and abhor this theory of dictation. And it remains for him to shew how the discovery of different readings in MSS., or the rejection of books as not genuine, which are now esteemed to be parts of the Canon, or even the detection of historical inconsistencies and mistakes in the inspired writers, would affect our belief. With regard to the new readings, just in proportion to our feeling of the importance and sacredness of the language, must be our desire to find what it really is. If there be no Bible, these investigations are idle and useless; if there be, they must be most interesting. The mental exercise in such inquiries must be most healthful, involving, if it be rightly conducted, the necessity of reflection upon the whole mind and scope of the text, a cautious and calm use of the judging faculty, a faith in the existence of truth, and in its willingness to reveal itself. Again; any person who really believes that there is a book, of which the distinct office is to explain the nature and conditions of a kingdom into which he has been actually brought, must enter upon the inquiry whether any one of the documents of which this book is supposed to consist be or be not genuine, in the same simple and honest spirit. The kingdom exists; he is not afraid of losing it or of

losing his place in it, even if God thought fit to take
away the book altogether.   Yet he has no fear that
He will do this, no doubt in the world that it is His
good pleasure to tell us what He is and what we are.
That this book has revealed these truths to himself and
to thousands of others for generations, he is certain;
whether he or they have been right in supposing that
a particular portion of it was necessary to the rest, he
is willing reverently and diligently to consider; nothing
doubting that He who upholds the kingdom and has
given the book, will not allow the ultimate continuance
of any intruder into it, or permit any integral part of it
to be taken away.   And if it be asked, But does not
this admission open a door to unlimited scepticism?
has not nearly every book been the subject of some
modern suspicion?—the answer, I think, has been
given already.   Let those talk to me about interpola-
tions in Shakspeare who know what Shakspeare is,
who have really studied his mind and writings.   I do
not care the least because Theobald or Pope may
determine that such and such passages are not suitable to their taste; neither do I care in the least
what may be the taste of the analysts or the modern
idealists about passages or books of Scripture.   Their
taste is no law of criticism.   I believe it to be a very
low and bad taste indeed.   Let them bring forward
external evidence and we will weigh it—cautiously,
because their taste is very apt to mingle with their
words, because they continually assume a maxim from
which we utterly dissent, as if it were part and parcel
of a fact which we may acknowledge; but still
earnestly and impartially.   I am not the least afraid
of touching a corner of the edifice because the rest

is likely to fall down; on the contrary, I believe it will prove to be a much firmer edifice than we have been wont to suppose that it is. The books which were thrown aside, even by religious men, at the time of the Reformation, because they seemed to have no direct bearing upon individual life, will be found to contain their own evidence, when they are looked upon as meant to develop the order and life of the spiritual kingdom.

The same principle precisely applies to alleged mistakes or inconsistencies in the admitted parts of the records. Suppose these mistakes and inconsistencies to be such as prove dishonesty in the writers —suppose them to be connected with any part of the revelation of the character of God or of the development of His kingdom—they fall under the last head, they become (*pro tanto*) arguments against the genuineness of that document wherein they are found. Suppose them to be merely accidental to the narrative, such as do not affect the meaning of the facts or the integrity of the writer, or such as may be corrected by comparison with another narrative of the same transactions, then I do not know that I have any right, *à priori*, to affirm from the existence of a Bible that none such will exist. I see no promise to that effect; I see no reason why it may not have pleased God to teach men by this very means; I mean, to permit the ordinary differences of opinions and eyesight which manifest themselves in the testimony of different witnesses of a fact, to be helps to us in the study of the real character of that fact; the ordinary confusion respecting points of detail to be the means of leading us away from those points of detail to that which is real and substantial. I say I can see no reason, *à priori,* either in the nature of a Bible or in the meaning of inspiration why this may not be so. I even fancy that I can see reasons in the analogy of the Divine dealings, and in the tendency of man to dwell upon the minutiæ of a transaction, not as helps to discover its real meaning and essence, but for their own sakes, why such a discipline may be most suited to us. If it should be found that this is not the case, I shall acquiesce most readily, but I shall have no more faith in the Bible than I have at present. For the Bible will not allow me to have any faith in it apart from faith in God, and whatever I find to be His way of training me and my race, that I hold to be the right way, and the way in which we may be trained to all goodness and all truth. I do not want to lay down a scheme or chart of the road in which it is fitting we should be led; that, I think, is presumption.

According to this shewing, then, the charge of departing from the ordinary rules which we apply to the study of other books, is far more applicable to those who urge it than it is to us. We claim that the Bible should be looked at as a fact, a most pregnant fact, in the history of mankind. It stands apart from other books; we wish to know why it so stands apart, what there is that differences it from other books, just as we wish to know what there is in the writings of Cicero that differences them from other writings, or what there is in the literature of Rome that differences it from other literature. And if we should discover that there is that in this book which entitles it to be called, as it has been commonly called, *The* Book, or

The Book of Books, we do not surely by such a name signify any contempt of books, rather a high appreciation of them. We declare that there is a book which directly and formally connects letters with the life of man, with the order of God; a book, which, just so far as it fulfils its idea, becomes the key by which all books may be interpreted, that which translates them into significance and determines the value and position of each. We declare, moreover, what is the temper and spirit in which a book should be studied. Nothing seems to me more preposterous than the notion that we can change our habits of mind when we turn from one subject to another. It is a flagrant violation of every ethical principle, that is to say, a flagrant tampering with our moral being, to suppose that we can be reverential at one moment and irreverent at another; that we are to be humble in the presence of this person, and proud when we are brought into intercourse with another. I perfectly agree, therefore, with the Rationalist, that to talk as some do of our right to sit in judgment upon all other books, and of the duty of submitting our judgments to the Bible, is not practical or reasonable. If we think that in reading Cicero or Shakspeare our proper position is that of judges, I am quite certain that we shall not be able to think otherwise when we study the Scriptures. And I am equally certain that while we do fancy that we are judges of Cicero or Shakspeare we shall not understand them. The posture of children or learners is the true profitable posture in all cases. It is not safe to propose to ourselves the end of being judges in any case. It is not safe for our minds generally, it is most

unsafe for the judging faculty itself. That is invariably
turned awry at first, blunted and stupefied afterwards,
if it be not sent to school, and if it do not carry through
life the docility which school is meant to give it. But
what is the schooling? We all know how difficult the
acquisition of docility is, how difficult in all days, how
difficult especially in our own. There are some books
which naturally tempt us to exercise the proud condemning spirit; feebleness is stamped upon them;
they themselves affect a right to judge others; we feel
as if here we might safely indulge our propensity.
Therefore we see the wisdom of the old notion, that
only the best books, only those which carry a kind of
authority with them, should be set before boys; when
they have been drilled by them into habits of deference
and humility, then they may venture, if their calling
requires it, upon the study of the worst, for then they
will have acquired the true discerning spirit, that spirit
of which the judging spirit is the counterfeit; the one
perceiving the real quality of the food which is offered,
the other, merely setting up its own partial and imma-
ture tastes and aversions as the standard of what is
good and evil. But even this is not sufficient, as
experience has proved. Starting from the study of the
meanest books, our modern critics have gone on to
higher books, and have asked why they may not
exercise their right of private judgment on one as
much as the other; why they may not pronounce
their sentence upon Herodotus or Livy as well as upon
any modern compilation. The Rationalist goes a step
further, and says, Why not pass our sentence upon
those which you call your inspired books as well as
upon Herodotus or Livy? It is good that such a

question should be proposed, because it brings the question to an issue.   It enables us to say, You have wanted to get rid of these inspired books, because, you have said, they were an affront to other literature; learn by this that they are the needful protectors to other literature.   If there be a book, of which we can say, Herein God is speaking to you; be silent and listen: we have the power of keeping down that saucy and insolent temper, which, so far as it is applied to anything, makes that thing unintelligible.   We have the power of cultivating our judgment, because we have the power of making it *not* a private judgment.   A private judgment means the judgment of a man who is cut off from his fellows, the judgment of a savage.   A man certainly has a right to such a private judgment, if by right you mean the power to exercise it.   For he has the power of being a savage; he has the power of saying, I will not be educated; I will not be led out of my own partial apprehensions, and the partial apprehensions of my age; I will not be a reasonable being, I will not be a man.   He may do this; I say also he may do something else if he will.   He may be taken under training and discipline, the training and discipline of God Himself, for the purpose of being led out of his private judgment, into a knowledge of the judgment and mind of Him who " weighed the mountains in scales and the hills in a balance."   He may have a book set before him, which unfolds the scheme and purpose of this universe and its Creator; he may be led by slow degrees to understand his own connexion with this universe, with those who lived in it, and with Him who is the author of it.   And if he will have this learning, if he will be taught out of this book, then every other book which he reads will be also a part of the same Divine institution.   God will be training him by that too; to trace out the course of His government, to see how different men have, consciously or unconsciously, cheerfully or involuntarily, been accomplishing some part of His designs towards His creatures; till having descended through different gradations of thoughtful inquirers, who, each in his own department, are humbly desiring to discover the meaning of their Lord, when He comes, at last, to the lowest point in the scale, to the last new criticism, or the last tavern speech in defence of the inalienable right of men to think what they like, he will find even in that something which is true, something which could not have been spoken if there were not a Bible in the world.

2. This view of the relation between the Scriptures and other books, may perhaps assist us in considering the question of miracles.   The analyst of the last century maintained that these miracles might be referred to natural causes.   The idealist of the present day considers them as inventions attesting that belief of something supernatural which belongs to men because they have spiritual faculties.   Both alike agree, that they are stumbling blocks and not helps to a belief of the doctrine and facts of Scripture.   I cannot regret that either of these opinions has been propounded.   Unphilosophical as I think them, they yet may clear our minds of a great confusion, and may help us in arriving at a great truth.   We have been used to speak of miracles as the chief evidences for the truth of

Christianity. Now if it is meant by this, that a miracle or prodigy, as such, proves the Divine commission of the person who enacts it, we have the strongest reason for rejecting such a notion, for the Bible commands us to reject it. We dare not believe anything, merely because something which strikes us as a departure from ordinary experiences or laws is done to confirm it: we are warned in Scripture, that we shall see such wonders, and that we are to beware of being deceived by them. Again, the Bible is remarkably a book of laws, a book explaining the Divine order of the universe; if it be not this it is nothing. Can we suppose that violations of laws, infringements of order, would be the great signs and witnesses in comfirmation of it? Surely, then, the eagerness of the analyst to get these miracles resolved into natural causes, that is, according to his notion, to get them connected with the general order of the world, is not surprising. But, once more, it is quite true, as the other class of rationalists affirm, that there has been a feeling, not at one time and in one age, but at all times and in all ages, after some power which is not circumscribed by the rules of ordinary visible experience, but which is superior to these rules, and can transgress them. He is quite right, that the acknowledgment of such a power lies deep in the heart of man, and that we are continually demanding instances and proofs of its exercise. Both these assertions are true; the difficulty is to reconcile them and apply them.

Now, supposing the Bible were the revelation of a spiritual kingdom or constitution of man, such as we have described; supposing it were the history of a Divine power for the redemption of man out of a slavery into which he had brought himself, we may perceive, I think, at least a dawn of light upon this controversy. I do find, unquestionably, in the portents recorded by Livy, the signs of a feeling in men's minds that there is something supernatural; that the powers of the world are not all with which men have to deal. But the feeling contradicts itself in the attempt to utter itself; it does homage to the powers of nature in the very act of seeming to rise above them. And, therefore, under such a system there could be no liberty for the human spirit, there could be no brave investigation into the mechanism or into the energies of the universe. Before these blessings could be attained, the sense of the supernatural in man must be justified and purified. He must know that when he is dreaming of something above himself, he is dreaming of a reality; he must know that nature is not that which he is dreaming of; that he is not to tremble before this, but to claim the dignity of a spiritual creature, to understand it and to subdue it. He must know that he is not the victim of a set of blind natural agents; he must have something more than a vague conception of what that power is, of which he is the servant. Such an effect, I say, the miracles of the Bible may produce upon him. Every one of those which is recorded in the Old Testament is recorded expressly as a witness, that the Jehovah, the I AM, the personal God, the Lord of the spirits of all flesh, is the King of the world, and that gods of sense are not its kings. Every miracle recorded in the New Testament is recorded expressly and professedly for the purpose of showing that the Son of

man is the Ruler of the winds and the waves; the
sustainer and restorer of animal life; the healer and
tamer of the human spirit; and that those who are
the adopted children of God in Him, while they are
doing His work, are not the servants of visible things,
but their rulers.   These miracles say to the poor man,
" Fear not the mighty unfathomable ocean, for your
King and Friend has calmly walked upon it; fear not
the powers of disease and sickness, for He who took
your flesh has mastered them; fear not the more
terrible powers that get the mastery of the understanding and heart, for Christ also hath cast out
devils; walk boldly and bravely over this earth, as
freemen united to this triumphant Deliverer; dread
only separation from Him; dread only that you should
not trust Him and cleave to Him sufficiently, and so
sink again under the bondage to nature and death,
out of which He, by His life and death, has purchased
you."   And do not they speak also to the better
taught man according to *his* necessities and temptations?   He does not so much want to be raised above
the natural fear of outward things; a calculation of
probabilities, or a habit of encountering difficulties
may easily give him that victory.   But the very means
of his deliverance are occasions to him of fresh bondage.
He acquires a drowsy, dull sense of an ever-moving
system of chances; he does not become an idolater
of the powers of nature; but he worships its even-
ness and persistency.   Most wretched and degrading
faith! far more to be loathed and dreaded than the
living and half-human idolatry of the peasant.   Yet
unless there be some demonstration that spiritual
power is superior to mechanical; that the world is

subject to God, and not to chance or nature; that there is an order, far more beautiful and perfect than that of sun and stars, in which men are intended to abide, and in which everything that is great and noble within them receives its full development;—I see not how this materialist superstition can fail to become the creed of every nation, and to bring about the decay of all institutions and political life, all feeling, affection, hope. With the other faith it has been possible for men to pursue physical science. The world has presented itself to them as a solemn, awful subject of study, but not as a tyrant before which they must bow. They have learnt that the mere customary links which connect a fact with its highest principle, may be suspended for the purpose of making that principle manifest. They have, therefore, risen above the slavish notion, that sensible experience is the law to which things are subjected; they have been able to set it at naught and defy it; not merely the astronomer, but every chemist who has truly investigated the functions and powers of material things, has moved on in this line, humbly asking nature to tell him her secrets, and receiving answers, the most satisfactory indeed, but the most contrary to our sensible anticipations and conclusions.

If, then, we are asked why we reject the analyst's doctrine about these miracles, our answer is, because by accepting it we should not be acknowledging the true order of the world, but we should be refusing to acknowledge it. We do not believe that the world is under the government of natural causes; we do not know what the phrase 'natural causes' means. We confess, and rejoice to confess, that there is an habitual appointed course of things; that each agent, voluntary or involuntary, has his proper place in the scheme; that no one link of this agency will be ever needlessly broken or dispensed with. But we say that no dishonour is put upon any of these agents, when He, who has assigned them their place, keeps them in their own relation to each other, imparts to them their powers, withdraws the veil which conceals Himself the prime worker, and so explains the meaning of His ordinances, the secret of their efficiency, the reason of their abuse. It is in this sense that we say the miracles are evidences of the truth of Christianity. If Christianity be the manifestation of a spiritual kingdom; if it be the satisfaction of the dreams of past ages; if it be that which was to exhibit through all the complications of after ages, what is the law which governs them, and who is the Giver of that law, then we cannot see how it could enter the world without miracles, or how those miracles should not be such as the Bible affirms that they were.*

3. The records of these miracles form such an integral portion of the Gospel narratives, that in speaking of the one I have necessarily anticipated many of the remarks which I should have made upon the other.

The real difficulty which has presented itself to

---

* Every reader of the Gospels will of course have observed that our Lord's signs did not satisfy the rulers of the Jews. They wanted another *kind* of signs, 'signs from heaven,' glaring tokens which the eye might recognise, not 'powers' exercised upon the inner man, and calling forth an effort of the spirit in answer to them. Beautifully do our Lord's words express the difference, 'It is a sinful and *adulterous*, or sensebound, generation which seeks after *such* signs.'

men's minds in the study of them has been this: 'How can we admit narratives which report such very strange stories to be true, without some higher evidence than belongs to almost any other writing.' This suggestion being once offered, of course every difficulty which harmonists have experienced, in bringing the parts of the different narratives into connection, every doubt which has been raised respecting the authorship of any one of them, every question about the existence of a common source from which they may have proceeded, has given new encouragement to scepticism. It has been said, 'so far from there being more evidence, it would seem as if there were less evidence for these than for the other parts of the record.'

Now our last inquiry seems to lead us to these conclusions. Either the strange stories spoken of are in accordance with the scriptural idea of the Founder of a spiritual and universal kingdom, or they are not. If they are not, no evidence whatever could establish the authenticity of the document containing them; for they would be self-contradictory; we should be bound to reject them because we believe in Jesus Christ the Son of God. On the other hand, if they are, we should require evidence to account for their omission in any record professing to contain the history of such a person. We should have a right to ask, Why did He give no signs that He came to connect the visible with the invisible world; why did He do nothing to break the yoke of custom and experience; nothing to shew men that the constitution which He pretended to reveal and establish has a true foundation? Take away the miracles, and there is an inexplicable chasm and inconsistency in these records, which it would require a vast amount of wit and ingenuity to explain.*

Now when this difficulty is surmounted, when the reader of the Gospels is not haunted perpetually with the thought, 'I wish that story were away ; I wish I could have the morality of these discourses, and the morality of the life of Jesus, without being perpetually asked to acknowledge something marvellous,' when he has seen that the marvel belongs essentially to the morality of the discourses and of the life, the other perplexities, I believe, will not be very serious. In the first place, he will see that all the failures of harmonists to bring the different facts of the different Gospels into connection or chronological sequence, have nothing whatever to do with the books themselves. They exist, they are facts, they have exercised a wonderful influence on the world in their present form, they have made known to men the same living Person. If they should be found to fit one into another, or to be contrived as supplements to each

---

* We are told sometimes that Mahomet understood the true nature of miracles far better than the Apostles of the Christian Church ; he said, 'The corn growing was a miracle, the rise of the sun was a miracle, life and death were miracles,' etc. Very likely he did, and they were very fine words no doubt. The question is, what effect have they produced? Have his best disciples been able, were they able even in the highest times of Arabian cultivation, to rise above the prejudices and illusions of sensible experience? But the fact of the difference *is* important. It shows how closely the kind of miracles recorded in Scripture belongs to the idea of the Incarnation. Rejecting that idea, Mahometans rightly reject the signs and forms which connect the visible with the invisible world. And *there* is the secret of their slavery.

other, I do not see that they would accomplish their purpose better. I am quite willing to listen to those who say they have discovered such an agreement in them, and to believe them if they make their point good. But I certainly am not the least troubled when I see them at fault.

A revelation to men of their Lord and King, must be something altogether wonderful. I could not the least conjecture beforehand how the records of it would be composed. They might come in the form of annals, no doubt. That is not the form from which one in general derives most knowledge of a character; oftentimes the story of a few days or hours brings it into clearer light; still this method might have been appropriate for such an occasion. But if another has apparently been adopted; if I am in possession of a set of documents, seeming to present to me a life in a number of different circumstances, all human and intelligible circumstances, the wonder lying not in them but in Him who is acting through them, and in the meaning He shews to be latent in them, and if I have the opportunity of comparing these documents, so that I may learn more of the meaning of the life, from seeing how the transactions which exhibit it appeared to different men, I am certainly not careful to disturb this order, for the sake of inventing another which I think would be much less adapted to us. So again, secondly, it should be remembered that the existence of these documents is not affected by any theories about their authorship or their construction. Omit all the names which we are wont to associate with them, or say that these names do not indicate any known persons, or that these persons were no eye witnesses, or that they were merely reporters of a current tradition, or that they all drew from a common tradition, or that they had communications with one another, or that they had none—still the books are; and the secret of their influence, and the strange impression which men have, that they do exhibit a real being to man, and that Being the Lord of man, the image after which he is created; this must still be explained, either by means of some one of these hypotheses, or without it. They may be all worth considering; each, doubtless, means something, and may teach something; but if they should all prove to be untenable, still the marvel itself is not got rid of. To that the theological student must address himself; he must look it fairly in the face, he must confess that all processes of his criticism must be preceded by the acknowledgment that there is something to be criticised. And however much he may be disposed to turn away from the common-place remark, that there is a singular absence in these records of those contrivances by which men usually try to set forth a hero; that the divinity which the writer believes he is exhibiting, does not occasionally but habitually exhibit itself in the simplest and lowliest forms of human life; that there is actually no exception to this practice in any one of these narratives, not one instance in all these traditions handed down by affectionate, credulous, ignorant disciples, of an attempt to establish their Master's celestial origin by connecting him with circumstances of outward greatness; however dull and dreary, I say, the repetition of such remarks may be, because they have been forced upon us all in books of evidence, because we have learnt them by rote, before they came out to us naturally and simply as characteristics of that which we were reading, yet they are true remarks, and can as little be passed over by any thoughtful reader, as any peculiarity in the style of an ancient classic. Therefore we find an evidently growing conviction in the minds of the more intelligent sceptics, that there must be a scheme for the purpose of explaining these difficulties. The whole history must be accounted for, not merely by finding fault with the details of the narrative, but by dividing the person of whom it speaks, according to his historical and his mythical attributes. This is the experiment which I have so often noticed. It may be applied to the Gospel narratives; but unless it will solve all the facts relating to a spiritual and universal kingdom which we have been considering it is worth nothing. Shew that there is no such constitution for mankind, and you have confuted the Gospels, for they are built upon the assumption that there is. But if there be such a kingdom, we must know who is the Head and Lord of it, and how He has established it. These Gospels have given that knowledge to men for many centuries; we believe that they have yet much more to communicate, which we have not been able to receive, but which the events of this time, and these very controversies, will make known to us. Feeling that they are given us, and that they have a deep reality in them, we cannot be unwilling that they should be submitted to any scrutiny. If there be anything in them which was not meant to be in them, we doubt not but it will be brought to light, and that He who brings it to light will make His own truth the clearer by the discovery. But that they contain that which no other books in the world contain, which no other parts of the Scripture contain, and which is a key to all that is written elsewhere; this, we believe, has been made and will be made only the more evident, by the questions which have been raised in these and in former days respecting them.

THE ROMISH SYSTEM.

I have contended, then, that a Bible without a Church is inconceivable, that the appointed ministers of the Church are the appointed instruments for guiding men into a knowledge of the Bible, that the notion of private judgment is a false notion, that Inspiration belongs to the Church, and not merely to the writers of the Bible, that the miracles of the New Testament were the introduction of a new dispensation, and were not merely a set of strange acts belonging to a particular time; lastly, that the Gospel narratives must be received as parts of the necessary furniture of the Church. Now is there not a manifest tendency towards Romanism in these positions? Do they not one and all belong to the system which I have denounced?

Let us consider:

1st. I have supposed the Bible and the Church to be mutual interpreters of each other. The Church exists as a fact, the Bible shews what that fact means. The Bible is a fact, the Church shews what that fact means. Now, what I complain of in Romanism, is that it has entirely overlooked the relation of these two parts of God's scheme to each other. It has concealed the Bible from men on purpose that the Church might be exalted. And it has proved

that the Church could not be exalted while the
Bible was hidden, that while there was no book to
explain to the whole body of the Church its own position, that position of necessity became unintelligible.
Men did not know what it was to be Churchmen,
because they could not learn it from this book, and
because no other was able to tell them.

2ndly. Hence we see, wherein my notion of the
powers of ministers differs from that of the Romanist.
He thinks that the minister has a power and commission to hide the Bible from the laity. I think he has a
power and commission to lay it open to the laity. I think
that every one has an appointed work to do; that when we
refuse our own appointed work, or do not acknowledge
the different appointment of another, we necessarily
miss some good which was intended for us. And
therefore I do not think that the laity, rejecting the
teachings of their appointed ministers, will understand the Bible. And I do not think, on the other
hand, that the minister, putting himself in place of
the Bible, and not encouraging the laity to read it, and
digest it, can be a true teacher, can exercise the
powers which God has committed to him.

3rdly. I believe, as I have said, that the Bible and
the Church were intended to raise men out of their
private judgments, and to guide each man who will
be guided, into the truth which is meant for all. The
Romanist claims an authority for the Church in opposition to private judgments. But it is not an authority to call forth the spirits of men—to draw them
out of the little narrow circle of private experiences
and conclusions; but an authority to crush the exercise of their spirits, to hinder them from obtaining

freedom.   And therefore this authority has itself become the tool of private judgments.   Half the inventions of Romanism are the inventions of private judgment, the fruits of a condescension on the part of the priest to the narrow-minded feelings and judgments of his subjects, or else the creations of his own judgment, both alike manifesting the need of that universal law and standard by which both ought to have been tried.

4thly. The presence of that Spirit who is the source of all inspiration, in the whole body of the Church, and in each of its members that he may fulfil his own appointed position,—this is involved in the idea of our baptism; disbelieving this, we acknowledge no Church at all.   In virtue of this gift, we are to believe that every member of the Church has a capacity for understanding the high privileges which have been obtained for him; in virtue of this gift, we believe that the ministers of the Church can educate their flocks into the apprehension of them.   Our complaint against the Romish system is, that it does not allow us to act upon the faith of this inspiration.   It supposes inspiration to be communicated to certain persons at certain periods, for the sake of certain startling effects.   It supposes an inspiration to reside somewhere in the Church, for the purpose of determining what men are, and what they are not, to hold, for the purposes of keeping down questioning, and giving a sense to Scripture.   But an abiding Spirit, one who will guide into all truth, and can tolerate no falsehood, one who can unfold the Scriptures to different ages according to their different wants, such a Spirit, such an inspiration, it will not allow us to recognize.

5thly. And, therefore, our difference on the subject of miracles is also very intelligible.   If you recognize miracles, as connected with the idea of a spiritual kingdom, and not merely belonging to a certain book, why, the Romanist asks, will you not recognize the miracles in which we believe ? why not suppose that they may occur in the nineteenth century as well as in the first? I answer, I neither affirm nor deny anything as to the question how often in the history of the Church or in what periods of it God may have been pleased to suspend the operations of intermediate agents, for the purpose of shewing that He is at all times the Author and Mover of them.   This question must be determined by a careful study of historical evidence ; upon the result of such a study I should be very sorry to dogmatize.   Those who believe that miracles are for the assertion of order, and not for the violation of it, for the sake of proving the constant presence of a spiritual power, and not for the sake of shewing that it interferes occasionally with the affairs of the world, will be the least inclined to expect the frequent repetitions of such signs, for they hold, that being recorded as facts in the former ages of the world, they become laws in ours, that we are to own Him who healed the sick of the palsy in every cure which is wrought by the ordinary physician, Him who stilled the storm on the Lake of Gennesareth, in the guidance and preservation of every ship which crosses the ocean ; and that this effect would be lost, if we were led to put any contempt upon that which is daily and habitual. Still, I should think it very presumptuous to say, that it has never been needful, in the modern history of the world, to break the idols of sense and experience by the same method which was sanctioned in the days of old. Far less should I be inclined to underrate the piety and criticise the wisdom or honesty of those men who, missing or overlooking intermediate powers, of which they knew little, at once referred the acts and events they witnessed to their primary source.

But these admissions only compel me the more solemnly to reject at least nineteen-twentieths of all the miracles recorded in Romanist books in later times. In reference to these, we are not bound to go into a careful collation of evidences. In general there is very little to collate, but where there is apparently the best and most respectable, there is a grand preliminary objection. I dare not believe such miracles as these, *because* I believe the miracles of the New Testament. I am expressly told in Scripture that there are miracles which I am not to believe, which are to produce no impression upon me whatever. I do not want to go into the question of the honesty or the dishonesty of persons who report them, that is a question between their own consciences and their Creator; they best know whether they are or are not lying for God. But it is the character of the miracle which determines my judgment of it. Is it to lead me into the worship of the Visible or the Invisible? Is it to deliver me from sensible things, or to make me a slave of sensible things?

Does the Romanist advocate say that I have no right to ask these questions? I know he says so— and I will tell him why he says so. He says so because there is a secret root of unbelief in his mind, a secret doubt whether anything *is* true, which finds refuge in the thought that everything *may be* true. This is a very prevailing tendency in our day; it is the natural reaction against the scepticism of the last century. A number of men in France and Germany, and perhaps quite as many in England as in either, have passed or are passing, not through any gradual stages, but *per saltum*, from universal doubt to universal credence. And they are able to carry the same habits of mind into both professions; they are able to say to themselves with great complacency, and with no little truth, 'we are not really changed, we do not acknowledge any standard now more than before; the only difference is, that we have substituted the new *pourquoi non* for the old *pourquoi*.' It does not the least surprise us to hear such men, men who twenty years ago would have laughed us to scorn for believing in the resurrection of Lazarus, now indulging in fierce denunciations of all who doubt the miracles in the Tyrol. The logic, '*where are you to stop short?*' was that which they used in their contemptuous manhood, and which still seems to them perfectly conclusive, in their not less contemptuous nor less really sceptical old age. We can only repeat, we stop short when we find ourselves arrived at the exact contradiction of that which we have believed. We have received our Lord as the Great Deliverer, who has led captive our captivity to sense; we stop short when we meet with persons who would bring us into that captivity again.

The Bible, we believe, is meant to cultivate in us a habit of distinguishing; faithfully and humbly used, it has that effect. If you, who have not used it or believed in it, shew that you have not acquired that habit, we have only another reason for giving thanks,.

that God has been pleased not to hide the blessing from us or from our children.

6thly. These last considerations apply very remarkably to the case of the Gospel narratives. It is said, "The Church has preserved to us these histories of our Lord's life; you receive them upon the authority of the Church. You know very little about the persons who wrote them, you accept them because they are given to you as parts of the canon. Well, but the Church has put its sanction upon many histories of the saints; she deems them also profitable for her children. Granted that they refer to inferior persons, that they never can be as important as the Gospels, yet where do you draw the line? You have admitted Church authority in one case, the highest case of all, why not admit it also in a lower case?" I answer, By the care of God's providence through his Church, these records of its Lord and Head have been preserved. They have been preserved, no doubt, for many great and solemn purposes, but for this especially, that there may be a standard in the world, by which all other acts and lives may be tried. Exclude the Gospels from our canon, let there be nothing there but epistles setting forth spiritual principles, and not only do those principles lose their meaning for want of a true personal object to which they may refer; but *this* end is wholly lost—there is no character set before men, which exhibits to them the image after which they were formed in connexion with the life of this earth. Now if the Church have preserved for me these books, and have told me the object for which they were preserved, I am not obeying her when I lose sight of this object; I am not obeying her when I am not bringing all other books and lives to this standard. I am not, indeed, to do this for the sake of condemning them, not for the sake of seeing what is wrong in them—I have no commission or powers for that purpose—but certainly for the sake of seeing how far I may safely follow them. If, then, I find records of different men, all professedly acknowledging this type or image as the one to which they should be conformed, I am bound thankfully to admire every feature of their lives which has been caught by reflection from it. I may very often go wrong in my judgment of these features; I may mistake a bad copy for a good one, or disown a true one because I have not sufficient spiritual cultivation to understand the circumstances of its form and colouring. Still, the more I study the original under such guidance as is given to me, the more I must believe and hope that the faculty will be cultivated in me, whereby I may discern the true from the counterfeit. And I must look to the Church to help me in this work, to be continually teaching me how to observe the traces of the Divine model in the human imitation, how to see what in it was produced merely by the accidents of the time, or by human self-will and frailness.

Such help I believe the Church, holding the Bible in her hand, is able to furnish to her faithful disciples; and my charge against the Romish system is, that it has hindered the Church from exercising this prerogative, and forced her to exercise a most different one. What I mean will be best understood by the use which has been made in this system of the word ' Saint.'

The Gospels teach me, the Church in all ages teaches me, to acknowledge our Lord as one who perfectly identified himself with humanity, with all its sorrows and sufferings, yea, with its sins ; because He was without sin, He was able to bear the sins of all men. This character of essential humanity, is so much the character which we feel to belong to our Lord, so much the character which did manifest, and which alone could manifest, His divinity, that it may be said to be the grand object of the Church, in her Advents, her Epiphanies, her Lents, her Passion Weeks, her Easter-Days, her Ascension-Days, to exhibit it. And it has been the feeling of every true saint in the world's history, that this was the character which our Lord would especially seek to produce in His disciples. A largeness of heart, a sympathy with all our race, a fellowship in its sufferings, grief for the sins which hold it down, these assuredly are qualities which the most conspicuous saints of the Romish calendar acknowledge as most high and Divine. Along with these are associated humiliation, suffering, indifference to good or evil report. But now comes in the counterfeit system : 'What a great and glorious thing it is to be a saint, to be above the rest of men, to be unlike them ! What a fine thing it is to be humble, self-denying, submitting to persecution and shame ! What glory do those get who can eclipse one another in this race ! What an honour it is to be enrolled in this calendar ; what fame we get here, what rewards in the life to come !' Who does not feel instinctively that we have here introduced a new image, the very opposite to that we were just considering. It has come in one knows not how, under the very names and words which seemed so sacred and beautiful; but see how frightful and deformed it is! Yet will anyone dare to say that there has not been a system, that there is not a system now, which sanctions this image, puts honour upon it, holds it up to imitation and idolatry?

We are not bound to say of any particular person, He has given himself up to this system, he has caught this image. We may believe, and rejoice to believe, that there have been multitudes in every age of the Church, that there are numbers in every country in Europe at this day, who, be their outward professions and symbols what they may, do in their hearts confess the true image, do in their lives conform to it. Such persons belong to the Catholic Church, they are witnesses of her permanence, and that she will one day come out bright and beautiful from all her corruptions, as a bride adorned for her husband. But the existence of such persons only makes us see more clearly and hate more fervently the system which has assumed the name and affected the powers of the Church; only makes us believe more surely, that it will be destroyed by the brightness of His coming, who is the true and only Pope and Potentate, the real King of Saints.

CHAPTER V.

ON THE RELATIONS OF THE CHURCH WITH NATIONAL BODIES.

SECTION I.

The Old Testament—Ancient Pagan History—History of Modern Europe—General Inferences.

THE question how the Old Testament dispensation is related to the New, has already come before us in several forms. But hitherto we have considered it only in reference to those signs which all Christians believe to have passed away; the Quaker merging them in certain spiritual ideas, we supposing them to have been exchanged for other signs betokening higher truths. When we speak of that which is commonly called the moral side of the Jewish economy, the controversy assumes another shape. One set of Christians strongly affirm that the precepts of this kind in the old Law are of permanent obligation and validity; others say that they have no authority except so far as they are re-enacted by, or involved in, the Gospel law of love.

The holders of the first opinion in general confine their assertions to the Ten Commandments. They do not positively affirm that the sacredness of the Divine Code may not extend to certain parts of the

Jewish institutions—that point they are content to leave open; but these Commandments stand out in clear and awful distinctness; they were proclaimed amidst thunders and lightnings; the Jews looked upon them as written with the finger of God; the sense of mankind has received them as Divine. On the other hand, their opponents see no reason for separating these Commandments from the rest of the ritual, either for honour or dishonour. 'The historian declares that both proceeded from the Lord; it is not on the ground of a difference in their authority, then, that you can distinguish them. Neither can you distinguish them by their character. The Sabbath is as much a positive institution as the cities of refuge; if you admit the distinction between that which is moral and that which is positive, you must acknowledge both to be transitory; if you reject that distinction, neither.'

It was impossible to consider this subject in the last section; yet perhaps some hints which were given there may assist us now. I have maintained that the Scriptures interpret to us signs which we discover actually existing amongst us, and which require an interpreter. The New Testament has explained to us the signs of Baptism, The Creeds, Forms of Worship, The Eucharist, The Orders of Ministry, as these exist in modern Europe. It has explained them to be signs of a spiritual and universal society. It has shewn us what such a society means; what place each of these signs holds in it. Supposing these signs to have perished, supposing there to be no longer a dream of such a society, the Scripture would be a very puzzling book; while they last it is an indispensable one to those who would understand their own position. The early parts of it were necessary in this point of view, because they discovered part of the meaning which each sign embodies, enabling us gradually to attain to a perception of its full import, and to look upon it as connected with the life of man. When, therefore, we meet in these early records with customs, institutions, ordinances which God has not been pleased to preserve to us, we presume that they are to be [contemplated historically, by the light of that which He has preserved to us. Or, if there be a question whether, perhaps, they might not be advantageously restored, we are in a condition to examine this point by the light which Scripture gives us respecting the whole dispensation. But supposing we find any signs which, amidst all changes of circumstances, have maintained their existence and have become identified with the life of modern society, we must desire an explanation of them, and must seek for it where it is to be had. If we belong to a different period of the world from that in which we first find these traces, it may be very important to know how the change has affected them, whether they exist under the same conditions now as heretofore : but the fact that they do exist is the first of all ; this compels us to ask, whence they are derived, and on what ground they rest.

Now anyone who considers these Ten Commandments, must perceive that they are definitive and conservative, not creative or constitutive. They presume the existence of certain facts, principles, and institutions, and it is the violation or forgetfulness of these which they denounce. The first presumes that the Jews had been brought out of Egypt by an unseen Being. He is their deliverer and Lord; as such they are to acknowledge Him. The second presumes the existence of Worship, a tendency in men to create the objects of it for themselves out of the things which they see and handle; a relation between the worshippers and the Invisible Lord; a government exercised by Him from generation to generation. The third presumes the practice of appealing to the Name of God, of invoking Him as one who knows whether a man be guilty or innocent. The fourth assumes the institution of the Week; explains whereof it is the sign; gives warnings against the forgetfulness of the distinction between the six days and the seventh day. The fifth presumes the existence of the Paternal Relation, and treats the respect for it as the condition of abiding in the land given to the nation. The sixth presumes the existence of a community which is interested in the Life of each of its members. The seventh presumes the institution of Marriage. The eighth presumes the institution of Property. The ninth presumes the existence of Tribunals, before which one may give witness respecting another. The tenth affirms the existence of a bond of Neighbourhood—the same bond which is supposed in all the rest—and declares that even the coveting of that which is a neighbour's is a violation of it.

That these facts, institutions, and principles, had a very close connexion with the life and being of that nation which was brought out of Egypt, most readers will acknowledge: but if they turn to ancient history, they find that some of them had a very close connexion with the being and life of every nation which it speaks of. The Greeks and Romans were remarkably distinguished from each other. But they were both alike distinguished from the slaves and barbarians, of whose existence we become aware chiefly through them. Wherein lay the difference? Apart from all intellectual superiority, (though it is hardly right to say, *apart*, the one characteristic was so involved in the other,) it is quite evident that they had a clear sense of certain great landmarks and boundaries in human society, the violation of which was an evil; that they believed these landmarks to have been fixed by an awful Unseen Power, and to be preserved by that Power: that among the chief of these landmarks they reckoned the sacredness of life, of the paternal relation, of marriage, of property, of appeals to the Divine name, of tribunals for rectifying wrong; the law of neighbourhood as binding those who acknowledged a common ancestry, and were living in the same locality; the majesty of law as preserved by the majesty of worship.

But two of the Commandments have no counterparts in the legislation of Greece or Rome. There was, I have said, a distinct recognition of an unseen Majesty from which it proceeded, and by which it was upheld; there was not the prohibition of confounding the unseen Majesty with things visible. There was the recognition of different sacred seasons connected with the course of the sun and moon: there was not the recognition of a Week; a division of time depending upon some other law than the astronomical; defining human life, by its two great principles of action and rest; connecting these two principles with the life and being of God; teaching that His rest and action are the patterns of ours, and yet that He is ever at rest while we are working, and ever at work on our behalf while we are resting; incorporating the Divine with the common, and yet hallowing the distinction between them; signifying that the palace and the hut, nay, the master and his cattle, are subject to the same government; making each nightly slumber the image of the final repose of the spirit and soul and body, each in its proper and appointed object. Let anyone consider how the political life of these nations was affected by the sensual tendencies of their worship; let him meditate upon the difficulty which every philosopher experienced in his endeavour to reconcile the idea of a living, acting God, with one continually resting in his own beatitude, the still greater difficulty of finding any point of sympathy between his own thoughts and those of common men who felt that the God they feared must interfere in all their transactions, and then let him say whether the second or the fourth Commandments do not receive as much illustration and confirmation from the human feeling and conscience of the old world as the sixth or the seventh.

Be that as it may, not only some of these institutions, but all of them, exist among ourselves. The Jewish order of time, so far as the week is concerned, has become as much a part of the institutions of modern Europe as marriage or property. All three may be regarded in different places with more or less of reverence; but they are recognized by every nation of Christendom, and incorporated with their daily transactions.

But on what authority do these institutions rest?

Here begins another difference of opinion. The ordinary statesman answers, 'They are national provisions, of more or less importance, deriving their sanction from the legislation of each particular national society, invested with a factitious and useful sacredness in the eyes of the vulgar by the tradition that they had a mysterious origin.' The ordinary religious man answers, 'They have nothing to do with the mere political or national life of any society; they are religious ordinances, appointed by God Himself, binding upon all because He has appointed them.' With the first I agree so far as this, that I do look upon these institutions as belonging especially and emphatically to particular nations *as such*, to England as England, to France as France, to Germany as Germany. I do not look upon them as universal institutions in the sense in which I have called Baptism and the Eucharist universal institutions; that is to say, as institutions which have nothing to do with the relations of space and time. And if the religious man objects to this distinction, I tell him that I must make it because the Scripture makes it. 'I am the Lord *thy* God'—this is the sanction of the code; clearly a distinct national sanction. But I differ with the statesman in this point. I do not think national society is a lie or stands upon a lie. If I did I should wish it to perish, and I should be sure it must perish. Now unfortunately he does think this, for he knows that he cannot maintain any of those institutions which he believes to be necessary for his nation, and for every nation, merely by his own rules and conventions. He is obliged to ask help from the faith which men everywhere have had that there is a Divine ruler, not only over men generally, but over their particular commonwealth; and this faith, he says, is a mere delusion. I believe that the imposition and dishonesty are in himself; that the conviction of mankind is a safe and an honest one; and that it will at last prevail against all the frauds which have endeavoured to support it, and have really made it weak.

In my conclusion, then, I agree with those who take the common religious view of this matter. But the difference in our premises is not a slight one, or one without the most practical consequences. I have partly explained wherein it consists, but I must endeavour to make my meaning more clear. We are first told that we must not look upon these Commandments merely as parts of a national institute. And yet they evidently are parts of a national institute. We are told that we must not receive them merely as of outward or formal obligation, for they contain the essence of morality. But they do seem to have a particularly outward and formal character. They refer, not one but all, to formal institutions; only the last even touches upon any internal habit of mind, and the exceeding definiteness of that one, 'Thou shalt not covet thy neighbour's wife, nor his man-servant, nor his maid-servant, nor his ox, nor his ass,' shews that the habit is noticed for the sake of the act, not the act for the sake of the habit. So far from wishing to overlook this characteristic, I am most anxious to notice it and dwell upon it; for herein I believe consists the exceeding importance of these Commandments, and the proof that they are not superseded by the new dispensation. They set the Divine seal upon that which belongs to man as a creature of flesh and blood, inhabiting a particular place, having a definite circle of human relations and earthly associations; they declare these to be settled according to a Divine order, and to be taken under a Divine cognizance; they bring acts, outward ordinary acts, into judgment.

By adopting this view, we seem to escape from some serious confusions. We are able to enter into the peculiar character of the Jewish nation, without losing our sense of its connexion with all mankind. We are able, by help of it, to connect our own lives with the lives of those people in the old world, of whom we read, and with whom we feel that we have such close sympathies, in spite of all differences of race, of language, of religious faith and knowledge. Above all, we are able to rid ourselves of the Manichæan notion (which it should be remembered has been always connected with a low notion of the Old Testament), that the outward and visible universe, and the ordinary social relations, are the creations of an evil spirit, to be esteemed lightly by all who have attained to the perception of a higher economy. That this last accursed doctrine, which cleaves most closely to the hearts of us all, and perhaps was never more threatening than at this day, will ever be fully exposed and scouted till we acknowledge the sanctity, the grandeur, the divinity of national life, I do not think that the history of mankind offers us the least excuse for believing. But, then, if we admit these positions, and have arrived at them by this method, other questions will necessarily force themselves upon us. We have seen that the objectors to the authority of the Ten Commandments found their most plausible argument upon the difficulty of separating them from the surrounding history. It has seemed to us that this difficulty is a very light one when we meet with records of that to which we have nothing answering among ourselves. Assume the fact of a nation, assume the Jews to be the specimen of a nation, and you assume, as a matter of course, the necessity of hundreds of regulations applicable to their condition, and therefore not applicable to ours. But if principles of national life have discovered themselves to us in the midst of these regulations, we must expect to find the history illustrating these principles, and thereby furnishing the key to facts which directly concern our own conduct. And this proves to be the case. We find it a part, not an accidental but an essential part, of the idea of a Jewish commonwealth, that Punishments should be inflicted upon transgressors, that in certain cases their lives should be taken away. The judicial Oath again belongs to the religion of the Jewish state; every Jew would have understood the third Commandment in reference to it. Still more obviously was the Jew instructed to look upon War, in certain cases, not as a permitted licence but as a solemn duty, to be undertaken in the full confidence that it was God's will he should engage in it, and that he should have God's help in carrying it through. Now these feelings and convictions belonged in like manner to every great nation of antiquity; belonged to them as nations, formed part of their religion, were the means of exhibiting those qualities in them which we are most compelled to admire. Courage, self-discipline, order, faith, all these moral attributes were connected in them with the conviction, that national life is a more precious thing than individual life, and that hundreds of thousands of individuals are cheaply sacrificed for the sake of preserving it. If it be said that these moral qualities were mixed with others of the most opposite character, and that these too found their gratification in wars and in judicial severity, no man in his senses will dispute the assertion. What I contend for is, that they were *opposite* qualities, however they might be intermingled; and that therefore, if we hate the one we must love the other, or else all moral distinction will become effaced in our minds. And what I say further is, that if we attach any sacredness to the Jewish history, as containing the Divine specimen of a national life, we cannot refuse to believe that the other nations of antiquity were justified in their deep inward conviction, that God has not given swords to men in vain, but that there are occasions on which the magistrate is bound, by his allegiance to God, to cut off the offender against the majesty of the law; on which the ruler of the land must invite and command his subjects to chastise the removers of landmarks, the corrupters of the earth, and the oppressors of mankind.

But even this discovery would not give us more than an historical interest in this part of the Jewish records. They are brought directly home to ourselves by the fact that every nation of Christendom resorts to judicial Oaths, imposes Punishments, in some cases capital, and believes War, under certain circumstances, to be a duty. The question, then, becomes a very important one; is this meant to be so or not? Is this Old Testament, this book which we have found to be a key to the main problems of our national life,

a justification of these convictions? It is in vain to
say that Jewish precedent will only justify oaths administered, punishments fixed, or wars undertaken,
under the express command of God. I have maintained that every nation ought to look upon itself as
having the Lord for its King; that if we do not
recognise that principle, the Commandments mean
nothing to us, the institutions of which the Commandments speak have no authority but that which they
derive from human convention. According to this
doctrine, the question what acts a nation ought to
perform and what it ought to omit, means, in other
words, what acts are in conformity with the purpose
for which God has appointed it, and what are not.
These acts need not be the same as those which the
Jews performed, because each nation has a purpose to
fulfil different from that which the Jews were to fulfil.
But these convictions which I speak of are common
to all nations as nations. They have been guiding
maxims assumed in the examination of particular
cases. The conscience of men has said, *Because*
oaths, punishments, and wars are in themselves autho-
rized by God, and can be only justifiable in those
cases and under the conditions which He approves,
therefore ought we to consider earnestly what these
cases and conditions are. The question is, whether
this primary assumption is or is not warranted by the
book which sets forth to us the Divine principles of
national society. It is idle to say, But where do you
find the authority for wars, oaths, or punishments in
the New Testament? I do not find the authority for
any of the distinct institutes of national life in the
New Testament. The Manichæans and Anabaptists

were quite right, when they said that there was no distinct precept respecting property in the New Testament; that the first sign of the existence of a Church was that of men not calling their goods their own, but counting all things common. Nor was there anything unnatural in their feeling, that since in the resurrection men neither marry nor are given in marriage, the kingdom of Christ, which is the kingdom of the risen life, must look with some contempt on the union of the sexes. Nor was it a surprising inference, from the continual allusions in the Gospels to our Lord's controversies with the Pharisees respecting the Sabbath day, that under the new economy, the distinction of days had been abrogated. If their first maxim was true, that we are to look for the whole law of man's life in the New Testament, all their conclusions, even though they might be contradicted by actual passages in it, were inevitable. If it can be shown that these, or any portion of our national creed, are *denounced* in the New Testament, we, of course, must abandon them, even though by doing so we involve ourselves in the most painful perplexities respecting the nature and the permanence of moral principles. Whether they are so denounced, I shall have to consider presently. What I am maintaining now is, that the mere absence of the same kind of language, in reference to these subjects, which occurs in every page of the Jewish Scripture, is no more a proof that they do not concern us, than the omission of any direct allusion to the principles of moral philosophy by a writer on political economy is a proof that he disbelieves them.

But, it will be said, these two cases are not

analogous, or, if they are analogous, it is because the writers on political economy *ought* to take cognizance of moral principles. If the universal society and the national society be both intended for man, any book which sets forth the character of either must touch upon the nature and laws of the other. Be it so : I am far from denying this assertion; it is one which I especially wish that the reader should feel the importance of. I do not expect to find the principles of the universal society developed in the Old Testament, nor the principles of the national society in the New. I do expect to find each illustrating and sustaining the other. I do expect that under one dispensation as much as the other, there should be signs that they are distinct but inseparable. Such signs force themselves upon me when I look into the Jewish records. We have seen how the germs of a universal society were planted in the heart of the Jewish commonwealth; how the existence of the priest, of the sacrifices, of the tabernacle, as much testified to the existence of that which is human and general, as the king, the judge, the law, testified to the existence of that which is peculiar and exclusive. The words at first sound paradoxical; to a Jew they would sound very paradoxical. He would say, ' Why, our likeness consisted in those features which you set down as peculiar, our difference in those which you set down as common.' Such a notion is plausible; I have already, I think, explained sufficiently why it is not true. The Hebrew was to be separate from all other people, in order that he might be the steward of a possession which was meant for all. He was cut off that he might witness of a Being who was not

cognizable by the senses, not material, not therefore
divided, not belonging to this or that locality. When
the member of the nation forgot that He was the
Lord God of the Hebrews, and sought to break
the chain of this peculiar polity, he failed to perform his function, he failed to be witness for a
God of the whole earth. When he refused to look
upon his covenant as capable of expanding to comprehend all nations, he lost his peculiar position, he
became the member of a sect, instead of the citizen of
a kingdom. This is unquestionably a paradox, but is
the paradox of Scripture, well worthy of our observation and study. I say, then, that there was a human
element in the national society, and that the methods
by which this element was incorporated with the
national element, and yet shewn to be distinct from it,
were very remarkable. The priestly tribe is one of
the twelve tribes, but it is cut off from all the rest,
placed under particular conditions, supported by a
particular species of property. From the very commencement of the commonwealth, the offices of the
priest and lawgiver are carefully separated. Both are
equally Divine, but neither may intrude upon the
functions of the other. And this is not because the
office of the priest is limited to what are technically
called religious services. He examines the leprous
man, and pronounces whether he is or is not fit to go
into the congregation of the Lord; he distinguishes
between the meats which are clean and unclean.
Whatever has to do with the direct oversight of that
which is internal, whether in the physical or the moral
life of man, this belongs to the sacerdotal part of the
commonwealth; whatever has to do with the outward

regulation of society, whether those regulations have reference to the bodily comfort or to the behaviour of men, this, it would seem, belongs to the legal part of it. Each presents the unseen Lord to the Israelites; the one as a Judge, taking cognizance of all their acts; the other, as one who spies out all their ways, knows what is passing within, deals not with crimes only, but with sins; who can take away the source of evil as well as its fruit. At the same time, as there is no division between the internal and the external life of man, no division in the character of God as the Lord of the outward and the Lord of the inward world, so neither is there in the Jewish economy between the offices which represent him in these characters. The sacrifice of the priest is necessary to hallow the troops which the king is leading out to battle; the king takes part in every ecclesiastical reformation. We feel that the Jewish commonwealth is one society, not a national body *plus* an ecclesiastical, but a body which could not be national if it were not ecclesiastical, or ecclesiastical if it were not national.

Now the counterpart of these signs we discover in both the two great nations in the pagan world. The difference between them is remarkable and characteristic. In the heart of each Greek state, we may indeed observe a priesthood, exercising some important functions. But the far more striking object which presents itself to our notice is the sacred ground of Elis, the common temple of Delphi. These were the signs and pledges of a fellowship between Greeks and Greeks, which the diversities of race, and the antipathies of democratical and aristocratical governments, could not sever. On the other hand, in

Rome, the sacerdotal influence is incorporated with all the national institutions, the name of every conspicuous office in the republic reminds us of the union. And it was this union which imparted so much solidity to the Roman society, after the principles upon which it was founded had been set at naught, after the Roman emperor had become "the king of kings and lord of lords," and his kingdom had been changed into one of those which are described in Scripture as Babylonian kingdoms, resting upon mere power, effacing national distinctions, exalting the visible above the invisible.

To this kingdom, we have considered the kingdom of Christ as the direct and formal opposite. The question, then, which we proposed before we entered upon the examination of its different signs, whether or no it resembled the Roman world in its hostility to national society, or whether it is meant to be, as it was in its embryo condition, the quickening spirit of national society, is one which we are bound to consider. We have seen that it had its cradle in a nation, that it appeared in that nation at a time when the old spirit had departed; when the Jews were calling themselves Pharisees, Sadducees, and Essenes; were striving to make their kingdom into a system or a sect. We have seen that the disciples of Jesus at once went back to the old language of their countrymen, refused to be spoken of as a sect of Nazarenes or Christians, proclaimed their Master to be the heir of David's throne, the King of Israel, declared themselves, and invited all men, to be his subjects.

Such a pretension was intelligible to the Jews;

by them it was denounced and persecuted: to the Romans it seemed utterly ridiculous. The Christians were one, perhaps the most extravagant, but certainly the least rebellious, of the Jewish sects; the Proconsuls in the different provinces were willing to protect them against the fanaticism of their countrymen.

It was a little different, when the professors of the new doctrine were brought face to face with the Cæsars. An instinct seemed to tell Nero that there was something in their position which was incompatible with his; what it was, however, could not be clearly understood till the Jewish polity had been destroyed. Then this body was seen still to remain, still to be adopting that language which was apparently derived from the old Jewish dreams now so signally confuted. The Christians still speak of themselves as members of a kingdom. The exclusiveness which had made the Jewish pretensions comparatively harmless was not preserved in them; they addressed themselves to all people in all provinces of the empire; they bound their converts together in a corporation, held them in one by a strange freemasonry.

The most philosophical emperors were least able to look with indifference upon such a fellowship. They might from benignity or contempt deal kindly with individual cases, but the society was an anomaly incompatible with the safety of the government. As that government approached more and more nearly to the character of a military despotism, the contest between it and the spiritual society became more flagrant, the necessity that one or the other should fall more evident. When Rome became almost Asiatic under Diocletian, the Cross had attained a power which the mild emperor might be inclined to tolerate, but which the state could not endure. But the most vigorous of all the persecutions failed of its object; the new kingdom could not be put down; under Constantine, the eagle did homage to it. Then the organization of the Church became connected with that of the empire; the civil dioceses became coincident with the jurisdictions of the Bishops, as well in Italy as in the provinces; the ecclesiastical officer acquired a civil position, the emperor exercised more or less of jurisdiction in spiritual affairs.

Here was the phenomenon of a superannuated despotism, based upon the acknowledgment of mere power, entering into union with a body based upon the acknowledgment of a King ruling in righteousness, whose strength both in himself and in his disciples had been made perfect in weakness. The alliance had not been sought by the Church; as a proof of her Master's dominion it was to be received with thankfulness; as a part of God's dispensations to mankind she was to enter into it, not as a state which could last, but as one which must hasten the coming of a new order of things. The change of the centre of government prepared the way for the approaching revolution. The Byzantine monarchy might be considered in some respects a new one, coming into existence at the very time Christianity was recognized, not necessarily established upon the old military maxims. But these maxims were implied in it; there was the same effort, however checked by other influences, after universal dominion. The dislocation of it by the Mahometan conquests proved that such a dominion is one which,

in conjunction with Christianity, cannot exist. In
the West the demonstration was still clearer. The
century after Constantine saw the dissolution of a
fabric which had stood for a thousand years. Charle-
magne re-established it as a Christian empire; in the
next generation it is again shivered into fragments.
But meantime the Christian Church was at work
upon the barbarian tribes. And what was the nature
of the operation? Had the Bishops of the Church
acted according to their own notions of what was
best, they would, of course, have reduced Europe into
one great society, having a common language, scarcely
acknowledging any territorial or political distinctions.
Such a dream would have seemed to be a most pious
one, carrying out the idea of the Divine commonwealth.
That they entertained it, and at different times strove
to realize it, and that they found the old Roman
jurisprudence a helpful aid in the experiment, the
history of the Middle Ages abundantly testifies. But
how was it defeated? I answer, *By the influences
which they themselves, when acting simply as Churchmen in their appointed vocation, and not as agents of a
preconceived system, brought to bear upon the tribes.*
The ecclesiastical society was the main instrument
in creating within each of these tribes a distinct
national organization, altogether different from the
ecclesiastical organization, though acting in concert
with it; by the ecclesiastical or Catholic spirit,
peculiarities in the character and intellect of each
one of these tribes were developed. The Bishops
called themselves an *Order*, said that they received
their commission from an invisible King, that they
were a link with generations past and generations to

come. When the chieftain who came into the land previously subjected to Roman government found this order established and submitted himself to it, he began to think differently of his own office, to consider it less as conferred by individual powers or cunning, to connect it less with the sword and conquest, more with some claim of religion. If these first notions of a government resting upon ordinance perished in the bud, or were extinguished by the ruder feelings of power with which they were associated, the tribe remained barbarous, became divided, and was overcome by some other more capable of receiving cultivation. If they bore fruit, (and this was more quickly the case when Bishops were the invaders of a ground previously pagan than when they converted the pagan invaders of their own,) the military chief over some district, or the bretwalda over several, was changed into the king anointed with oil, doing homage for his authority to Christ, transmitting his kingdom in a hereditary line. He has, of course, his council of chieftains, the sharers with him of the soil which he has conquered. The Bishops, as possessing greater wisdom and a character of sacredness, are invited to take part in the deliberations of this council. Gradually the whole council begins to look upon itself as an Order, bound together by another tie of allegiance to their sovereign than that of mere fellowship in arms; holding their lands by another tenure than that of mere conquest, recognising relations between themselves and their dependants. Here is the first form of a national society. If it merely stays in this form, it will be still only a feudal society: but it may gradually develop itself under the same moral influence, till one and another portion of the community shall have felt itself also to be an order, shall have become an integral part of the nation. But while this process is going forward, we find indications that the spiritual society itself has acquired a national position. It had established itself already when it was a missionary body first in some great city, which became the home of its Bishop or overseer; then it had sent forth its presbyters into different districts. The Bishops become permanently connected with the cities, the districts are *parishes* acknowledged by the civil body as connected with an ecclesiastical jurisdiction. The owners of the soil do homage to this arrangement; a part of its produce is appropriated to the teacher of the district in which it is found. The wealth of individuals is voluntarily contributed for the purpose of establishing permanent endowments in particular districts, or for the use of particular districts in certain diocesan centres. And it begins to be felt more and more that the spiritual officer is, as he was among the Jews, conversant with all that is internal, all that lies beyond the sphere of sense. This conviction gives rise to schools and universities; first, some enlightened ruler establishes them, then some noble or commoner, interested in the welfare of a certain neighbourhood, provides funds, which may enable the objects of his peculiar care to share in the general education of the land.

I am not aware that any of these statements are exclusively applicable to any one nation of modern Europe. Under different modifications, this is the history of the formation of modern society. The modifications are very

interesting and very important, because they illustrate
another point to which I have alluded; the way in which
the characters and institutions of the nations received
their distinct form, so that there should be vastly
more difference between Englishmen, Frenchmen, and
Germans now, than there ever can have been between
Saxons, Franks, and Burgundians twelve hundred
years ago. Still they were only in part the cause of
these differences. A similar tillage, working upon
different soils, will educe all their latent peculiarities,
will make it manifest what each was meant to bring
forth. This tillage has been carried on by the universal society. It has not, as we have seen, acted
according to its own notion; it has not cast Christendom into the mould into which a Churchman would
have naturally tried to cast it. There has been
evidently a higher will, another power at work, cross-
ing human calculations. But if we trace the history
of modern Europe, we see, that by some means or
other, a witness has been borne to that very constitution which Scripture makes known to us. The
form of national society which the Old Testament
invests with so much sacredness, is reproduced by
that other New Testament society which seemed to
have displaced it. As before, a spiritual element was
proved to be necessary to uphold a legal society, so
now, a legal element, a body expressing the sacredness
and majesty of law, is shewn to be necessary in order
to fulfil the objects for which the spiritual and universal
society exists. In what way each is necessary to the
other, what kind of duties each has to perform for the
sake of the other, this has been the question which men
have constantly asked themselves, and to which they

have invented the most opposite answers. Those who have gone along with us in our earlier inquiries, will feel that this question, instead of being obsolete, never occupied men's thoughts so much as at the present time. And they will feel too, perhaps, that though the speculations of men may have done comparatively little, the experience of the world has done much, in supplying an answer to it. The legal power can no longer help the spiritual power by persecuting and putting down its enemies; the spiritual power can no longer help the legal power, by throwing a fictitious sacredness around it. On the other hand, the spiritual power cannot make men feel that there is a Being who is the Judge and punisher of evil acts, unless it can shew that His authority is somewhere impersonated; the legal power tries in vain to convince those who are subject to it, that there is a Being who can renew and mould the will, unless it can shew how that mighty influence is exerted. The Church wishes to make men feel that they are subjects, but its own influence is one which especially aims at setting them free; the State wishes to have a free intelligent people, but it has itself only the power of keeping men servants. If any great work is to be done for man, if God's gracious purposes to him are to be fulfilled, one would think that these two powers must be meant continually to act and react upon each other, and to learn better, by each new error they commit, their distinct functions, their perfect harmony.

Sermon on the Mount—Different passages in it considered—Provision
for Ministers.

THE Quaker objects to this whole statement: formally, to that part of it which treats of war, oaths,
and punishment, and of a national provision for the
spiritual body; practically, to all the principles upon
which these institutions have been defended. 'Our
arguments,' he says, 'may sound plausible enough
to worldly men; those who take the Gospel simply,
and try to form themselves according to its precepts,
find them directly and in terms contradicted by the
Sermon on the Mount. The highest of all authorities
has said " Swear not at all;" "resist not evil;" "love
your enemies." We choose to say that the practices
of statesmen, who set these precepts aside, are reasonable and religious. He has in the plainest words
annulled the maxims of the old dispensation in
reference to these points; it pleases us to affirm that
they are still binding. But it is not in our power
to make bitter sweet, or evil good, though we may
call them so; men will be judged by Christ's commands, not by our glosses upon them. Our theory
however, is consistent, if not with the language of
our Master, at least with our own practice. We
wish worldly men to receive us into their houses;
it is fitting that when they are in debt one hundred
measures of wheat to their Lord we should bid them
take their bills and write fourscore. If we become
pensioners on the nation's bounty, we must make the
best of the nation's sins. The Apostles followed

a different rule. They lived upon the love of their flocks; they took what was cheerfully given them by those whom they served. We have not only become hirelings instead of shepherds, but we actually boast of the change, and think ill of them who will not submit to it.'

I. As the first class of these charges turns primarily upon the interpretation of the 5th chapter of St. Matthew's Gospel, I will enter at once into an examination of that portion of Scripture. We are accused of violating the spirit of it, of perverting the letter of it, of lowering the high standard of duty set forth in it. I shall think my case not established if I fail in bringing home each of these charges to the Quaker himself.

1. It is impossible to read the first sentences of the Sermon on the Mount, without feeling that they must be in some measure a key to its whole purpose. The series of blessings upon certain states of mind compels us to feel that we are in the presence of One who is come to establish a kingdom in the inner man; to deal with the principles of things; to lay the axe to the roots; to baptize with the Spirit and with fire; to reform the fruit by reforming the tree. We cannot help feeling, that however little worth there may be in the notion or superstition of an intended parallelism between the mountain on which the trumpet sounded long and loud, and that on which Jesus opened his mouth and spake, the principle implied in that parallelism is exactly true.

2. The words, "Ye are the salt of the earth, ye are the light of the world"—the exhortation to see that the salt possesses that quality by which it hinders

putrefaction in other bodies, and do not contract their tendency to corruption; to take care that the light be not quenched by the inner darkness which it is meant to penetrate, and thus be prevented from manifesting itself outwardly to men;—these exhortations are in exact accordance with that which has preceded them, and shew forth the nature of the authority with which the new teacher spake, and which distinguished Him from the letter-hunting Scribe. In all these passages we observe, moreover, that the effects which are promised to follow from these states of mind, are of the same kind with themselves,—are distinctly spiritual effects; the poor in spirit shall understand what it is to be brought into a kingdom; the mourner shall be comforted; the meek shall have the government of the earth (shall have the joy, the greatest he can know, of making other men happy); the merciful shall obtain mercy; those that hunger and thirst after righteousness shall obtain righteousness; those that are peace-makers shall be called the children of Him who is the great Peace-maker; the pure in heart shall see God; the privilege of him who preserves the salt within him from corruption, is that he shall preserve the earth from decay; of him who keeps the light alive within him, that men shall glorify their Father which is in heaven. I am anxious to make this remark, because it is my object to shew how carefully our Lord preserves the characteristics of His kingdom, and its rewards, from all secular mixtures; how He transports men into a region entirely unlike that with which they are ordinarily conversant, and yet their own native region, the region of their own true and proper being.

3. But how is this distinctness preserved? Is it by denying the existence of a lower outward region? Is it by setting aside that lower outward region as being in itself evil and impure? Is it by absorbing all influences into the one paramount, transcendent influence? Or is it precisely by taking the opposite course to this, by recognizing the fact and reality of that outward world, by shewing how it is provided for in God's economy, by shewing what relation it bears to the invisible and celestial atmosphere which informs and encompasses it? Our Lord's next words answer these questions, "Think not that I am come to destroy the law and the prophets; I am not come to destroy, but to fulfil. Verily I say unto you, Till heaven and earth pass, one jot or one tittle shall in nowise pass from the law till all be fulfilled." It may be as well to remind the reader, since every word in this memorable passage is important, that the word 'fulfil' is not the same in these two verses; that it would be better to translate the last clause of the eighteenth, "until all things have been done, or have come to pass." I suppose it is our inconvenient version which has given colour to the notion that our Lord speaks here of His own personal obedience to the law, as that which should practically abrogate it; as if He had said, "I am come to fulfil the law, and when I have fulfilled it, then indeed it may pass away; but not a jot or tittle of it till then." But such an exposition as this, destroys the connexion of the passage with all that preceded it and all that follows it. The sentence, "Whosoever, therefore, shall destroy one of the least of these commandments, and teach men so, shall be called least in the kingdom of heaven,"

could not have been added, if the law were spoken
of as destroyed by the work of Christ; for the
kingdom of heaven is that kingdom which His work
was to establish. Our Lord must therefore use the
word *fulfil* in its most strict and ordinary sense; he
must mean, that he is come to give that which fills
up the husk of the outward law, its kernel, its substance. He must mean further, that this kernel or
substance will not destroy the husk; that that will
remain still in all its dryness and literalness; not one
jot or tittle of its enactments abolished, not one jot
or tittle of its authority diminished, until all things
be done, or have come into their perfect estate and
condition; till formal law have lost its application to
the universe, because its meaning and spirit are
accomplished in every human creature. Till heaven
and earth have passed away, till the whole existing
economy of things has ceased, so long as there is
any evil to be prevented in it, so long as there is
flesh in any man which is not subject to the will of
God,—so long law in its outward character must exist;
and he is the least in the kingdom of heaven, he has
least spiritual intuition, who shall try to abridge it
of its precepts or its terrors.

4. Thus far everything in this sermon of our Lord
would seem to negative the opinion, that He came to
repeal one set of rules, and establish another. Everything would seem to shew, that He came to confirm
rules existing before: to shew the ground, the inward
righteousness, of these rules; and to lead those who
were willing to be His disciples into the possession
and enjoyment of it. The next words greatly
strengthen this conclusion: "Verily I say unto you,

Except your righteousness exceed the righteousness of the Scribes and Pharisees, ye shall in no case enter into the kingdom of heaven." There are but two ways of interpreting this passage. The one treats the righteousness required of the disciples as something different in *degree* from that of the Scribes and Pharisees; the other as different in *kind*. If the former notion be adopted, then, indeed, it will follow inevitably, that our Lord comes to set aside the decrees of the Mosaic law, and to establish another set of stricter decrees, more difficult to be complied with, in their place. And no doubt there is a feeling, indicated in this way of considering these words, which ought not to be despised. It is so common to believe that the Christian economy is a system of mitigations and allowances, mainly valuable because it dispenses with troublesome restrictions upon self-indulgence, that it is no wonder honest men should be startled into a violent reaction against this notion, and should be eager to press all Scripture into a proof that the requirements of the perfect dispensation are really higher and severer than those of the imperfect. But, after rendering full honour to the truth implied in this exposition, we are bound to say, that its fruits have been most pernicious; that it has turned the Christian race into a selfish contest who should gain most of the rewards of a future state; that it has wholly blinded men to the nature and quality of these rewards; that it has destroyed all high, pure, disinterested morality; that while it has depraved the principles of those who seemed to be aiming at the highest ends, it has done infinite injury to the practice of those who were content with lower achievements, in making them suppose that there is not a universal standard to which all men must be conformed, but a peculiar standard, which men may choose for themselves; that it has been the parent of useless superstition, ecclesiastical oppression, on the one hand, and of utterly lax and reckless habits on the other; in fine, that it has more utterly contradicted the whole scope and meaning of the Sermon on the Mount, than any other opinion which has prevailed in the Christian world. We are driven, then, to the other, which is the interpretation of all good commentators,—that the righteousness which exceeds that of the Scribes and Pharisees, is one which is spiritual and not literal, the conformity of the life and character to the original mould after which all outward laws are fashioned,— the pattern on the Mount, and not the mere conformity of conduct to any precepts. And, seeing that the Pharisees notoriously had the idea of supererogation, seeing that they did themselves suggest to their disciples a more exalted righteousness than that of the multitude, nay, that their sect was based upon the profession of such a righteousness,—we might expect our Lord to shew the difference between this sort of superlative morality and His own; we might expect to find Him shewing how the one actually set aside the law in attempting to refine upon it, how the other sustained the law while impregnating it with a new life; we might expect to find Him shewing that every attempt to adapt or modify the law, for the purpose of reforming and exalting the inner life, was utterly hopeless, because it existed for quite another purpose;— because the principle to which it was the finger-post was something quite different from the mere exterior command, and could not be extracted from it by any twisting of its formulas. But we should certainly not expect to find Him, after so many cautions, after so careful a declaration of His object, undertaking to annul any of the precepts, which He was not to destroy but to fulfil, or introducing any new legal dogmas instead of them, when He came to bring in a righteousness that is above all dogmas.

5. Let us see, then, whether He disappoints our anticipations in this respect, or whether every passage which follows is not a clear, consistent, and beautiful illustration of the preface. "Ye have heard that it has been said by them of old time, Thou shalt not kill, and whosoever shall kill shall be in danger of the judgment; but I say unto you, that whosoever is angry with his brother without a cause shall be in danger of the judgment; and whosoever shall say to his brother, Raca, shall be in danger of the council; and whosoever shall say, Thou fool, shall be in danger of hell fire." What consequences would follow if we supposed that the formula, "It has been said by them of old time, but I say," meant in this case, "I am about to tell you something which annuls or abolishes what has been said of old time?" In that case the expressions, "He that says to his brother, Raca," "he that says, Thou fool," must be taken in just the same formal and legal sense in which the words, "Thou shalt not kill" are taken. Words which are meant to supersede and abrogate other words, must be construed as they would be construed. If the command, "Thou shalt not kill," points to a definite, specific proceeding, the words, Thou shalt not give this name to thy brother, must point to a specific, definite proceeding also. Now,

who does not see what a shameful limitation of these sublime precepts, what low superstition, what vile hypocrisy must be the result of such an interpretation as this? And who does not know that men have actually fallen into all these evils through the attempt to ascertain what exact amount of slander and vituperation in their own language answered to the Greek μώρε, and the Syriac Raca, and in what degree of danger they therefore were of the judgment, the council, and hell fire? If these doubts and cases of conscience have only now and then expressed themselves in this monstrous form; yet it is easy, from many indications, to perceive that they have been haunting the sin-darkened minds of men, and that they would have haunted them much more, if there had not been teachers to tell them, "These words are not addressed to your outward, but to your inward ear; the words 'Raca,' and 'Thou fool,' are merely significant indexes of certain states of mind; the anger without a cause, is the commencement of the disease; it has become chronic when it finds vent in words of fury; it has become radical, it has infected the vitals of your constitution, when it finds vent in words of settled scorn. The first state of mind subjects you to a judgment; you experience separation from God and man; you cannot feel with the congregation; you cannot pray to your Father. This condition of mind may pass away, if 'thou agree with thine adversary quickly whilst thou art in the way with him;' if the accounts between thee and thy conscience (thy adversary) are settled, which thou knowest that they cannot be till the outward account with thy brother is settled too. But take care that thou do not let it harden into the second condition,—that will subject thee to the council,—a more complete, thorough alienation from all heavenly feelings, all peaceful hopes, all capacity of entering into communion with God. Still God's discipline may work a cure of this also; but there is a period when all discipline has been tried in vain; when the sentence on the soul is, 'Let it alone,' then must it be left to those raging and consuming fires, which could not be quenched by the love of God, of which the fires burning without the city of Jerusalem, to consume its rubbish and its offal, are the only sufficient emblems."

Such is the meaning, so spiritual and so awful, which we are allowed to put upon our Lord's words, while we feel that they belong to us in our highest, most responsible, and most perilous condition of immortal and spiritual beings, taken into covenant with God, brought into fellowship with our brethren, submitted to the government and education of His Holy Spirit. Such is the meaning which we must abandon, in favour of some barren, hungry interpretation, fretting to the conscience, profitless to the heart, the moment we forget our Lord's words, that He came not to destroy the law but to fulfil it; the moment we permit ourselves to imagine that His work was to substitute one formal precept for another, and not rather to stanch the fountain of evil in the heart, whence had proceeded all those crimes against which the outward law was the true and permanent witness.

6. The next two passages refer to the Marriage-bond; one to the prohibition of Adultery by the law, the other to its toleration of Divorce. In the first

case the meaning is evident. Our Lord comes not to
destroy, but to fulfil. He leaves the precept against
adultery as He finds it, and stamps it with new authority. Still it belongs to the 'old time.' He has a
message to the inner man. He aims not at the crime,
but at the sin. "Look not upon a woman to lust after
her;" "If thy right eye offend thee, pluck it out;"
"If thy right hand offend thee, cut it off." Be
willing to sacrifice the exercise of powers which God
meant thee to exercise, the enjoyments of sense which
God has given thee, if thou findest them to minister
to thy inward corruption, and so to hinder thee from
attaining the higher joys of the spiritual kingdom.
For it is better to enter into life halt and maimed, to
have the spirit itself pure and free, at the cost of some
of its tools and ministers, than having two hands and
two feet, having all thy powers and thy senses at
liberty, to be cast into hell-fire, to be consumed by
tyrant lusts, and an ever-renewing remorse. This is
the very principle and illustration of inward spiritual
discipline.

The next clause is, at first sight, more puzzling.
Our Lord seems to be repealing the Mosaic law
of divorce, though He expressly disclaimed the
intention of repealing any jot of it. But, if we
consider a moment, we shall perceive that there
is no inconsistency. The Law of Moses was not
meant to encourage divorces. It was meant to throw
obstacles in their way. For the Jew, instead of
being allowed to send away his wife whenever he conceived a displeasure against her, was obliged to resort
to a legal instrument; he must have a bill of divorce-
ment. Thus much the law could do to witness for

the sanctity of marriage. More it could not do, because of the hardness of heart in those with whom it had to deal. Prohibitory or penal enactments could not of themselves preserve that primal law of creation which God established, when He made them male and female. To fulfil the end which they wish to compass, the new dispensation exhibits marriage as a lower form and image of its greatest mystery, imparting to it a sacred and only not sacramental dignity.

7. And now we are come to one of the points of dispute between us and the Quaker. "It has been said by them of old time, Ye shall not forswear yourselves, but ye shall perform unto the Lord your oaths; but I say unto you, Swear not at all, neither by heaven, for it is God's throne, neither by the earth, for it is His footstool, neither by Jerusalem, for it is the city of the Great King, nor by your head, for you cannot make one hair of it white or black."

Now, I do not say that the Quaker may not be able to prove that this passage forbids all oaths, judicial and religious, as well as vituperative and conversational. But I do say, that this is not the view of the text which would suggest itself to any literal interpreter who reads the whole sermon, and seeks to interpret one part of it by another. No literal interpreter could treat with indifference the repetition of the formula, " It hath been said by them of old time, but I say unto you," or, without the strongest reason, could affix an opposite meaning to it in one place from that which it evidently bears in three others. No literal interpreter could disregard the circumstance, that not one of the oaths which our Lord instances as illustrative of His prohibition is a judicial oath; that every one of them is just the kind of oath which, from the analogy of other nations, we should suppose would be used in familiar discourse. No literal interpreter would be heedless of the circumstance, that the communication (λόγος), which is to be yea, yea, nay, nay, cannot, without a most strange use of language, imply a formal, legal procedure. While, therefore, I am far from assuming that the Quakers may not be able to overreach all these à priori arguments against their view of the passage, I maintain that they have not the shadow of a plea for putting themselves forward as strict interpreters, and for denouncing our laxness. They are bound to shew some cause why our Lord should in this instance have violated the method and coherency of His discourse ; why He should introduce this instance of an old law, in seeming illustration of His principle, " that He has not come to destroy but to fulfil," when it is a direct exception from that principle ; why He should have connected it, by the use of a common phrase, with two other cases, which did most remarkably enforce and expound it.

The only effort, so far as I know, which they make to defend their theory against these apparently powerful presumptions, consists in such assertions as these: —" That the words, ' Swear not at all,' are clear and obvious words, spoken for the use of poor and ignorant people, by one who came to preach the Gospel to the poor; that, let commentators say what they will, any ordinary man taking up the Bible, and finding such a command as this, would suppose it to govern all possible cases, and not a few particular cases; that it is impossible to discover any line of moral distinction between an oath in private, and an oath in a court of justice; and, lastly, that the prohibition of private, conversational swearing was superfluous,—no one in old time, or in any time, supposed that to be lawful." With respect to the first of these arguments, I shall not stop to inquire with what grace it comes from those who have particularly prided themselves on the discovery of meanings in Scripture, which do not present themselves to the ordinary, thoughtless reader, but which commend themselves, as they say, to the spiritual man. I do not ask whether they are just the persons to complain of us for not adopting the most superficial, outside view of a passage which presents itself; but I at once grapple with the difficulty. I take an ordinary English peasant, possessing just so much intelligence and religious feeling as makes him capable of attaching any meaning at all to the passage; I say that such a man would not be nearly so likely to suppose that our Lord meant him to abstain from judicial oaths, because he said "Swear not at all," as he would be to think that our Lord meant him to injure some of his members, because He said, "If thy right hand offend thee, cut it off, if thy right eye offend thee, pluck it out." Not nearly so likely, and for this reason, that he would have a practical test of the meaning in the one case, which he would not have in the other. This peasant knows perfectly well, that the feeling with which he goes into a solemn court of justice, and in the presence of men in solemn official costume, calls God to witness that the words he is about to speak are true, is as different a feeling from that by which he is influenced when he takes the same holy name into his lips, to confirm some chance word which he has uttered over his cups in the tap-room, as any two that ever dwelt in the same individual can possibly be. It would never occur to him for an instant to compare the two acts together, except, indeed, in this way;—he has seen, that the persons who are most in the habit of using oaths, and trifling with the name of God in common conversation, are those on whom an oath judicially administered has least effect, and who are most likely to forswear themselves. If, then, it is meant that the real wayfaring man will be particularly likely to discover any perplexity or contradiction here, I believe it is a mistake; I do not say that he may not, because I do not say that he may not be perplexed with any passage of Scripture. I have urged already, that a personal ministry is just as necessary to him, and has been just as much appointed for him, as the Written Word itself, and that one is not in general intended to profit him without the other. All, therefore, that I need maintain here is, that my view of the passage, when it is set before him, instead of seeming to be more difficult, more contrary to his previous expectations, will be much more intelligible, and much better interpret to him his own experience. For instance; to a congregation of English country-men I should speak, with the most perfect confidence that what I said would approve itself to their hearts and understandings, some such words as these: " My friends, the assizes are to be held to-morrow in the county town, three miles from our village. Several of you are summoned to be witnesses there; now, that you may understand what you have to do, and in what spirit you ought to go about this work, I shall explain to you this morning a passage out of our Lord's Sermon on the Mount. You know I have told

you very often that the Bible is not a show-book,
written about things which have nothing to do with
you, but one that concerns all your common business
and tells you how to set about it in a right way. Well,
then, attend to this passage. It begins so :—' It hath
been said by them of old time, Thou shalt not forswear thyself, but thou shalt perform unto the Lord
thine oaths.' Now, first, you would like to know who
it is that said this in old time. If you look back a
few verses in this chapter, you will see it is written,
' It has been said of old time, Thou shalt not kill; '
and again, a few verses lower, ' It has been said of
old time, Thou shalt not commit adultery.' These
commands were given of old time to the Jews.
You know who gave them. Just now I was reading them to you from the altar, and before them
all I read, ' God spake these words and said; '—
God declared himself to the Jews as their King, and
He told them amidst thunders and lightnings that
these laws were His laws; that when they broke any
of these laws they disobeyed Him, and that misery
and destruction would follow. I have often talked to
you about the history of the Jews. You know they
tried whether it was true or not that misery and
destruction would follow if they broke God's commands; they tried, and found that it was true. Misery
did follow, till at last they were sent away into a
strange land. Well! as God commanded the Jews
not to kill and not to commit adultery, so He commanded them not to forswear themselves, but to
perform unto Him their oaths. Our Lord, you see,
puts the same honour upon all these commands. He
speaks of each of them as ' what was spoken in old

time;' that is to say, what God spake of old time to His people, and what they had preserved as His commands. And I tell you, my friends, that if the Jews had forgotten this command, they would have been just as ill off as if they had forgotten either of the others. They were held together as a people by having God's name put upon them; therefore, when they came together as a people, to have any solemn transactions with each other, they were bound to remember that they were in God's presence; that God was looking on their words and intentions; and that He would be avenged on them if they did not act honestly by each other. An oath in a court of justice says this, 'We are in God's presence, and we know He is a witness whether we speak truth or lies, and He is a God of truth, and will be avenged upon us if we speak lies.' If the Jews had forgotten that they were to perform unto the Lord their oaths; if the rulers of the land had not enforced oaths upon them, they would have been guilty of a great sin; they would have refused to bear witness for God, as He told them to bear witness of Him; and I say again, it would have fared as ill with them, the nation would as much have fallen to pieces (because there would have been no fear of God, no feeling that He was near them), as if they had committed murder or adultery. Yea, what is more, they would have committed murder and adultery, because the thought of God, which keeps men out of these courses, would have departed from them. Now, my friends, our nation of England acknowledges God for its King, just as much as the nation of the Jews did. We call Him, in our prayer for Queen Victoria, 'King of kings and Lord of lords.'

Just as He was the King over King David, so He is
the King over our Queen. And our laws which say,
'Thou shalt not kill, thou shalt not commit adultery,'
are God's laws; they are not the Queen's laws; she
did not make them, nor any king or queen that was
before her. She and her servants execute them, and
she and they are answerable to God how they execute
them. But they were made of old time,—God made
them, and God enforces them; and we are to perform
all our transactions as in His presence, knowing that
He is the witness of what we do. And our rulers are
bound to tell us this; to put us in mind of it, and on
all solemn occasions, when we meet as in a court of
justice, they must urge us to say out boldly, that we
know and feel that the eye of the unseen God is upon
us, and upon what we do, and upon what we say, and
upon what we think. Remember this when the book
is put into your hands to swear; remember that you
are declaring then, in that court, that God's eye is
upon you, and that you believe He will teach you to
speak truth, and that you believe He will be avenged
upon you if you lie. But I have something more to
say to you yet. I have told you often, that all the
laws in the world will never make us good men. They
are 'a terror to evil-doers, and a praise and protection
to them that do well.' But they will never put one
right thought into your heart, they will never make
your heart pure and holy. The laws cannot, but He
who gave the laws can; and this is what the second
part of our Lord's words is about. He says, 'It has
been said by them of old time,' (that is, in other words,
I, the Lord Jesus Christ, said in old time, for it was
He who gave the law, He was King then, He now),

' Thou shalt not forswear thyself, but thou shalt perform unto the Lord thine oaths. But I am not going to tell you this again. It has been said once, and it lasts always. I have now a new message to you. There are some of you who think that you must be very careful of using the word God in your familiar talk, because God hath set apart that for solemn purposes; but you do not think much of swearing by heaven, or earth, or by Jerusalem, or by your head,—you do not care how lightly you use these oaths. Now, whether you know it or not, this arises from want of reverence for God. You think it is just the name that is sacred. Oh, no! Everything is sacred. Look up to the wide heaven over your head; the sun speaks of God, the moon speaks of Him, the firmament speaks of Him. Look at the earth; every tree, and plant, and flower speaks of Him. Go into Jerusalem; there is the Temple in which God has promised to dwell. Think of your own head; there is a witness for God; it is He who preserves every hair of it. I say, then, Swear not at all. If you trifle with an oath, you trifle with God, in whose presence you are living, and moving, and having your being.'

" My friends, these are the words of Christ's new covenant. They were not spoken to the disciples only, they are spoken to you who are under this covenant. You are baptized men, children of God, members of Christ, heirs of heaven. Christ has other, better, higher, more acceptable words for you than those which He spoke in old time. He tells you that He has brought you into God's immediate presence, that He has adopted you into His family, that He has sealed you with His Spirit. He beseeches **you to**

remember that you have this high honour, this unspeakable glory; and therefore He says to the heart
of each one of you, 'Swear not at all.' When thou
goest forth to thy work in the morning, look cheerily
and reverently up to heaven and say,—'That sky
under which I am to labour to-day is my Father's
throne; it is a holy thing; I must not trifle with it.
This earth, which I am to till with the sweat of my
brow, is my Father's footstool; He cares for it; He
causes it to bud and bring forth: this, too, is a holy
thing.' When you go into the town to market, look
up at the churches and say,—'This, too, is my Father's
dwelling-place; these are witnesses that I am a citizen
of the New Jerusalem, that I belong to an innumerable
company of saints and angels, and that all these men
who are about me are of the same family. The city
and the men in it are holy.' When you return home
at night, and lie down on your bed, and no one else is
near you, think that 'in this body of mine God hath
said He will dwell, and make it His temple: this, too,
is a holy thing.'

"Yes! it is your privilege as Christians, to have
these calm, happy thoughts wherever you go, whatever
you are doing. These are the thoughts of new men,
who believe themselves redeemed to God by the blood
of Christ. Think how contrary to them every idle
oath is! What pride there is in it! What contempt
of God! What setting up of ourselves! And, in
general, what cruelty to our brethren! Depend upon
it, every such oath makes men feel God's oaths less
sacred, makes men more likely to forswear themselves
when they are sworn in a court of justice. If you think
it would be very horrible to commit such a crime—if

you wish to obey Christ's first command, 'Perform
unto the Lord thy oaths;' see that you attend to His
second command, by not swearing at all in your communications one with another; see that you get the spirit
of these commands into you, by remembering at all
times, in all places, that you are in the presence of a
Father who loves you, and that all things testify of Him.
Then you may go to court to-morrow with free, clear
spirits; you will not have to think as slaves and
cowards think—I must not tell a lie, for then I shall
be prosecuted for perjury, or be turned out of my
place, or be pointed at by other people—but you will
speak the truth, and the whole truth, and nothing
but the truth, because God is truth, and because you
know that they who tell lies cannot stand in His sight;
but that every true-hearted servant and child of His
He will help and bless, and bring them on farther
and farther in the knowledge of Himself."

I think there is nothing in this which a plain man
would reject as unintelligible, or an honest man as
sophistical. It marks out a great moral distinction
between two acts, which Quakers have hastily confounded together, merely because they have a common
name. It shews that there was a reason for giving
this command against conversational swearing in this
place; for though the Jews had not argued that they
might trifle with oaths because they were directed
to use them on the most solemn and sacred occasions,
—that was a subtlety which never suggested itself
to their minds, ingenious as they were in finding a
plea for their evil practices by a tortured application
of the letter of the law, they had persuaded themselves that, if they abstained from the dreadful name

of Jehovah, they did not invade the awfulness of
oaths by using them familiarly. And in striking at
this hypocritical notion, our Lord was able to throw
a new and brilliant light upon His own dispensation,
to shew how it was that He came to bring men into
the very presence of God, to hallow every place with
His presence, and to bind together the awful feeling
of a distinct personality, an unutterable name, which
had possessed the heart of the Hebrew with that
feeling of a God everywhere, which had been struggling
with it in the conceptions of the Greek Pantheist.
This prohibition was not a superfluous thing for that
time, or for any time. It associates a rule of daily
life with the most deep principles of our being. Adopt
the Quaker notion of the passage, and our Lord says,
in a sermon especially addressed to the hearts and
consciences of men,—" Once, without a reason, I told
you to do a certain act, now, without a reason, I tell
you not to do that act." Adopt our view of it, and
we see the eternal grounds of these precepts in two
principles, alike involved in the constitution of man,
each developed in its due season, (one by the teacher
who had the veil over his countenance, the other by
Him who came to shew forth the express image of
God in human flesh,) each to be upheld for the sake
of the other, each losing its own stability when the
other is forgotten.

8. The Quakers, and those who adopt their theory
respecting the Sermon on the Mount, make scarcely
any distinction between the two following paragraphs.
The two old sayings, " An eye for an eye, and a tooth
for a tooth," and " Thou shalt love thy neighbour and
hate thine enemy," are taken to be proverbs of nearly

the same import, expressing generally the savage character of the ancient dispensation, for which Christ substitutes the mild spirit of the new. Surely that interpretation must be intrinsically vicious, which confounds together two maxims, as different in their objects and application as any that ever were expressed in human language. The first manifestly applies to the judicial proceedings of the commonwealth, the second to its external relations. Whether good or evil, barbarous or gentle, they do not mean the same thing; and every person who really wishes to interpret our Lord's words strictly, will examine them separately.

To begin with the words, "An eye for an eye, a tooth for a tooth."

The feeling of retribution and compensation,— that every injury should have its just recompense, that the evil suffered shall be proportionate to the evil done,—you see working in the heart of every savage, you see secretly prompting and justifying his acts of blind fury and punishment. To be sure he constantly passes the limit; he makes the satisfaction exacted far exceed the wrong committed, and for that *excess* his conscience reproaches him. Confused as his perceptions are, you may make him acknowledge that it was an evil spirit which drove him to take more than the equivalent; but it is in vain to urge him farther; I believe it is not *right* to urge him farther; it is tasking his conscience to a work for which it is not prepared; it is making him doubt the reality of its testimony, so far as it goes. And why is this? Why is a man who really approaches his brother's soul with fear and trembling, knowing what an awful

thing it is; knowing how wicked it is to displace one
true, sound conviction in it; knowing that most
tenderness is necessary where the good is weakest,
least guarded, most surrounded with contradictory
elements,—why is such a man careful of impairing
or destroying this idea of adjustment and retribution
in the heart of a savage? Because he believes that
every transgression *does* and must receive its just recompense of reward; because the absence of all sense of
this truth in the savage mind, would indicate the
absence of all feeling of a law; because the presence
of it may be the means of leading him on to the
acknowledgment of his own subjection to law. It
is then, I conceive, the very essence of a lawgiver's
duty to take this principle of God's government, which
each man is feeling after and clutching at, and making
the excuse for acts of violence, (acts that keep alive,
aggravate, and harden into a habit, the inward hatred
which conspired with this right feeling to produce
them),—to take this principle, I say, and make it the
rule of his own proceedings, and by strictly enforcing
it, lead men to feel that there is a power ruling over
them, which redresses the wrong that each has so
impotently and mischievously endeavoured to redress
for himself. It is the business of the lawgiver to say,
"You are all members of one body; the law cares for
each of you distinctly; it feels every wrong inflicted
upon every one of you as a wrong to itself; it will
require from every man who injures another man,
that he shall make compensation and satisfaction for
that evil which he has done. It proposes to itself
this end, and will endeavour, as far as it can, to reach
it,—of making every wrong-doer feel that he suffers

in that kind, and to that degree, in which he has offended.

I maintain, then, that the principle, "an eye for an eye, a tooth for a tooth," is a principle which lies at the foundation of a State, and perhaps more than any other, explains to us what a State is. It is a righteous principle, I had almost called it *the righteous principle;* for it is that which presents to us the most complete image of the order and moral government of the world; it most exhibits the rights of each distinct person, in connexion with that order and government. Vengeance must be somewhere—"It is mine, saith the Lord;" and the State is that which teaches each man that there is a Lord, an invisible ruler, and judge, and governor over him, whose authority he is bound to acknowledge, and upon whose authority every act of private vengeance is an infringement.

Thus much the law *can* do, and, what is more, nothing but a law can do it. No spiritual principle, acting upon the life of man, reforming and regenerating his heart and will, can bear this witness for a God who punishes wrong-doing, can bring men into an apprehension of the system of retribution which is established in the universe. If we have not a power distinctly standing out and saying, "An eye for an eye, and a tooth for a tooth," "As you have done so shall it be rendered to you again,"—distinctly standing out, I say, and embodying this principle in acts of regular, anticipated, proportionate punishment, there is nothing in the secret operations for moulding the character of a man into the Divine image, to suggest the belief that man is actually subjected to such a Divine government. When these operations are exclusively regarded, all feelings respecting God are absorbed into the one, that He is the renewer and sanctifier of our lives; the belief of Him as a judge, which is in fact the belief of His personality, is in hazard of being lost altogether. On the other hand, it is equally certain, that this law, with its scale of retributions, cannot approach the heart and spirit of any man, cannot go one step towards producing that tone of feeling which yet it shews to be most necessary. The law may say to a man, "Vengeance is mine, vengeance is the Lord's; all acts of individual vengeance shall be themselves accounted crimes;" it may even do much to convince a man that his private fury is a very inconvenient thing for himself as well as his neighbour, that it is a monstrous outrage upon the order of society; but it can do nothing towards taking the principle and desire of vengeance out of man. It cannot make cheerful citizens, with minds recognizing its righteousness and delighting therein; it cannot even provide against the outbreaks which the will of man, rising superior to the rules of his understanding, is continually producing. To hinder these, it must resort to some spiritual influence, and this spiritual influence may be of three kinds:—It may be mere discipline, such as was adopted in Sparta; discipline excluding education, compelling all the faculties and energies of the spirit into one direction, making them consciously feeble and helpless when they venture into any other. It may be an education of the calculating faculty merely, a skilful experiment to destroy every thought and feeling which interferes with the hope of direct and tangible advantage; but this experiment is possible only in a thoroughly enervated age, and possible then only for a short time. Lastly, it may be that kind of spiritual influence which acts directly upon the will, which despoils it of its selfishness, which conforms it to the perfect will of God. To employ this influence, the lawgiver must seek the aid of Him who said, "Resist not the evil;" "if any man will take thy cloak, let him have thy coat also;" and who, in saying these words, shewed that "He was not come to destroy but to fulfil the law"—"an eye for an eye, a tooth for a tooth."

Thus, then, we come back upon our old doctrine. I say that the law protests against the selfish, individual principle, and raises a standard against it; and I say that the Gospel comes to exterminate that same selfish principle out of the mind and heart of the man. Upon the same ground, therefore, that I hold tribunals for the rectification of social evils to be of godlike institution, and to carry Divine authority with them, I hold the principle to be godlike, and carrying Divine authority, "that whosoever shall smite thee on thy right cheek, thou shalt turn to him the other also." The most patient endurance of private wrongs and indignities, the most entire willingness to abstain from any acts of recrimination, or even of self-justification, are parts of the Christian character, after which, I conceive, every Christian should seek, and without which he should feel that his profession is maimed and imperfect, that he is not acting out the idea of his baptism. No toleration of selfishness in himself will he for one moment plead for, but be most anxious that all indications of it in him should be detected and exposed, in

order that the thing itself may be exterminated.   He
has no fear of carrying out our Lord's commands too
far, and thus sacrificing his civil duties to his Christian.
The law will not thank him the least for being liti-
gious; he does not confirm its authority by turning it
to his private advantage; but just so far as he com-
municates any portion of his spirit to the world, (and
he knows that the higher his standard and his practice
are, the more of that spirit he will communicate,) so
much better will the law be observed, with so much
more of cheerful reverence will all its subjects behold
it.   Observe, however, it is a principle to which he is
binding himself, not a rule.   He determines, by God's
help, that he will never resist evil for a selfish purpose,
because he knows this to be our Lord's meaning.   He
does not say that he will not resist evil; for if he did,
he would say that he would not be like his Lord, whose
whole life on earth, and whose whole life in His members, is a constant resistance to evil.   He determines
not to go to law to avenge himself, or get himself
profit: he does not determine that he will not go to
law, if the dignity of law be assailed by some illegal
power.   It is most mischievous to think that there
can be the least departure from a great principle of
morality; it is most ridiculous to affirm that the most
opposite methods may not at times be necessary to
uphold that principle.   When Hampden resisted ship-
money, I think he complied far better with our Lord's
precept than if he had paid the tax; for he was
sacrificing his own interest for the sake of the dignity
of law, not using the law for the promotion of his
own interest.   The conscience of mankind recognizes
the distinction, (in cases where private interests

do not interfere,) as most broad and palpable;
and the conscience of each man, guided by the
Spirit of God, and seeking light from the Word of
God, will be able to carry it out into daily practice,
when private interests do interfere. Thus we allege
this case also as an illustration of our Lord's fundamental proposition, that He does not destroy but fulfil.

9. There is one remark which I would make as
introductory to our consideration of the next passage,
the last which concerns our present subject. It is,
that the whole argument against war, so far as it is
gathered from this sermon, or, I might add, from the
New Testament, must turn upon it. After what I
have just said, it is obvious that no attempt to extract
a condemnation of war, or any allusion to it from the
words, " Resist not evil," " He that smiteth you on
one cheek," &c., can be successful. The application
of the new doctrine must be determined by the application of the old; if the " eye for an eye, and tooth for
a tooth," refers to judicial proceedings, the words, be
they of repeal, or of confirmation, must point in the
same direction; and it is most manifest torturing of
their letter, and a gross perversion of their spirit, to
connect them with another class of cases, which our
Lord has himself treated of distinctly. Let it be
clearly understood then, that the words on which the
question turns are these :—" It hath been said by them
of old time, Thou shalt love thy neighbour and hate
thine enemy: but I say unto you, Love your enemies;
bless them that curse you, pray for them that despite-
fully use you and persecute you, that ye may be the
children of your Father in heaven; for he maketh His
sun to rise upon the evil and the good, and sendeth

rain on the just and on the unjust. For if ye love
them which love you, what reward have ye? Do not
even the publicans the same?"

There is one other observation that may also be
necessary for the satisfactory examination of the question. The words which our Lord attributes to the men
of old time, do not appear, *totidem literis*, in the Old
Testament scripture. Hence it has been urged, that
in this particular passage a traditional maxim of the
Scribes—a gloss, probably, on some text in the books
of Moses—may be denounced, and not a dogma carrying with it the authority of inspiration. I must think
that the commentator who can deliberately avail himself of this subterfuge, has not yet learned that honesty
and plain dealing are as much required in criticism as
in the affairs of common life. He does not find the
words in any text of the Bible. Does he not find the
meaning in a hundred? Can he read the five books of
Moses, the Kings and Chronicles, above all the Psalms,
and say that if a scribe invented this phrase, he did
not very happily embody in it the feeling of the old
time, or that our Lord does not evidently sanction his
representation of it?

But, leaving this phrase for the present, let us
observe the ground on which our Lord bases his new
precept. "That ye may be the children of your
Father in heaven, for He causes His sun to shine upon
the good and the evil, and sendeth His rain upon the
just and the unjust." Here we perceive at once the
whole principle of God's dispensations. To restore
the Divine image in man is the end of these, and
therefore every precept or command to man is connected with a revelation of something in the character

of God. He is not required to exhibit any qualities in himself which have not first been presented to him in their original and archetype. This doctrine being assumed, we may deduce two or three corollaries from it. First, we see that a precept of universal love to men, and especially of love to them in their character as sinners, could not be delivered except in the way of hint and preparation, till there had been that complete manifestation of God in the person of His incarnate and dying Son, as connected with all men, feeling for men in their present condition, caring for the most vile and abject. Secondly, that every previous duty imposed upon men, as a test of their faithfulness and obedience, must have corresponded to something in the character of God which had been made known to them. Thirdly, that since these two revelations of God's character cannot contradict each other, since the qualities attributed to Him must in some sense or other be compatible, the corresponding duties required in men cannot be contradictory, must in some sense or other be compatible. Fourthly, that unless one of these revelations of God can be shewn to merge in the other, so that all the qualities attributed to Him in the first shall be actually, if not apparently, contained in the second, the duties founded upon these separate revelations cannot be merged in each other, but must continue distinct obligations. A very few words will be sufficient to illustrate each of these points, and shew you their application to the subject in hand. In the first, it is distinctly admitted that Christ came to establish a universal dispensation, which did not exist previously; that this dispensation is grounded upon a manifestation of God as absolute, universal love; upon the fact that He has entered into relations in the person of His Son with man as he is; and that to men so united to His Son, He gives His Spirit, that they may be endowed with that same universal love which is His own essential nature, and which has been displayed in the acts and sufferings of a real man. This revelation and this command lie at the foundation of the Christian Church; this is expressed in our baptism, "into the name of the Father, and of the Son, and of the Holy Ghost." They who enter into this state are bound to love their enemies, are bound to love all men, because they see that God loves all; they love those who hate and persecute them, because for these enemies and persecutors Christ died. They love even the enemies of God, because they regard them as creatures still bearing the flesh which Christ bore, not yet finally separated from Him, not deserted by His Spirit. They keep the command given in His Sermon on the Mount strictly, fully, spiritually, for the reason which the Lawgiver Himself lays down, because they "are the children of their Father in heaven."

Our second corollary affirms, that every duty enforced upon the Jews as a proof of their zeal and faithfulness was grounded upon some declaration of the character of God. God is declared to be the King over the Israelites, to watch over them, to care for them as a father careth for his children. They are His chosen nation, His appointed witnesses; therefore they are to care for each other. They are to feel themselves members of a nation distinct from other nations; they are to feel for each other as they do not feel for other men; for they are called to a distinct office, they have a distinct position, which it is a sin for them not to maintain—"they are to love their neighbours." Again, God is revealed to them as carrying on a war against evil in the world, and upholding the law and order which He has established. In performing this work, He sends judgments upon nations, sweeping away by pestilence and famine whole multitudes; vindicating the truth and order, which are the only happiness of mankind, at the expense of the lives of individual men. He requires of His chosen people that they should feel as He feels; that they should hate violations of law and order as He hates them; that they should be ready to be the executors of His purposes; to maintain the principles of order and truth; to be avenged of those who violate them; not to shrink from the sacrifice of individual life, sacred and awful as it is, for the sake of maintaining that without which life is a mere miserable lie. They are to look upon their nation as established for this very end; to be a witness against evil; to carry on a warfare within and without against those who break down landmarks, set up might against right, turn the world into a wilderness, denying righteousness, denying God. It was not always to be fighting; its witness was oftentimes to be a silent one; but there were occasions when it was to draw the sword and fling away the scabbard; at all times it was to maintain its own God-given position; it was to resist the invaders of the land until the death, unless, indeed, a time should come in its history, an awful time, such as did actually arrive in the days of the prophet Jeremiah when it was a witness for God no longer; when to

resist the invader was merely to assert the continuance
of a self-willed power, which had thrown off the Divine
yoke; when allegiance was dissolved, society at an
end; when it was a duty in each man to surrender,
that he might have his life for a prey. But so long
as the nation was a nation, so long as it owned God
and God owned it, the maxim, "Thou shalt hate thine
enemy," expressed a duty as real, as binding as the
other to which it was appended, "Thou shalt love thy
neighbour."

Our third corollary affirms, that the revelation of
God as universal love is not inconsistent with that prior
revelation of Him, as the Being who is carrying on
continual strife with whatever in our world resists and
opposes law and order; and that, consequently, the
duty of loving our enemies, which is grounded upon
the one revelation, must be in some way or other compatible with that duty of hating our enemies, which is
grounded upon the other. Only think to what the
idea of a Being of perfect love must reduce itself—to
what it has actually reduced itself—when men have
contemplated these two Divine attributes as contrary
to each other. What does love become, but a weak,
contemptible tolerance of that which is unlovely, a
merciless mercy, which now and for ever can permit
the creatures it has formed to be as sinful, that is to
say, as miserable, as they will. Does not every man's
conscience vehemently resist the decree of his carnal
understanding, that there is any strife between the
idea of a law of love and a Being who is determined
to carry that law into execution? Does not he feel,
that if he parted with either side or aspect of the
character, the other would straightway become prac-

tically unintelligible? Well, and is it not the same, must it not be the same, with our judgments of ourselves and our fellow-creatures? Do we not feel that that love of good is a very paltry thing, which is not accompanied with a hatred of evil? And do we not feel that hatred of evil is a mere name, if it is not willing to go forth in acts for resisting and extinguishing evil? And do we not feel that that man has a very poor love of his kind, and of each individual man as a member of that kind, who does not regard as his enemies those who hinder the good and help forward the evil, and who does not, in that character and capacity, hate them? These are no sophistical refinements; they are the common, honest judgments of mankind, triumphing over sophistical refinement, getting through the mere resemblances of names and words into the essential resemblances of things, and thus even unconsciously justifying the ways of God, and asserting the harmony of His dispensations.

Our fourth position affirms, that unless the view of the character of God presented by the Jewish economy be comprehended in that view which is presented by Christ in the Sermon on the Mount, the duties required of the Jew remain binding on the Christian, and are not swallowed up in the duties specially and characteristically appertaining to him as the heir of the New Covenant. Our Lord says, " Love your enemies, for your Father in heaven causes His sun to shine upon the good and the evil, and sendeth His rain upon the just and the unjust." Here is a fact of His providence introduced as an illustration of His character. But there are other facts of His providence existing side by side with this, not interfering

with it. He who gives rain and sunshine, sends also
plagues and pestilences. These come not, indeed, to
distinguish between individuals, not to determine
which are good, which evil; but yet, certainly, for
discipline; certainly to teach the nations the effects
of indolence, intemperance, sensuality; certainly to
lead them gradually to distinguish truth from falsehood, the good from the evil. If, then, these facts
exist together, and exist as distinct signs of distinct
though perfectly harmonious purposes in the Divine
mind, men, who are meant to be the images of God,
should have some way of distinctly expressing each
in their own minds and procedure. Christ comes to
bring men into closer connexion with God, to endow
them with the power of completely fulfilling His will,
to make them complete vicegerents in executing His
purposes towards the world. Surely He does not
come to depose them from the office of executing any
part of the work to which He once called them;
surely, if He does not cease to judge and to punish,
because He admits all into His kingdom of love,
neither can it be meant that they should cease to
judge and punish under Him, because He has appointed
them under Him to publish His Gospel, and open the
doors of His kingdom. And the only remaining question is, How can both these forms of character be at
once preserved? How can these two sets of duties,
apparently so opposite, be fulfilled? Clearly, there
is the greatest danger in omitting either; there is
the greatest danger in confusing them. What weak,
ineffectual lovers we are, when love is separated from
law, we have hinted at already; what monstrous per-
verters of the Divine law when we set up law against

love, it requires no words to explain. But, do we fare much better if we try to keep up a balancing system in our minds? Not too much love, lest you should grow lax—not too much law, lest you should become cruel. Will this kind of see-saw satisfy any man who wishes to be honest to himself and his fellow-creatures? Not too much love! How can there be too much, if dying for love was not too much? Not too much law! How can there be too much, if the destruction of cities and empires, yea, of a world, for the sake of it was not too much? Then, I say, if it be so, there must be some distinct Divine scheme for asserting the dignity and glory of each; for upholding love in its fulness lest law should perish; for upholding law in its fulness lest love should perish. By acting in concert with each of them, a man shall find that the feeling of God's universal love in himself does not clash with the feeling of God's eternal and unchangeable law; that his perception of his own duties, inward and external, and of the perfect compatibleness of those which seem most opposed, waxes clearer and clearer; and, by refusing to act in concert with each of these schemes, he shall find one set of duties continually interfering with another, the peculiar temper of his mind determining which he shall prefer, which neglect. The words, then, "Thou shalt love thy neighbour and hate thine enemy," are not destroyed but fulfilled by the words, "Love your enemies, bless them that curse you."

The reasons of my difference with the Quaker, I hope, are now sufficiently explained. I do not contend for any abatement in the strictness of his views, I only want them to be less narrow. I do not wish him to have a less spiritual conception of Christian morality, I want him not practically to exhaust it of its spirit by depriving it of its body. Above all, I want him to perceive that the scheme which he has set up in the world for the purpose of establishing peace and charity in it, is a far less effectual one than the scheme which God has set up in it for the same end. The Quaker's society has contained self-denying and brave men, who have borne witness for the truth that we are not to resist evil but when we are smitten on one cheek to turn the other also. Such men must have done good. Everyone who lets the world see that selfishness is not his law, that he can obey a principle, that the arm of God is more to be trusted than the arm of flesh, will certainly do good. But there is nothing to hinder the Catholic Church from bearing such testimonies, many in all ages have borne them. It is the other kind of Quaker testimony, his negative testimony, which seems to me of no worth at all, except so far as it may obtain some worth from its mixture with the acts I have just spoken of, nay, which in itself is seriously mischievous. There is much in the worst feelings of men, especially in our day, which sympathises with the Quaker language respecting war and punishments. There is a cowardly shrinking from mere physical suffering, a great disposition to talk about the expensiveness of national honour, because money is a visible, honour an invisible thing : there is an unreasonable, uncharitable, and superstitious notion, that a soldier, so far as his profession is concerned, is of this world, and that a man who dies on the field of battle is necessarily less prepared for his change than one who dies in his bed. All these feelings, which have tended sadly to degrade and impoverish the mind of modern Europe, to cultivate the trade temper, to make armies what they are told they must be, and therefore to make them dangerous by depriving them of any high restraining principle, have been greatly encouraged by the tone which religious men of our day have adopted from the Quakers. What is such language doing for the promotion of permanent and universal peace? It is the greatest hindrance to any high understanding of the words, to any hopeful expectation of the thing. For whoever translates· the holy name 'Peace' by carnal security or luxurious ease, desecrates it, and makes every scriptural application of it unmeaning. Whoever teaches civilians to love their pelf above all things, or military men to believe that they have no vocation but a murderous one, helps to make the one so weak that they must be ready to quail before any physical force, the other so wicked that they must be ready to exert it. And the loss of all national spirit will lead, as it has ever done, not to a golden age of Christian fraternization, but to a military despotism. Far otherwise, as we have seen already, has the Church of Christ worked in the world. It has been the instrument of putting down military despotism, the instrument of evoking national feeling. The sins of its ministers leading them to exalt their own position and to make it extra-national, the sins of the national rulers, in seeking to put down that spiritual power within it which seemed to interfere with their projects, have thwarted the gracious design of Providence, but they have only made the character of that design more evident. They have shown that it is His will to establish peace; first, by creating in the heart of every nation a witness of what the true order and universal fellowship of the world is; next, by using the society which embodies this fellowship as an instrument for cultivating the spirit of each nation, for awakening each to the perception of the object of its existence, for destroying in each the motives which lead to strife and division, (the worst and strongest of those motives being the trade temper;) finally, by putting into the hands of the national ruler a sword for the chastisement of those who love war rather than peace, a sword not to be sheathed or to grow rusty till all things be fulfilled.

II. It remains that I should say a few words respecting those objections of the Quaker, which refer to a national provision for Christian ministers. We shall derive great help in understanding this subject, from the remarks which have been already made in this section. We have found that there are two societies, both organic, both forming part of the same constitution; both related to man under different aspects of his life; both bearing witness for God according to different aspects of his character: the one expressed in such institutions as Sacraments, which directly concern man as a spiritual being; the other in such institutions as Property, which directly concern him as a creature of this earth. We have seen that the first and higher of these societies has been, under our dispensation, that which has called the lower into life. Now nothing is more true than the assertion of the Quaker, That all the provisions made for ministers of the Gospel in the first ages,

were made by the love of their flocks. He is most
right in asserting that this was so, because the
principle of the Gospel is a principle of love, because
the power of the Gospel is one which acts immediately
upon the spirit and the will of man. He is most right
in asserting, that since we are under the same dispensation of love as the Apostles were, the principles
which governed the Church then are to govern it
now. But he has overlooked one point; he has
forgotten that love is not a thing which looks at to-
day or to-morrow, but which stretches its thoughts
into the future, which brings all ages together in its
embrace. The love of the early Church was not
shewn to St. Peter and St. Paul chiefly for their
own sakes, but as stewards of the mysteries of God,
as the representatives of a kingdom of which there
was to be no end. Therefore it was inevitable that
this charity should be exercised in providing for
the wants of the time to come, for the service of
God and for the benefit of men in generations
unborn. I ask whether this far-looking spirit of
charity be not more indicative of a dispensation,
than that which can only see present objects, can only
think of those to whom it is personally obliged? And
yet it is this charity which is the foundation of all the
complaints of Quakers against the principle of an
ecclesiastical property. That property is expressly a
fund of which particular men, in particular ages, are
merely the stewards; which is a fund for all ages.

But I grant that whatever may have been the
origin of such a fund, it is a most dangerous possession for anybody, providing the ends for which it
exists are not very clearly defined. Now, the effect of

the union of the Church with the nation is precisely to
define these objects, to make the property which is
bestowed upon the ecclesiastical society as such,
available for certain clear, intelligible purposes. The
Church establishes itself in a particular district, sets
up its buildings, carries on its services by the processes which I have spoken of already; the people,
among whom it comes, acquire a national consistency,
begin to have more distinct notions about their relation to each other, and about this matter of property.
What they do with reference to this ecclesiastical property, is to give it the security which belongs to individual property, and by different arrangements to
make it available for the education of the nation from
age to age. What further they do, is to exact from
the owners of the soil a direct acknowledgment that
their own property, though assured to them individu-
ally, is a trust from God, for the good of the nation,
and must contribute a portion of its produce to the
general fund. This is the simple history of Church
property, and of its connexion with national property.
It was increased afterward by voluntary gifts and
bequests, the fruit in many cases of superstitious
influences, but of influences acting upon the will, and
therefore not destroying the character of the benefac-
tion. On the other hand, the influence of the nation,
as everybody knows, was exerted in the Middle Ages
to prevent this accumulation of wealth, to make these
gifts and bequests difficult or ineffectual. Nothing,
therefore, can be a greater perversion of history than
to speak of ecclesiastical revenues, as if they were the
fruit of union with the State. The State has been a
great instrument, in God's hands, for preventing the

mischiefs which might have accrued to the Church, and which did accrue to it at different times, from its influence over the minds of men. On the other hand, it has been a great instrument in pointing out to the Church the purposes for which its wealth has been given it, and may be most profitably exercised. And if we are asked to shew what tokens there are of its being the will of God, that a fund should exist for the teaching of the nation, which should be exempt from the assaults of individual avarice, and which should not be diverted to mere selfish uses, I will mention three.

First, the shameful inclination which the clergy have often shewn to turn this wealth to purposes of selfishness and luxury ; the witness which it has borne against that sin, the strong feeling and conscience in men, that because the clergy were stewards of this property selfishness was a greater sin in them than in others; the heavy judgments which have followed upon the exhibition of it. Secondly, the greedy disposition which the nobles and gentry have shewn to plunder this property ; the proofs they have given that this disposition was part of the same which led them to be careless of their tenants and dependants, to live lives of self-indulgence, to say, ' The soil is our own, who is Lord over us ;' the miserable habits which they have cultivated in themselves and transmitted to their descendants, whenever there has not been such a fixed and continual testimony as Church property furnishes against these wicked imaginations. Lastly, the utter incapacity of Quakers, with all their charitable tendencies, acts, and protests, to convince the world that they do not estimate wealth far above its value; that they do not look upon the acquisition of it as the main end of life. I do not say the impression is a true one; I do say that a society which exists to bear a testimony against that which is secular, has utterly failed in making mankind understand the testimony, and has failed precisely because it has treated property as a thing necessary and yet evil; to be toiled and watched for, and yet not to be redeemed from temporary and servile uses for the continual service of God and man.

SECTION II.—THE PURE THEOCRATIST.

UNDER this name I comprehend various sets of men differing from each other in many respects, but all distinguished by a certain Jewish spirit, the spirit most directly opposed to that of the Quakers. The Scotch Covenanter is one, perhaps the most remarkable, specimen of the class. The Fifth-Monarchy Man exhibits a very different modification of it. Some of its more general features may be traced even in the Nonjurors of the seventeenth and eighteenth centuries, who regarded the Puritan factions with so much contempt and horror. It has reappeared under at least two different forms in our own day. On the whole it may be pronounced rather characteristic of Great Britain, on which account I shall be the more brief in my notice of it here.

The Theocratist believes, as I do, that the Old Testament is the great key to the meaning of national society. He believes, as I do, that the Lord is the King of every nation as much as He was of the Jewish nation. He thinks, as I do, that a nation is to undertake wars, to administer oaths, to inflict punishments, in the name and under the authority of its unseen Ruler. From these premises he proceeds to deduce certain inferences, which are various, according to his other feelings and tempers and beliefs, but which are all apparently sustained by the same scriptural authority.

The Covenanter says that the Jew existed to witness against idolatry; for the putting down of idolatry he was to unsheath his sword. The modern nation exists for the same object, and is to use the same means for effecting it. By its obligation and oath to God it is bound to extirpate all forms of faith, which are either idolatrous or tend to idolatry.

The Fifth-Monarchy Man does not see in any existing nation the pattern of a theocracy. But one is on the point of being established, one which shall fulfil the prophecies respecting that kingdom which was cut out of the mountain without hands. He is not very clear whether this society is to be universal or national, a Catholic Church, or an Ancient Israel. He finds some of the features of both in the Bible, and he strives to unite them.

The Nonjuror recognises the Church and the nation as distinct, but the nation exists in the person of its king, for the purpose of supporting and propagating the Church and putting down heresy. This was the function of the old Jewish king, this should be the function of the king now. For this purpose he is anointed with oil, his person is sacred; he may not be deposed or set aside for any offences.

After what I have said in my remarks upon the

Sermon on the Mount, the reader may perhaps understand my main point of difference with all these classes.
But it will be well to bring it out in reference to each
side of the doctrine. The Covenanter has surely the
strongest warrant for his assertion, that the Jewish
Commonwealth was in all its parts a protest against
idolatry, that the moment it forgot that protest it
virtually ceased to exist. And I think he is right in
saying that every nation exists under the condition of
its bearing this protest. Sensual worship is its
destruction. The acknowledgment of an absolute
unseen Being, a rigid exclusion of every thing which
tends to confound Him with the works of His hands,
are implied in the very nature of law, and are the only
terms upon which law can be enforced.

A nation, then, must by all means strive against
idolatry; but how must it strive? Under a national,
legal dispensation, where law is the first thing, and
spiritual principles are looked upon as the support of
law, the ordinary means which a nation resorts to for
the punishment of other offences must be resorted to
for the punishment of this. Idolatry and all forms of
false worship must be crimes to be punished by the
State. There are manifest inconveniences in such a
course; but it is inevitable, the existence of the nation
depends upon it. Under a spiritual dispensation we
escape from this necessity; idolatry is raised from the
circle of outward crimes to the circle of inward sins;
the sword of the Lawgiver is felt to be inadequate to
reach it; the sword of the Spirit is known to be more
effectual; it claims this as part of its province; it
leaves to the legislature only outward crimes, of which
idolatry, if not extirpated out of the heart, must be

the cause. The Covenanting doctrine, therefore, that because the Lord is our King, our National King, we are bound to treat offences directly against Him as offences against the law, is applicable only to a State existing without a Church. Neither the honour of God nor the safety of the Nation binds us to take any particular method for avenging the one or preserving the other; and if we believe, as those who believe in a Church must, that spiritual methods are the most Divine, and as readers of history must, that they are the most effectual, we have no excuse for following Jewish precedent at the cost of sacrificing principles which are·implied in the Old Testament and expounded in the New.

It will be evident, I think, from these considerations that the Scotch Covenanter was seeking to establish a Jewish and not a Christian nation; that is to say, a Nation professing Religion, and not a Nation which recognises a Church as the ground and vital principle of its own existence.

Of the Millennarians I will only say, that the records of their thoughts are by no means unworthy of study. Their confusions respecting that which is distinct and that which is universal, that which is spiritual and that which is legal, are only the same confusions concentrated into a small compass, and divested of restraining and correcting influences, which we find scattered through all ecclesiastical history. And in the writings of Sir Harry Vane, if he is to be considered one of them, we may detect very deep principles and remarkable distinctions indeed, which need only the acknowledgment that they were embodied ages before in the Catholic Church, to make them as practically important as they are profound.

It will seem most strange that I should impute to the Nonjuror, who is usually spoken of in England as the highest of High Churchmen, the same legal, anti-ecclesiastical spirit which we noticed in the Covenanter. But the fact seems to be this : he conceived the Church to be little more than the Canon Law embodied in a set of persons and institutions. This law he set very much above the national law, and resisted as Erastian any attempt to bring one under the yoke of the other. But of the Church, as a spiritual, sacramental body, constituted not in laws but in a Person, exhibiting the principles and essence of laws, and therefore not to be circumscribed by their formalities, he seems to have had little idea. How, therefore, the Nation could serve the Church, except by propagating its opinions and putting down its enemies, how both might be employed to fulfil the purposes of Him who is the absolute Love and the absolute Righteousness, towards a spiritual creature who is dwelling here under visible and earthly conditions, he did not much consider. And it would seem that the same habit of mind which must have so much obscured the New Testament to him, did not help him greatly in his interpretation of the Old; otherwise he must surely have perceived that, however unlawful it may be for subjects to depose kings, the King of kings is often said in Scripture to exercise His own prerogative in deposing them. And if we are living under His government, as the Jews were (which is their own doctrine), we must have a right to inquire whether He has, on any occasion, exhibited His displeasure against any monarch who has broken a national covenant, by setting him aside, and by appointing another. For it may be, that in refusing our allegiance to that other ruler, or in denying that he is rightful as well as actual king, we are making light not of the privileges of subjects but of the authority of God.

SECTION III.—THE SEPARATIST.

BY this name I designate those who say that the Nation and Church ought to be separate bodies, while yet they do not, with the Quaker, look upon national life as an evil thing. They state the reasons for their opinion thus: 'The State is secular; the Church, if it be a true Church, is anti-secular; to unite a secular and anti-secular body is monstrous. The effects of it are an invasion of the rights of conscience, continual disputes between the two societies, an impossibility of reformation.' These are the doctrines generally maintained by the successors of those English Puritans, who were themselves such vehement assertors of the religious character of the State.

It is not necessary to reply to them at any length. I have admitted their premises as fully as they can desire. A secular and an anti-secular society can exist together only as deadly enemies. If the State be secular, the Church must desire the extinction of the State, for she lives that she may destroy that which is secular. Our difficulty is to understand how Christian men can speak with so much toleration of that which they describe by an epithet so purely evil.

For, if they do not use the word *secular* in an evil sense, where lies the point of their antithesis? How is the Church anti-secular except as she is opposed to something wrong, something ungodly? If by the word anti-secular is understood merely *spiritual* as opposed to *legal*, then the whole phrase is a cheating one. For we deny that there is any contradiction between that which is legal and that which is spiritual; and those who use this language will join us in the denial. They say continually, that the Law and the Gospel are not contrary to each other, though the Gospel is able to do that which the Law, being weak through the flesh, cannot do. They resist, as we do, the doctrine that what is evangelical is anti-legal, while they assert, just as we do, that it is something entirely different from that which is legal, because it has an inward and not merely a literal power. What I have been endeavouring to maintain is, that a nation just so far as it is a nation, is anti-secular in one way, just as much as the Church is anti-secular in another. Both are God's appointed instruments for resisting the evil, rebellious, disorderly principles, which make up the scriptural notion of 'this world.' Both are liable to invasions of that principle, which they are appointed to resist; both have been infected with it. The Church has become secular when she has attempted to realise herself as a separate body; the Nation has become secular when it has tried to realise itself as a separate body. But each does so, by violating the law of its existence, by refusing to be that which the Scriptures affirm and history proves that it was meant to be.

After what I said under the last head, it is scarcely

necessary that I should say much about the charge of
this union being unfavourable to the rights of conscience. How such a notion has gained prevalency I
think I have explained. A nation, I said, if it is to
preserve its own existence, must put down that which
is undermining it. It finds that principles lead to
acts, that notions about the Supreme Being lead to
evil conduct towards men; therefore it must extirpate
those principles if it can. Nations in union with the
Church have used their swords for this purpose;
Churchmen may have encouraged them in such acts:
but the act was not necessary for the nation, the
Churchman ought to have known that he had powers
more adequate to the repression of such evil. He
ought to have warned the statesman not to meddle
with his province, and to have told him how very
impotent his arms would prove when he tried them
against spiritual enemies. But whether he has done
this or not, the incorporation of his spiritual power
with the national power is the great, the only witness
for this truth. Separate it from the State, and the
State ruler, let his notions be as liberal as they may,
must and will use his power for keeping down opinion.
You may preach to him about the sin and folly of the
attempt, but you will preach in vain. He cannot
shut his eyes to the fact, that opinions do divide his
subjects, do make them rebellious, do lead to the most
open mischiefs. He cares nothing about them in
themselves, but if he is an honest man, he cannot be
stopped in dealing with them by such means as he
has, when the interests which are committed to him
are at stake. You say he should leave them to
spiritual influences. What influences? You denied

that the spiritual influence had anything to do with the nation. You said that the statesman was to treat it as something entirely unconnected with him.

I have spoken in this instance, as I wish to speak in all others, to what I believe to be the real feeling of those who raise the objection. They feel that there is a Conscience in man, to be reverenced as the witness of God in His creature. There is no truth I am more anxious to assert than this. If there were no conscience, no ear within to receive the voice without, I do not know what the Law would address by its terrors, or the Gospel by its promises of life. Without it, I do not know what a Nation could mean, or a Church could mean. But is it not curious that those in our day and in our country, who talk most about the *rights* of conscience in their speeches, are least willing, in their more learned discourses, to admit the *fact* of a conscience; nay, actually denounce the idea of a conscience, as inconsistent with the doctrine of human depravity? And to this point I believe all must come who do not think that there is a constitution for man, and that his depravity is shewn in his refusing to abide in that constitution; in his choosing to be a separate self-willed creature. We say that his Conscience is continually protesting against his self-will; that the office of the Nation is by stern and righteous punishment to restrain that self-will when it breaks out into acts; that the office of the Church is, by gracious and loving methods, to bring out the true free-will of which it is the base counterfeit. In like manner we say, that the office of the nation is to punish those overt acts of folly, proceeding from man's private judgment, which disturb the order of

the commonwealth; that the office of the Church is
to teach men how they may rise above their private
judgments, and attain that clear manly judgment
which is one of the best qualifications of a good
citizen. Sad is it when men are *taught* to indulge
their self-will and their selfish judgments, and when
these qualities of the evil nature are invested with the
awful name of *conscience.* Sad is it for national order
and for spiritual life.

The complaint that the relations between the
Church and the Nation have always been productive
of conflicts, I have considered sufficiently in a former
part of this chapter. The fact is undoubted; the
Nation has tried to usurp the prerogatives of the
Church, the Church has tried to usurp the prerogatives of the Nation. All history is full of such
records; so also it is full of disputes between parents
and children, brothers and sisters, kings and subjects.
Undoubtedly, if we could get rid of relationships, we
should not have to read continual accounts of their
being violated. But can you get rid of them unless
you unmake God's world, and turn it into a wilderness? Can you cause that that which speaks to man's
inner life should not stand in some connexion with
that which speaks to him as an inhabitant of this
earth? Has he not both a spirit and a body? Does
the fact that they are continually at variance, prove
that there is no law of fellowship between them?

But the union of the Church with the Nation is a
hindrance to the reformation of the Church when it
becomes corrupt. The evidence of this fact from
history is particularly weak. There have been great
attempts at reformation in the Church, conducted

in opposition to the civil power. Such, for instance, was the reformation attempted by Hildebrand in the eleventh century; such were many of the reforms attempted by the religious orders. There have been other reformations carried on in conjunction with civil rulers. Such was the Lutheran reformation, in Saxony; the Zuinglian and Calvinistic reformation, in Switzerland; the reformation in Sweden, in Holland, in England. In all these last cases, the civil rulers were the patrons and promoters of reformation. I can see evils in all these changes; those carried on by the Church against the civil power, and those carried on by the civil power. But is the English dissenter prepared to say that the first were in their conduct and results very much better than the last? If he is not, he must abandon his principle, that the Church has no chance of being purified from her irregularities except when she stands wholly aloof from the State. If he is, he must defend himself as well as he can from the charge of Popery. To me it seems clear, from experience as well as reason, that the State is an excellent admonisher to the Church respecting her inward corruptions, because it comes in contact with those outward evils which are the fruits of them, even as the Church is a most excellent admonisher to the State respecting its sins, because their effects in destroying the Nation's heart are most evident to the spiritual man; but that each will do mischief if it attempts, according to its own maxims, to set the other right.

Section IV.—The Patrician.

Idea of a Golden Age.—Allegorical Interpretations of the Old Testament.—Church Discipline.—Extrusion of Heretics.—Catholic Unity amidst National Peculiarities.

THERE is still another class of objectors to my statement, whose opinions are entitled to great consideration. They do not look upon the union of the Church with the civil power in different nations as a positive evil. It was God's ordinance, to be submitted to like everything else which He appoints. 'But to say that the Church is better for this state of things, that its circumstances in modern Europe are better than its circumstances were in the first five or six centuries, is false and dangerous. The age of the Fathers is the pattern on the Mount—the true model of a Catholic Church; in which there was fellowship in faith and worship, discipline for moral offenders, separation from wilful heretics. Since that time the Eastern Church has been separated from the Western, Protestants have divided themselves from Romanists; heresies have been tolerated, discipline made light of, the idea of national Churches substituted for the idea of a universal Church, in each particular nation the Church regarded as part of the civil establishment. This is a condition of things to be borne with humiliation and patience, not to be spoken of with triumph.'

1. The feeling that there has been a golden age of the Church to which we may look back, and for the restoration of which we may pray, has been so deeply rooted in the minds of men, in the most various circumstances, and holding the most va-

rious opinions, that he must be a very thoughtless
Christian indeed who could treat it lightly. Nor
can those who would restrict this age to the times
before Constantine, or those who would confine it
within the lives of the Apostles, fairly complain
against the eulogists of the first six centuries. For
it is clear that, in one sense, even the most limited
period cannot be called a period of purity. As
long as the Epistles to the Corinthians and the
Galatians remain in the Canon, nay, till every
epistle be weeded of some of its most striking
warnings and exhortations, we must be content to
admit (everybody has practically admitted), that
there were spots even then in the feasts of charity;
yea, that every form of corruption, every habit
which threatens apostasy, might be found in the
infant family of Christ. Do we, then, betake ourselves to the notion, that the glory of the apostolic
period is to be sought in the ministers of the Church
though not in its members? The epistles to the
angels of the seven churches come in to perplex this
conclusion. Some of these had lost their first love,
some did not exercise discipline, some were guilty of
tolerating a heresy, (which a moderately well supported
ecclesiastical tradition would trace to one of the seven
Deacons,) some had a name to live and were dead,
some were neither hot nor cold. Are we, then, ready
to give up altogether the feeling that the apostolic
periods were different from other periods? If not, I
think we must resort to some such hypothesis as this,
which will perhaps really satisfy the minds of most
men, who will give themselves leisure to consider it:
That there was a more distinct and evident conflict in

*the age of the Apostles with different forms of evil,
both without and within the Church, than there ever
has been since.* It was a critical period, one might
say, *the* critical period in the history of mankind, and
therefore was one which brought to light all dark
images side by side with the perfect light to which
they were opposed. And this, it may be, is the true
idea of the golden age; at all events, the only one
which the past history of the Church presents to us—
not an age of innocence, but an age of conflict; not one
which was holding itself up as a model to the world,
but which was bringing out the idea of the Church
as a body belonging to no age; as the permanent
witness against that secular spirit which would always
make some period of time, and not the principles
exhibited in that time, the object of its admiration.

Now surely the history of the Church for the
first five or six centuries does present the Church
in the same kind of struggle as this which we
have discovered in the apostolic time. The battle
is somewhat changed in its character after the
accession of Constantine, but who will say that it
was less severe? Or who will venture to affirm
that the Divine image was less brought out through
these strifes in such men as Athanasius and Chrysostom, than it had been in Ignatius or Justin?
The whole history of this century is a book of the
wars of the Lord; most precious, surely, because it
shews how the principle of strength made perfect
in weakness was working itself out in individual
men and in the whole of society; because it shews
how the shouts of the soldiers of the Cross were
laying low the highest Babel tower that was ever

raised in this world; because it shews that the scheme of God was to prevail, and that nothing was to withstand it. But surely this is the picture which that time presents; not a picture of still, beautiful, pastoral life, but of great crimes and great virtues—oftentimes appearing in the same men, yet always illustrating each other; always enabling us, if we look, to see what man is with God and without Him. He has been pleased to exhibit to us this age, not in particular specimens of virtue and excellence, but as a whole; as a whole it is precious to us. We lose the blessing of it, we lose the idea of the Church which it presents, if we omit any of its darker features. Let us consider, then, what we do when we desire that this age, so invaluable as a portion of history, should be restored to us in fact. If we ask that the age in which St. Paul preached may come again, we ask that Nero may come again; if we ask that we may be transported back to the glorious period of Athanasius, we ask to live under the tyrant Constantius, to have the world almost wholly pagan, to have the Church almost wholly Arian. If we long to sit at the feet of Chrysostom, we long for the infamous corruptions of Antioch and Constantinople, for the government of Eutropius, for the horrible villanies of the eunuchs of the palace. If we reckon that it would have been a blessing to live under the teaching of Augustine, we must be content to see Rome sacked by one set of barbarians, and the Church in Africa threatened by another; we must get our learning from a race of effete rhetoricians; we must dwell amidst all the seductions and abominations of Manicheism. These are very commonplace con-

siderations; but as they are true, it is very advisable
for the honour of the Church and of its Head, as well
as for the removal of a certain fantastic habit of mind,
which is most alien from the temper of the early
ages, that we should occasionally dwell upon them.
The effect of doing so cannot be to make us fall into
any contempt of the Fathers, or to adopt those notions
respecting them which have been propagated of late
in this country with so much more of self-conceit than
learning, and which could only have gained currency
through some weakness in the theory to which
they were opposed. Unquestionably, if we are reasonable men, the more we look at that mass of evil in
society, which the Church was sent to decompose, the
more we shall admire the power which decomposed it,
and be thankful for the instruments by whom He
worked.

2. But, then, can we do this, and not see something
more than a permission of those national societies which
the Church called into being, and with which, in the
Western world, she became identified; must we not
believe that this was a mighty step in the development
of the Divine scheme, in the establishment of the
Divine kingdom upon earth? The Church had been
brought out as one body existing in different places,
to try its strength against the Roman world, and it had
prevailed. It had made good the principle upon which
it stood against the most terrible odds. What so
reasonable as to believe that it was to carry on its
work of creation, in the very line in which the world's
work of destruction had been carried on ; that as the
Roman empire had swallowed up all nations into itself,
its mighty antagonist was to make them breathe again,

to shew each what its proper place and function
was in God's kingdom and commonwealth? Are we
told that this doctrine savours of those modern
theories respecting progression, which are so godless and intolerable? I care not what ill name may be
given it, provided it justifies the ways of God to man,
and shews that the Church has not existed for nothing.
But if by this charge it be meant that we are supporting a notion of progress, which is inconsistent with
the permanency of God's order and truth, there never
was one so ill supported or so unfortunate. *They* are
the innovators, *they* are the deniers of the permanence of God's order, *they* would make the Church
merely a growth out of foregone and exhausted states
of society, who maintain that national life, upon
which so much honour was put in the old world,
has been discarded as worthless in the new. We
say that there was no such alteration in the counsels
of the Divine mind, that the history of modern Europe
proves there was not. We say that the constitution
of the Church, as it was exhibited during the conflicts
with the Roman empire, was simply a universal constitution; we rejoice that it was so; hereby such a
constitution was shewn to exist, hereby the meaning
of past history, which had all been leading to the discovery of it, was made evident. But we say that this
constitution was necessarily imperfect, for it left all
the relations of men, as held together by the bonds
of neighbourhood, as distinguished by race and language, unaccounted for; it did not bring these
relations under Church influence. And we say that,
seeing these relations are especially developed in the
Old Testament, it was the necessary consequence of

x 2

this imperfection, that one aspect of that Testament should be lost to the first age of the Church. I know that I am using language which will shock some good persons, and therefore I will endeavour to explain myself.

3. It is commonly said that the Fathers must be looked to as the interpreters of Scripture, in consequence of their proximity to the Apostles, the opportunities they might have had of hearing the very words which they uttered, etc. I confess I have never been able to understand this doctrine of proximity. It would seem to me to prove that Athanasius, or Ambrose, or Augustine, must be of far less value to us, as an elucidator of truth, than Hermas or Ignatius; and I do not think that this has been the practical feeling of the Church in any age. It would have seemed to me rather, that the great worth of the Fathers arose from their being placed by God in circumstances which especially enabled them to apprehend certain great truths, especially those foundation truths which concern His Being and the order of the Universal Society. Adopting that view, I can believe that each had his own special merits; that the Alexandrian might see that which the Latin could not see; that one principle would be brought out in mighty power by him who struggled with Arians, another by him who, in his own heart and in the world, had done battle with Manicheism. Adopting the other, I think that I shall not only be in danger of making an age into a Church, but of exalting particular individuals of that age above others, to whom perhaps a more important work was committed.

But whichever of these views be adopted, it will be difficult to prove that the Fathers had any better means than other men of understanding the circumstances of the *Jewish* nation. They had no *proximity* with the Fathers of that nation. The Jews with whom they could converse were either those in whom the national feelings had been merged in more general Catholic sympathies, or those who were trying to set up their old national distinctions against the Church, or those who regarded their whole past history as little more than a collection of allegories, or the development of a Mosaic philosophy. Again, their circumstances could give them no sort of sympathy with the old national life of the Jews; the temple was gone, the city was laid waste; these events had been necessary to the establishment of the universal Church, and that Church stood in the midst of a great empire, in which there was no nation "that moved the wing, or opened the mouth, or peeped." Would it not have been most reasonable to expect, under such circumstances, that so far as they were polemical, they might be able to prove clearly that the Jewish Commonwealth was meant to be the seed of a great tree; so far as they were experimental, that the Jewish saints had struggled with the same internal enemies, which were assailing themselves; so far as they were mystical, that there had been an invisible guide and teacher, training man to know Him through all past ages of history: but that whatever belonged to the common, daily, human life of the Jews would be utterly puzzling to them, would seem quite out of place in a Divine book, and would therefore of necessity be translated into cabalistic lore? I say, would not any one expect this from the position in which the Fathers were placed? And if the facts should be found exactly to accord with these expectations, if every Christian of the present day who looks into them should be puzzled and perplexed by curious and subtle spiritualisations of facts, which simply as facts have been his delight as a child, and which, as he grew to be a man, have seemed to connect themselves with what is passing in the world around him; if there be a use of this spiritualising method, which the Church even of that age has itself condemned, if yet this extravagant use of it was justified in the practice of the most learned and laborious of all the Fathers, and if it be most difficult to find where the point is at which he transgressed the legitimate rule, is it more wise and pious, and more respectful to these holy men, to say that they *could not* take in the literal meaning of the old Scriptures, so as to give that literal meaning any life, and that it was not intended they should do so; or to determine that we will make out a case for them by renouncing all our own advantages, by resolutely praising a system of interpretation which our consciences and hearts are continually repudiating; and then, after all, to give up the defence of it when it is clearly and consistently worked out?

I will not stop to remark, what must be obvious to every person who considers the foregoing statements, that the ideas of the Fathers respecting marriage, property, every institution which belongs in the first place to our earthly condition, must have been exceedingly affected by their views of the Old Testament generally. In all cases they will have sought for the highest, most transcendental ground upon which such ordinances were to be defended; since they must exist, they will readily have looked upon them as types of something higher; but how to connect the type with the actual fact, how to avoid the conclusion that that which is not directly of heaven belongs in some sense to human depravity, it was impossible for them to see. It will be impossible, I believe, for us, if we do not feel something more than a grumbling acquiescence in the scheme of God for the education of our race, if we do not acknowledge, that by restoring national life through the means of the Church, He was carrying out the law of redemption, and shewing how everything that belongs to man and his position here, everything that does not involve the violation of that position, is comprehended under it.

4. But it is affirmed that the discipline of moral offenders was recognised by the early Church as essential to its existence, and is almost lost sight of since the Church entered into fellowship with the nations. I admit at once that the principle of spiritual discipline, of a discipline for the rectification of habits and principles, a discipline far more deep and subtle than any which lawgivers can exercise, is implied in the constitution of the spiritual body, and that it was first manifested to the world, like all the other principles of the Church's polity, in its first ages. I admit, further, that in connexion with this highest power, there is one implied in the very existence of every society, (but especially necessary to such a society as the Church,) of noticing the more outward and flagrant transgressions committed by its

members, and of determining how far they exclude the offender from its privileges. This power, I conceive, was not only exercised by the early Church, but was almost the only witness to the degraded and sensualised slaves of a military despotism, that there is any authority in heaven or earth competent to punish the offences of the high as well as of the low. One such example as that which St. Ambrose gave, in his sentence upon Theodosius, was for its practical effect worth all the tomes of the Roman jurisconsults. But yet the history of that transaction, and of all the other transactions of that period, proves that the Church was utterly unable to deal with the accumulated mass of profligacy which was to be found among those who had been admitted to its fellowship. Councils might determine that such and such crimes excluded the offender for five, or six, or twenty years from the Eucharist, yet we know that crimes of the blackest character were perpetrated by clergymen as well as laymen. And it must occur to every one sometimes to ask himself whether the Church, while she was claiming such lofty and heavenly powers, was not frequently compelled by the circumstances in which she was placed, to degrade these powers, and to assume far too much the character of a mere spiritual police.

Now I readily allow, that the effect of the restoration of fixed, positive national law, and of outward formal tribunals for the punishment of crime, has been to make men less sensible of the meaning and of the need of spiritual discipline. And the more strict and definite this law has become, and the more men in general have been brought to acknowledge it as a fixed necessary element in their lives, so much the less has the sense of another kind of government, one reaching to the feelings and character, prevailed; nay, there has been a desire to get rid of it altogether. But none of these facts convince me, that the establishment of outward law, the formation of national societies, were not parts of God's great scheme for developing more fully the nature and character of Christ's kingdom. Looking at the question in the most obvious way, if I compare the state of any nation in modern Europe, I would include even Russia, with that which we know to have been the state of the Roman and Byzantine empires during the first seven centuries, I should really tremble for my own ingratitude, if I did not wonder at the change which God has wrought. And this change, I affirm to be not merely one in outward and material happiness, but one connected with the very ends for which the Church exists. It does seem to me, in the first place, a positive good that the Church should not be looked upon at all in the light of a police, that there should be another body performing that function, and leaving it to find out its own. And next, I believe that every circumstance in the later history of Europeans has been enabling the Church in each nation to discover if she will what her powers are, how much greater than those of the statesman—how indispensable to the statesman. In the first age, spiritual discipline tried to be everything. Since that time outward law has tried to be everything; the existence of spiritual discipline has been forgotten. I shewed, in my first part, how clearly and awfully it has been demonstrated that law cannot do what it wishes to do and pretends to do. Thus, then, I think we are coming to a time, when the spiritual side of Christ's kingdom must come forth into a prominence which it has not yet assumed; when the education and discipline which the Church exercises will be demanded by each nation for the preservation of its own existence. But the Church, I believe, can only profit by this great crisis in the history of mankind, if she be ready to acknowledge that according to the will of her Author and her Lord she is not meant to have an independent existence; that she is not meant to be extranational; that she has no commission or powers which dispense with the necessity of positive, formal law, and with outward government; that her highest honour is to be the life-giving energy to every body in the midst of which she dwells.

5. 'But the Church in old times was able to cast heretics out of her bosom. When she becomes connected with the nation, it either undertakes the punishment of them by its own vulgar methods, or else entertains them and tolerates them, without paying the least heed to the Church's sentence.' Here, again, I believe the same observations apply. The character and constitution of the Church in the early ages were, I think, manifested in its contests with heretics. One or another partial theory was broached, one or another article of the Creeds was set aside or pared away. The Church, often against terrible odds, asserted the integrity of her constitution; asserted that spiritual unity which is the ground of her existence. That there might not be divisions, she was driven to draw subtle distinctions, submitting oftentimes to the charge of logomachy, that she

might maintain the realities which logomachists were making void; often seeming to puzzle the wayfarer that she might preserve to him his inheritance. This was her conflict at that time; for this end it was necessary she should have her individual champions and her general councils. I have no doubt this was the work of the early Church, and that amidst all the sins of even her best and bravest members, she fulfilled it as it was meant to be fulfilled.

But does not everyone feel in reading ecclesiastical history, that this position, though in some respects a glorious one, was in many an unfortunate one? In these struggles with those who would have divided her, the Church was maintaining her character as a kingdom, cohering by its relation to an awful name, which it was bound to assert and defend. And yet the impression of her having this character was in no slight degree impaired by the strifes into which she entered for the sake of it. These led men more and more to fancy that the battle was for a set of dogmas or opinions, which the particular set of doctors called Catholics had agreed to maintain against the world, but which, unfortunately, they could not settle among themselves. Supposing Pagans or Jews had taken up this notion, it might be a matter of regret; but if Christians and Christian teachers fell into it themselves, the very existence of the Church was put in peril. And it is evident that this was the case. The Greeks especially, priding themselves upon that gift of subtlety which has in all ages been committed to them, seem to have lost unawares the entire substance, every part of which they were able with such accuracy to dis-

tinguish; to have called forth new heresies by the
very zeal and decrees which suppressed the old; to
have felt less and less that the Church was anything
but a school, even while they were resorting most
unscrupulously to measures which could only be
justified to their consciences by the belief that it was
the one human fellowship. I think we must all feel
it a relief to escape from this Greek world of controversy into the Latin world of business and enter-
prise. There may be much evil there, too, but there
is a practical work going on; societies are growing;
the Church is felt to be herself a society, governed
by certain laws, informed by a certain principle.
Who can help feeling, that amidst all the contradictions
of the Middle Ages, the sense of a common bond, the
feeling of a one spirit and a one object, were far
more realised than they had been except by a very
few of the highest minds in the age of the Œcumenical
Councils? And this is surely what one would expect,
if one really believed that the Church was under
God's government, and that He was making its
meaning and power manifest, amidst all the perplexities
and distractions of men's self-will. Now, however
strange it may appear, the connexion of Church polity
with national polity was certainly the means of
keeping this feeling alive. The Greeks could not
look upon the Church as a kingdom, because they
had nothing to teach them what a kingdom was; they
were living under a despot with whose government
they had no sympathy, who ruled by creatures and
tools, not as the centre of a social order. And this
assertion is confirmed by a fact which seems at first
to interfere with it, and to supply a better reason for

the character which I have attributed to the Western Church. The Pope, it will be said, made the Middle Ages conscious of their Church unity, and yet the Pope was the great antagonist of national societies. I answer, it was the feeling of national life that grew up in the countries of the West, which made it possible that there should be a Bishop assuming the position which the Pope assumed. When once the national feeling had been strongly developed, it was impossible to view the Church in the light of a mere learned school; men were obliged to look upon it as a kingdom, for it was exercising the powers of one, and in no other character could they have paid it homage. Hence it was possible for the Bishop of Rome to give an outward formal character to this kingdom, to put himself at the head of it, and though amidst continual reluctations and manifestations of independence to act as the feudal superior of the different societies into which Christendom was divided. But mark under what conditions this was possible. The Pope himself becomes the sovereign of a state; he does honour to the very principle he is setting at naught. I feel of course all the anomaly of this position; but it explains, I think, clearly, how truly it was the will of God that the Nations should come into being, and how necessary this was, not for the chastisement of the Church, but for its development. And to return to the point immediately under our consideration, it is in this way that the new position of those who differed from the doctrine or order of the Church is explained. In the first age they are pronounced guilty of violating the tradition and creed of the universal society; in the second age, they are treated as invaders of the order and unity of the particular state in which they are found, or of the states generally, so far as they feel themselves united for a common object; in the third age, the state feels that it consults its own peace better by leaving them alone, by allowing them a settled position, by treating them as the rest of its subjects. I have already said why I believe that each state will continue to do this only just so long as it maintains its relation with a spiritual society; why, the moment it becomes a mere civil body, it will of necessity resort to force again for the putting down of opinion. But now I am looking at the question in another light, and I would ask whether this is not a most important step in the plans of God. First, the spiritual society in her general councils took cognizance of the schisms and heresies, but in doing so she ran the risk of seeming to be herself only the maintainer of a certain system of opinions, not the pillar and ground of truth. She inadvertently cultivated the very spirit of disputation which she wished to check. Next, the particular states shew that they are interested in the repression of these schisms and heresies, hereby testifying that they are of a practical character, that they do really interfere with government and order. But in bearing this testimony, the states were also doing a great injury to the Church; they were putting themselves into its place; they were using vulgar visible arms, for the accomplishment of an invisible and spiritual end.

Lastly, the states have forborne, or are inclined to forbear, from these experiments, having found them to be ineffectual. But in turn they are inclined to look upon all spiritual matters as transacted between quarrelling schools and sects, with whom the national government has little to do,—except, when they become very violent, to keep peace between them; at other times leaving them to carry on the work of mutual destruction. Now, I say, if there be a Church in the world, these are circumstances in which she can produce an evidence of her reality which she could not produce in either of the previous periods. She cannot cut off heretics from her communion, for they have cut themselves off—they do not care for her communion. But she can shew that she has that secret power within her which may unite them; that those nice distinctions of Fathers and of councils were not really distinctions meant to cause separation, but to prevent it; meant to preserve truth in its fulness and completeness against a time when men, having tried their different plans and methods of thought, should begin to desire that which would reconcile them, and when they should acknowledge no higher evidence of a Divine mission in any body than this, that it satisfies that aspiration. The Church, again, cannot make civil rulers perceive that she has a power of the same kind which they possess, for when they have fought her with her own weapons, they have prevailed and she has been foiled; but she may prove to them that she has another power, entirely distinct from theirs, far higher than theirs, to which they must resort, or perish in their feebleness.

6. I will conclude this head with one or two remarks upon the alleged impossibility of recognising a one Catholic Church under the distinctions

and limitations of national bodies. 'How,' it is asked, 'can a Church be one if it have no visible tokens of unity? Those who dream with the Quakers that the Church is a purely spiritual unseen body, may perchance think that all ceremonial uniformity is of no worth. But the defenders of National Churches are very far from any such notion as this. They require that the ecclesiastical organization should be strict and formal. Yet, according to them, it must have a different organization in every country, for there can be no general councils, seeing that everything is subject to the will of particular princes, and seeing that even provincial synods and national convocations are regarded with great jealousy by the civil power. What can happen, then, but that the Church should lose all the features by which its identity is ascertained in different parts of the earth, that it should gradually become more and more accommodated to the habits of particular districts; till at last it becomes more proud of that which separates it from other communities in other parts of the world, than of that which it has in common with them.'

My answer to these arguments is this: I have maintained against the Quaker that there are certain permanent *ordinances* in which the character and universality of the Church are expressed; she does not, therefore, depend for her unity upon the faith and feeling of her particular members, but bears a constant and abiding testimony against the want of faith or feeling in any or all of them. If this be a true doctrine, if it be the will of God that *these* ordinances should denote the universal and spiritual society, we should naturally expect that

He would manifest the distinction between them, and everything which is but accidentally connected with them. Evidently there are some accidents with which they must of necessity be connected. Baptism and the Eucharist must be administered in *some* mode; there must be rules about the jurisdiction of Bishops. If there are forms of prayer there must be given forms. There may also, of course, be a number of accidents which are not necessary, but which, from particular reasons, have obtained sacredness in different parts of the Church, or through the whole of it. Now the effect of the general legislation which the Church possessed in the early ages was unquestionably to connect together a particular mode of treating these ordinances with the ordinance itself. I do not say that this was the wish of the early Church: on the contrary, I believe that the study of the proceedings and decrees of councils would lead us to trace a very cautious and often subtle wisdom in discriminating between that which was merely of needful ecclesiastical institution, and that which was of the nature of the thing itself. And there was a higher wisdom than this, directing the practice of the early Church, and actually hindering different portions, even of such an empire as the Roman, from adhering to one ritual or one set of observances, with that fidelity which they observed in preserving the Creed and the ordinances. Still the result of œcumenical government in some degree to those who lived then—in a much greater degree to us who merely read their history,—is to efface this distinction, and to prevent us from contemplating the Divine sign in its own simplicity and integrity,

as separate even from the most desirable and indispensable arrangements respecting it.

When the Bishop of Rome tried to perpetuate
in his own person this œcumenical legislation, the
peril became infinitely greater. The most fearful
confusion arose between the signs of the Church
and the ecclesiastical appointments which had been
devised to make these signs effectual. Nothing
could so obscure the Divine origin and constitution
of the Church as this confusion. The eagerness of
the Church to claim the power of legislating in
emergencies hid from view the fact that she was
resting upon any principles, or that God had legislated
for her. At the same time she could not practically
maintain a strictly universal legislation; the habits,
maxims, and precedents of different localities interfered with it :—only to make the confusion of authorities and obligations more complete. Then came the
Reformation, asserting the law of God as something
paramount to the law of the Church, and, when its
maxims were perverted, suggesting to men that their
wills or their notions were superior to either. Meantime, however, the Church within each nation had
begun practically to claim for itself the power of
decreeing rites and ceremonies. That claim, properly
considered and used, was the greatest witness which
could be borne against the notion that ordinances and
ceremonies are the same. It did homage to the former
as the gifts to the Church universal; it treated the
latter as needful provisions to be taken cognizance of
by the spiritual body, this body having at once the
strongest obligation to teach men by outward evidences
that they were members of one family, and not to

permit its own theories or notions of what was suitable to this end to mix themselves with the great principles of God's government. Various causes, however, interfered to mar the effect of this proclamation. As the ecclesiastical body in any particular nation found itself checked by the self-will of individuals unwilling to submit to the regulations which are necessary to the existence of every society, and which acquire an especial sacredness in one which is meant to be the pattern of a human fellowship, it was inclined to put forth its pretensions more strongly, and to identify that which it decreed with the very being of the Church. This temper was especially likely to prevail in nations which had acquired a strict civil organization, and which were continually exercising their powers of legislation. The ecclesiastical body would naturally catch the habit of looking upon itself as merely existing to legislate, and would be more proud of the rules which it was laying down for its own government, than of all the influence it was exerting upon the heart of society. Supposing such a tone of mind to become prevalent, I can conceive no greater mercy than that the civil power should step in to put a stop to clerical convocations, or to discourage provincial synods. But for such violence, I cannot conceive how any national Church could have learnt what its own peculiar powers were. I think it must have been crushed under the weight of its own decrees; and, above all, that it must have lost sight of the only grounds of unity which it can have with the members of other nations. On the other hand, it seems to me that by this discipline it has been manifested wherein the substance and essence of a national Church consist;

that its substance is given it by those ordinances which belong to it in common with Christians elsewhere; that its essence consists in those powers which belong to it in common with the different parts of the body, and which are to be exerted in the first place for the benefit of its own country. When this lesson has been well learnt, I have no doubt but that each national Church will recover its synods and its convocations; for then she will know how to use them. Not with the lust of legislation, not in the hope of accomplishing her chief objects by decrees, but for the purpose of satisfying scruples, of leading men away from the restless study of what is external by not compelling them to arrange and deliberate about it for themselves, of determining those ceremonies which to a people of a particular climate, character, and constitution best express the great ideas of the Church, of more effectually establishing and directing discipline and education, of promoting fellowship with national Churches which are willing to acknowledge themselves as parts of a great Catholic body.

Whether when national Churches begin to understand their own position they may not once more send their representatives to a general council, and whether the princes of the different nations may not feel such a measure helpful instead of injurious to their objects, I will not inquire. I see no reason why, if we follow God's method, we may not arrive at such a result, though I can see the strongest why, if we violate that method and seek to have an independent existence, no councils, no compacts, no projects of union, can ever be otherwise than evil in themselves and pregnant with mischief.

Ought we to say then, that Church unity belongs to the first six centuries, and that since national distinctions began, there have been no traces of it? We have, I think, been able to perceive, that the separation of the Greek from the Latin Churches, which is so frequently lamented over, and which ought to be a great cause of shame and humiliation to both, has, nevertheless, led to very blessed results, by separating the Church from a cruel and mischievous tyranny, and enabling it to develop its powers under freer and happier conditions. In like manner, if we consider the subject calmly and solemnly, not omitting repentance for our sins nor thankfulness for our mercies, we shall, I believe, perceive, that but for the Reformation in the sixteenth century, European society must have sunk into the condition of an infidel world, nominally ruled by the intriguing head of a little Italian principality; really divided into a number of warring states, each aiming at the most selfish objects, each only looking to religion as the means of accomplishing them. From that time it has been evident to thinking persons, that there are two principles struggling in Christendom for supremacy: the one, that which is embodied in Protestantism, resisting the claim of the spiritual power to any extra-national domination, and always tending to set at naught spiritual authority altogether; the other, that which is embodied in Romanism, resisting the attempts of the particular states to divide their own subjects from the rest of Christendom, continually striving to uphold the Church as a separate power, and to set at naught the existence of each particular nation. These principles have fought together in Europe for centuries. If it be really the purpose of God in our age to reconcile them, and to cast out the element in each which is contrary to His will, and which has been introduced to it by the perverseness of men, shall we whine about the loss we have sustained by not being born at a time when the Church was making its first struggling efforts to assert its own unity? Shall we not rejoice and give thanks, that we are born in these latter days of the world, when all things are hastening to their consummation, and when the unity of the Church shall be demonstrated to be that ground upon which all unity in nations and in the heart of man is resting?

Section V.—The Modern Statesman.

Such statements as these, however unacceptable to many Churchmen, will not avail to conciliate modern politicians, or to remove the fears which they entertain of ecclesiastical influence. Perhaps they will be inclined to say that the power which I claim for the spiritual body is really a more dangerous one than that which I renounce. 'To admit the existence of a dominant hierarchy is the necessity of a statesman's position; nay, he has not much right to complain of the necessity; it helps in common times to keep other sects quiet, and clergymen indifferent. But when you say that this hierarchy is the proper educator of the land, you are not content that it should be entertained with a bauble. You wish it to become practically and politically mischievous. That power which can educate a land must rule over its families, over its arts, its literature, its science, its ethics, its philosophy, nay, in one sense, as the head of the professional classes, over its law and its medicine. These are pretensions which no government in this day can tolerate further than as it is compelled to tolerate them by circumstances. The religious bodies in every country must undoubtedly affect its education for good or for evil; but they are happily broken into fragments, and it is the statesman's business to see that they act, one and all of them, as religious bodies, and in no other character. The general education of the land he must gradually (for unquestionably there are many difficulties from old prejudices and institutions which he must remove before he can fully accomplish his desire) take under his own direction. If he allows it to be superintended by any ecclesiastical body, that body becomes just as dangerous as the Jesuits have ever been. For where has lain the real power of the Jesuits? Not in their government over courts, but over schools; not in the poison they have been able to infuse into the ears of monarchs, half so much as in the maxims of ecclesiastical submission and craft which they have communicated to children along with their primers and their grammars.'

In the first division of this work I have endeavoured to trace the history of some of those political and philosophical movements, which have led men in our day to contemplate education as the only adequate means of preserving government and society. I shewed that the course of thought by which we had arrived at this opinion was altogether at variance with the practical results to which it seemed to be leading. The statesman demands education as a power for acting upon the spirits of men. But the statesman of our day has distinctly and formally repudiated the notion that he can deal with the spirits of men; he has blamed his forefathers for assuming any such authority. It seemed to us, therefore, that when the statesman claimed himself to be the educator of his land, he was involved in a strange contradiction. Yet it was a contradiction into which he had fallen most naturally. He found that a set of warring religious bodies were not competent to exercise the kind of influence over his subjects which he feels to be necessary for them. He wants them to be united and harmonized; a sect-educator sets them at strife. He will therefore do what he can. He will leave to these religious bodies the right of teaching their own dogmas; whatever else is included in the idea of education must be taken under his own immediate cognizance. And this course, awkward and inconvenient as it evidently is, nay, destructive of the very idea of education, seemed to us the only one which is left for the modern statesman, unless there were some spiritual body existing in the heart of his nation, which was as organic as the civil body, and able to perform those functions which by its own confession the civil body is incompetent to perform. Our subsequent inquiries have led us to believe that there is such a body; that it has established itself in the heart of every European nation; that it has been the teacher of every nation; that it has incorporated itself with the civil society; that the statesman finds the society with which he has to deal everywhere bearing witness of its existence; that he is obliged to depose this body from its functions before he can commence schoolmaster for himself. Such is the state of the question at present. I shall not enter into it at large, because it has been discussed elsewhere. But it is necessary for our present purpose that I should offer some indications of the difference between the effects of an education given by a national Church which understands its own powers and responsibilities, and one given—first, by the State; secondly, by a set of different sects; thirdly, by an ecclesiastical extra-national order, like that of the Jesuits. That I may follow the method in which I have supposed the objections to arise, I will speak very shortly of these kinds of education as they affect family life, science, art and literature, popular ethics, and philosophy.

I. 1. I have already had occasion to speak more than once on the first of these subjects. I have shewn that a mere religious body, such as that of the Quakers, of the Calvinists, etc. though it may regard family life with reverence, though, at certain stages of its existence, it may even have preserved family life in great purity, cannot connect the institution of the family, as such, with its religion. The religious man is one who chooses for himself; who at a certain time has been led to seek for a new life, and a new fellowship expressive of this new life. Such is the notion in which a sect begins. It becomes exceedingly modified when the sect has established itself. Hereditary feelings and sympathies develop themselves; to desert the faith of forefathers begins to be spoken of as an evil. But still the religious society subsists upon this principle. Those who are admitted into its privileges do not grow into them. The religious body is looked upon as something different in kind from the family. And therefore it is the common complaint in all sects, that wherever the hereditary habit has begun to prevail, the religion becomes a matter of course, its power is exhausted; some violent

efforts must be made to revive it. Now such influences
as these, I maintain, cannot by possibility cultivate
the family life of a nation. They do not bring the
spiritual life into any direct relation with the life of
natural kinsmanship. And in a day when so many
influences are threatening household sanctities, when
so many schemes of universal society exist which cast
them aside altogether, the statesman who has no better
means of protecting them than that which is afforded
by the teaching of religious sects, must be prepared
to see them perish altogether. Where there are no
political influences and motives at work, no trade-
temper, no grand philosophical generalizations, the
religious men in the sects may hope to keep alive the
habit of respect and attachment among their children.
Where these are abroad, they must tremble ; at all
events, he who believes that the existence of the
nation depends upon the preservation of domestic
relations must tremble if these be their only guardians.

2. But what can the statesman himself do by his
education to protect these relations ? Nothing whatever. Ought I not rather to say, that of necessity he
must do much to shake the confidence in them, and
to impair their sacredness ? It is no fault of his,
it is the necessity of his position, a part of his duty,
that he should aim at making men citizens. He
cannot teach them to be sons and brothers, he is
obliged to interfere with the duties which belong to
them in these capacities. He must have his schools
established upon the express principle, that the parents
are not competent to teach, or to choose teachers
themselves. He must treat the authority of the father
as if its sacredness depended upon the authority of the

law. All wise statesmen of antiquity felt this difficulty, and rejoiced to avail themselves of such means as they had of escaping from it. Modern statesmen should surely ask themselves with some earnestness, whether any helps for this purpose are within their reach.

3. That the Jesuit is not exactly the person to whom one can safely confide the custody of family life and relations, most of the persons with whom I am now arguing will acknowledge. And perhaps they will agree with me in thinking, nay, may wonder that I should make such a concession, that the evil of the Jesuit's influence does not arise solely, or perhaps chiefly, from the particular opinions which he inculcates; that if there could be a Protestant order of the same kind, it would be almost equally mischievous. And wherein, then, upon my principle, does its evil consist? Precisely in this: I believe God has established a universal Church in the world, which grew out of a family, which embodies the idea of family life in its highest possible expansion. That idea, I believe, is preserved in freshness and reality, just so long as a strict unbroken connexion is kept up between its highest form and its lowest; so long as the application of the word Father to Him who was, who is, and who is to come, is felt to be no figurative abuse, but rather the only possible explanation of its most ordinary application. And I believe that Ignatius Loyola established a universal order of his own upon a principle altogether different from this Divine principle, nay, subversive of it; that such an order cannot be the means of preserving any part of the true constitution of society; that it must be con-

tinually interfering with it, and substituting something else in the place of it; that, above all, family order and this pseudo-ecclesiastical order must be perpetual, irreconcilable enemies.

4. If this be the case, I need not spend any words in proving that the spiritual and universal society of which we have discovered the signs, seeing that it assumes the family to be taken by baptism into God's family, seeing that it supposes all civil duties and relations to grow naturally out of these first duties and relations, and seeing that it looks upon the highest ecclesiastical duties and relations as connected with the ordinary social duties, should be the great instrument for accomplishing that object which divided sects, the civil power, a seemingly universal fellowship cannot accomplish, that of building up and sanctifying the domestic society of every nation.

II. 1. How far religious bodies or sects can be trusted with the *scientific* education of a nation, may be judged from the difference of the feelings with which they have regarded science at different stages of their history. Almost without exception, the impulse of every sect, when its religious faith and sympathies were most strong, has been to look at science as something wholly alien from the nature of faith and not to be reconciled with it. Whether this has arisen from a Manichæan horror of the outward world, or from a dread of it as something too holy to be touched, or merely from a dislike of the slow and cold methods by which a knowledge of its secrets is obtained, or, as in the case of the Quakers, from a certain dim intuition of a link between the laws of physical and spiritual investigation which ordinary philosophers had overlooked, the result has been the same. In a generation or two the case becomes altogether changed, at least to all outward appearance. Persons arise out of these sects who shew a genius for physical speculation, and devote themselves wholly to it; a notion pervades the members of the body generally that such pursuits can no longer be discouraged, as they were in the days of their fathers; a few sturdy Protestants still remain to warn younger men against perils which a sure instinct tells them are most real; others, who fancy themselves more wise and enlightened, and yet withal very religious, explain what lessons respecting the Divine wisdom and goodness may be gathered from natural discoveries. This last change strikes some as a very promising one; to me it seems that the old state of things was far better. The old teachers were acting out a principle; they believed that the business of man's life is to acquaint himself with his Creator, and to do His will; they did not see what these studies had to do with this great end, therefore they rejected them. Their descendants, when they first enter upon these pursuits, do not complain that the application of the maxim was narrow, they complain that the maxim itself was narrow; that men, if they attend properly to their religious duties, may bestow a fair portion of their time upon pursuits which have a different aim and motive. Soon, of course, these pursuits are felt to be genuine and real, the religious duties artificial and traditional; if the former are not wholly followed, and the latter neglected, there is, at all events, no sympathy between them. Then if there should come a religious revival, and the feelings which are embodied

in the different sects should be able to influence public
opinion, and to create what is called a religious world,
the expedient is resorted to, of making sciences tell a
tale about the truth of the Scriptures, and the being
and attributes of God. A moral is wrung out of its
facts, by fair means or by foul, often by most dishonest
construction of evidence, often by positive suppression
of that which has been proved. If any fact is brought
to light which opposes a current notion in theology or
a current interpretation of the Scriptures, it must not
be fairly looked at; the question is raised whether
there ought to be such a fact, and, therefore, whether
we may recognise it supposing it should be one. The
scientific men are rightly disgusted. They see that
not only the cause of science but also of honesty is at
stake; they begin to suspect an hypothesis the more
for its gratifying religious feelings.

2. And here comes in the civil power, and says,
'This we cannot permit; our subjects must be taught
science fairly and truly. We must have railways and
steam-engines. In the present state of society, our
very handicraftsmen must understand something of
the regulations of that machinery which they have
to work; the knowledge of a multitude of subjects
unknown to their ancestors is needful for them; your
religious men may impart what corrections or draw
what inferences you please, we must teach the
things, we must give our countrymen a scientific
culture.'

I have nothing to say in answer to this determination, but that I believe it will defeat itself. This
teaching of a multitude of things is not, I fancy,
scientific culture, but is fatal to it. The favourite

name with those who defend this sort of education is the name of Bacon. Oh, that they would devote some real pains to the study of Bacon! They would find him denouncing as one of the main hindrances to scientific knowledge and scientific progress, the desire for facts which should be "fructiferous" and not "luciferous," which should lead to mere results, and not to the search for higher principles. The whole object of his writings was to teach how in facts one may seek for laws; not how, out of a heap of observations, one may make first a theory and then a machine. To the passion for mere effects, and what are called practical results, he attributed most of the delusions and crimes of the alchymists. And unquestionably, if he were to reappear in our day, and were to hear himself eulogised as the man who had taught how much nobler a thing it is to make shoes than to seek for principles, he would believe that the very mischiefs out of which he had been the means of delivering his countrymen, were coming back upon them through the abuse of his own wisdom. Yet this is the doctrine which the statesman, who is merely a statesman, does inevitably adopt; this has ever been, and must ever be, the maxim of a State education.

3. The Jesuits cannot be accused of neglecting to give information on physical subjects to their scholars. Nor does it appear that they attempted to restore old theories on these matters, or to teach any other opinions than those which had the general sanction of philosophers in their day. As the Dominicans and the Franciscans were the means of reversing the papal decree against Aristotle, so it seems as if the

Jesuits had practically reversed the decree against Galileo, rather eagerly availing themselves of the direction which men's minds were taking towards physical inquiries, to turn them away from inquiries into subjects more immediately concerning themselves. Here, as everywhere, their instruction proceeded upon one principle, and in one regular, coherent system. Teach everything, be it physics, history, or philosophy, in such wise that the student shall feel he is not apprehending a truth, but only receiving a maxim upon trust, or studying a set of probabilities. Acting upon this rule, they could publish an edition of the "Principia," mentioning that the main doctrine of it had been denounced by the Pope, and was therefore to be rejected; but, at the same time, recommending the study of the book as containing a series of very ingenious arguments and apparent demonstrations. There was no curl of the lip in this utterance, strange as it may seem to us, nor, in the sense we commonly give to the word, any dishonesty. The editors did not believe that Newton *had* proved his point. They had not enough of the feeling of certainty in their minds, to think that anything could be proved. All is one sea of doubts, perplexities, possibilities; the great necessity is to feel that we cannot arrive at truth, and that therefore we must submit ourselves to an infallible authority. This was the habit of their mind; whether it was a true one or no the religious man will be able to resolve when he has considered its effects in producing the scepticism of the eighteenth century; the scientific man, when he thinks how hopeless of progression those who cherish it must be.

CHAP. V.] THE CHURCH AND THE NATION. 337

4. Now a national Church, which believes that it exists for the purpose of cultivating the inward man, just as the civil power exists for the sake of the outward man, which believes that it has a commission and vocation for this end, must be a continual witness against all these notions of education. She cannot tolerate for an instant the sectarian notion, that the study of the laws according to which God has framed this universe is not a solemn and religious work, to be carried on reverently, in connexion with the study of the laws upon which He has constructed the moral universe. As she believes that there is a method for arriving at the knowledge of the one constitution, so she believes that there is a method for arriving at the knowledge of the other. There may be a connexion between these two methods, but they cannot be the same. The spiritual method is not honoured when you compel the physical facts into obedience to it; you are certain that they cannot contradict it; you are sure they will, at all events, illustrate it ten thousandfold more than all your moralities about them ever can. A national Church must believe in the highest sense that what *is* is right. This is the pillar of her own existence; this is what she opposes to the maxim of the world, that things are right which we make so by our rules and conventions; therefore she must teach her children to ask bravely and boldly, " What is ? " encouraging them by all means to expect an answer; teaching them in what frame of mind to wait for it, to receive it, to give thanks for it.

But this lesson is very unlike that one which the civil power seeks to inculcate in its education. The spiritual teacher in his own sphere is occupied in leading men into the secret heart of things, in teaching them the laws of their own being, and their direct relation to the Creator. In this sphere of physical science he must act upon the same principle. He cannot merely teach facts and opinions, he must seek to guide his pupil into the knowledge of laws. This method he will follow with the higher or professional classes who are submitted to his discipline. He cannot change it, though he may alter altogether his scheme of instruction, when he is occupied with the lowest classes. For these, too, consist of men; of men who want to know, and who have a right to know, what that order is in which they are placed; what the meaning of the things which they are doing is; who must not merely be taught what they are to do, or merely be furnished with rules for doing it.

And therefore it is almost needless to say that such a teacher looks upon authority, not in the way in which the Jesuit does, as a substitute for truth, but as that which is to put us in the right way of searching after it. A national Church believes that she is set in the midst of a nation by Him, "who for this end was born, and for this end came into the world, that He might bear witness to the truth," in order that she may bear witness of it, and may rebuke the slavish and godless tempers which hinder men in any direction from seeking it; and that by leading them to know it she may make them free.

III. The treatment which literature and art are likely to receive from these different classes may be conjectured from the remarks which have been just made. Sects in their infancy reject both as worldly

and heathenish, in their manhood and decline tolerate
them as necessary indulgences, or endeavour to make
them religious by sugaring them over with a Christian
phraseology. The civil power encourages both, because
they furnish certain measures of diversion and entertainment to different classes of the community; but
determines their value by the degree in which they
minister to immediate utility. The Jesuit favours all
that kind of literary diligence which exhibits itself in
laborious compilations, annals, chronologies, etc.; all
that kind of art which may help to connect devotion
more closely with the senses. So that in each of these
forms of education, there is from different causes the
same tendency to give to human utterances, whether
in books, or pictures, or sculpture, or music, or archi-
tecture, an artificial, outward, fictitious character: to
make them insincere expressions of that which is
actually in the hearts of men; or else to make those
hearts themselves insincere, by leading them constantly to aim at the production of some effect to
which the names, "moral, useful, religious," by a
great abuse of language are applied. But if there be
any body which really believes that it has a commission
to cultivate the mind and spirit of a nation; to call
forth in it that which is truest and noblest; to awaken
the reason, the understanding, the affections; to give
them their key-note, to bring out their different
harmonies; such a body will feel that the men to
whom God has given the power of expressing their
own minds and the minds of their age, whether in
words or in sensible forms, have a high vocation and
a mighty responsibility; that the influences of the
world are likely to choke their powers and prevent

z 2

them from freely and happily expanding; that the spiritual mother is to brood over them with tender and affectionate care; to cheer them on amid outward and inward discouragements; to give them the soothing food and medicine of peaceful devotions and outward images of serenity and quietness; to stir them up by heroical examples, to make them conscious of their relation to the past and the future; to hold forth high and distant ends, that they may not be crushed by the influences of their age, or be tempted to court its approbation; to humble them that they may be exalted; to teach them how they may discover the invisible in the visible, instead of confounding them and bringing the higher under the conditions of the lower. While thus training the more illustrious citizens of the commonwealth, she is really marking out the course by which all should be trained who are to be citizens indeed; for to each God has committed some trust, which may be fulfilled for His glory and for the good of the land.

IV. 1. I will conclude this subject with a few words upon the subject of ethics. Strictly speaking, the sectarian does not recognise the existence of such a study. For he looks upon the religious man as taken into a position altogether different from that which other men occupy. He and they are not under the same law. There is a set of rules and maxims which they must observe, in order that they may be members of the family and citizens of the community to which they belong. The religious man submits to these, but he is subject to another set of Gospel influences, with which the ordinary man has nothing to do. Christian ethics mean the religion of the heart according to the Bible, they apply only to the converted; worldly ethics mean the regulation of the conduct according to the rules and maxims which are received among worldly men: these apply to the unconverted. Upon this shewing a morality for man as man does not exist.

2. Accordingly the statesman interferes, and says in this case as in the others, 'Then you shall teach that morality which belongs to your position; I will teach that which belongs to mine. Men must acknowledge some rule of life. These subjects of mine, call them converted or unconverted, must be trained to some sense of their relations to each other. Mere legal penalties are not sufficient for them, they must be taught some reason for their conduct, some method of self-government.' Of course these reasons and these methods must turn upon maxims of self-interest. How can they turn upon any other maxims? The statesman has been warned off the religious ground, this is all that remains to him.

3. Of Jesuit ethics I need not speak at length; they are in sufficiently bad odour among us, and probably in most nations of the Continent. What I wish to remark is, that all the evil which is in them has flowed from that first principle of establishing a universal order upon a human calculation of what is expedient for the preservation of the Church and of religion. Once construct a society of such power and of such coherency as the Jesuit society, and it is impossible, in the nature of things, that the preservation of this order should not begin to be regarded as the one great end, to which every other is subordinate. To keep this great machine in motion, to make it

effective, everything must be sacrificed. I do not think that there is one pernicious maxim in the Constitutions which may not be legitimately deduced from this primary assumption. The Jesuits feel about morality, as about science, not that it *is* but that it *has been made,* and, therefore, that it may be remade for a higher object. The world has framed its maxims to keep itself alive; he may frame his maxims in order to keep the holy religious order alive. The object is surely better; the ways in both cases are determined by arrangement and convention.

4. Once again I say a national Church exists to protest against these outrages upon that which is the very ground of a nation's existence. It affirms morality to be universal, in its highest form to be meant for all men and to be attainable by all men, seeing that the covenant of Baptism takes all who will receive it into the highest state which a man on earth can enjoy; the state in which he has all helps for resisting the powers of the flesh, the world, and the devil, which are seeking to rob him of his human privilege. It affirms morality to be in direct opposition to selfishness, not in its highest forms merely, but in its lowest; the penalties of the lawgiver, the prayers of the Church, being alike directed against this sin; one denouncing its outward effects, the other aiming at the extirpation of the internal disease. It declares morality, not in its highest forms only but in its lowest, to be grounded upon the character and will of God; subjection to that will being the lesson inculcated by the law, conformity to that character being the effect produced by the power of the Gospel. And, therefore, of necessity it must hate and curse all such schemes of

morality as the Jesuits have sanctioned; schemes
which pervert the truth that each individual case has
peculiar points and delicate complications of its own
which require wisdom and refinement and a freedom
from rash habits of judging in the person who deals
in them, into the confounding doctrine that there is
no common law of right and wrong, or that no conscience for perceiving that law exists in the creatures
to whom it is addressed.

I have but two remarks to make before I conclude this head of my subject. The first is, that I
believe all the defects in national Churches, and in the
education which they have communicated, may be
traced to a notion which has prevailed far too
generally in the members and ministers of them:
either that their position is sectarian, that they are
merely civil bodies constructed for certain civil
ends; or, on the other hand, that they are merely
parts of a religious society or order existing for
purposes wholly foreign to those for which the civil
power exists. Should therefore any opponent produce
facts which illustrate the weakness and inefficiency of
these Churches, or of any one of them, I shall be
most willing to consider his statements. I am satisfied
they will all tend to the confirmation of mine, that
they will all tend to prove the inherent viciousness of
those schemes of education which have at different
periods suggested themselves as most plausible and
satisfactory, that they will furnish another reason why
every national Church should understand its own high
position, and should zealously assert it. My other
remark is addressed to the statesman. He has felt in
most countries of Europe, he feels still, the peril of

Jesuit influence, and the necessity of guarding himself against it. But what can he do? If he tries to get rid of the idea that there is one Catholic Church in the world, and treats religion as if it were merely a matter of private sectarian opinion, he will not hinder the Jesuits from entering his dominions and becoming masters of his schools. His tolerant maxims will make their settlement more easy; the earnest cry which will be raised throughout a land left to sectarian influence for some united body, some organic fellowship, will cause their appearance to be hailed with delight. Will he, then, in despair, resort to his own peculiar powers? Will he proscribe and banish the intruders, or put them to death? These methods, he knows, have been tried and tried in vain; the crushed order has risen again with all its other influences made stronger by the credit of persecution and of martyrdom. One barrier, and one alone, this subtle and Protean society knows that it cannot break through. A national Church, strong in the conviction of its own distinct powers, paying respectful homage to those of the State, educating all classes to be citizens by making them men; this is a spectacle which the Jesuit regards with wonder and despair. Where there is such a national Church he may be safely allowed to walk up and down in the land; the sting of his order is taken away; he may become a worthy and respectable member of the commonwealth. If the statesman be convinced that the maiming and ultimate suppression of such a Church is the true object of his policy, he must invent some new charm for laying this enemy. None has yet been discovered.

SECTION VI.—THE MODERN INTERPRETERS OF PROPHECY.

THERE is one class of persons for whom I entertain a sincere respect, who may, I fear, be offended by some of these observations: I allude to the modern interpreters of Prophecy. First, they will think that while I have professed great reverence for the Old Testament as containing the national history of the Jews, I have overlooked one of its most remarkable features, its promise of permanence and restoration to God's ancient people; that hereby I have shown an indifference to the words of inspiration, and a preference for my own theories. 2ndly, they will say that my notion of a Divine constitution already established, which is not merely spiritual and universal but national, practically sets aside the doctrine of the second coming of Him who is to make all things new. 3rdly, that when I have spoken of the Romish system as distinct from the Latin Church, I have overlooked the clear declarations of the Divine word respecting the judgments upon the apostacy and the ultimate excision of all bodies which belong to it.

1. I agree with those who look forward to a national restoration of the Jews, that much of the language which is commonly applied to their views, is the result of prejudice and misapprehension. I do not, for instance, understand what is meant by the word *'carnal'* when it is used in connexion with the doctrine that other privileges exist besides those which belong to the Church as a spiritual body, and that of these the Jews were formerly and shall be hereafter the possessors. If I am right these privileges are just as

necessary witnesses against carnality (when by carnality
is meant the inclination of that flesh which is not
subject to the law of God, neither indeed can be), as
those which directly appertain to us as children of
God and inheritors of the kingdom of heaven; nay,
in one sense, they are stronger witnesses against this
carnality, for they come more directly into contact
with the acts and proceedings of our earthly life,
which are wont to call it forth. And so far from considering this witness as less belonging to our age than
to previous ages, I believe it is our characteristic
infirmity, that we are disposed to place religion in a
middle region, and that we will not understand it
either in its most transcendent character or in its
application to common doings and daily occurrences.
I cannot help, therefore, suspecting these phrases
about carnality; they indicate a tendency which the
sight of a national commonwealth constituted as the
Jewish Commonwealth was, might counteract more
effectually than anything which one sees at this time,
or perhaps has seen at any time in the Catholic Church.
Neither, again, do I understand how the reappearance
of such a commonwealth on the very soil which was
the original seat of it, could be other than a very
marvellous and glorious testimony to the mighty
scheme which God, whose works are known to Him
from the beginning of the world, has been carrying
on, and which no human self-will can frustrate. To
me it seems that everything is tending towards this
result; that so strange a body as the Israelites are
could not have been permitted to exist for so many
generations unconnected with any country or polity,
if such a destiny were not in reserve for them; that

it is a strange and painful effort for the mind even to imagine all traces of national distinctness lost in men who, in their glory and depression, have been for nearly three thousand years witnesses for the existence of such distinctness; that this miracle would be infinitely more startling than the establishment of a Hebrew commonwealth in Palestine; but that the first miracle would be in violation of all the analogy of God's dealings, the other, the natural consummation of them.

These conclusions seem to me so reasonable, that I cannot help asking myself why I have had so much difficulty in arriving at them, and why so many persons, less hindered than I may be by prejudice or want of faith, should still experience the same difficulty so strongly. And I cannot help feeling that the mode in which the claims of the Jews are ordinarily stated has been, at all events, one great obstacle to our acknowledging them. At one time it would seem as if the modern interpreters of prophecy expected that the Jewish nation should take the place of the universal Church; at another, as if they expected Jerusalem to be the centre of that Church in the next age, even as Rome has tried to be the centre of it in this; at another, as if they believed that in the restoration of all things, the Jews were to furnish the one specimen of a true and godly nation. Now it is very possible that none of these views may really be entertained by those who use language which appears to imply them. But surely the very approximation to such notions may well inspire good men with some alarm. If we are to relapse into a national dispensation, if the idea of the universal Church is to be absorbed in that of an exclusive society, all the promises made to the Fathers, it seems to me, are set at nought; the very truth of which Old Testament history was pregnant has come to nothing; the mighty conflicts of St. Paul, to prove that it had actually been brought into light, were idle and vain; the last eighteen centuries have been a dead blank in the annals of mankind. If, again, the principle be admitted, that in any corner of the universe, in profane land or in holy land, the spiritual Church can find a visible capital for herself, the principle of Romanism seems to be confirmed, and all the sad experiments which have demonstrated it to be an ungodly principle are set aside, as of no worth. If, lastly, the Jewish nation or the Jewish Church is to exalt itself in solitary greatness over the ruins of a fallen universe, it seems to me that Isaiah and the prophets were wrong, and the Pharisees in the days of our Lord's incarnation strictly right. I do not mean merely that Isaiah and the prophets looked forward to a universal dispensation, to a Church which should develop itself out of a particular nation; but I mean that they uniformly speak of Judea, even in their time, as the centre of a set of countries, each of which was (or was trying to be) a nation. The burden of the 'Valley of Vision' stands not alone, it is connected with the burden of Egypt and the burden of Moab, with the burden of Tyre and with the burden of Damascus. The Jewish nation interprets to each of these what it ought to be. But each is looked upon as standing in some relation to the Lord God of the Hebrews; each as connected with His scheme of judgment and mercy, each as threatened by the same Babylonian power. This feeling had been wholly lost

by the Pharisee; their only desire was that Judea
might be supreme as Rome was supreme, that it might,
in fact, be that Babylonian monarchy against which
it had been for so many generations bearing testimony.
But supposing all these views of Jewish restoration
were abandoned, then I think, that the way in which
I have spoken of *the state* in this chapter may possibly
strike earnest and thoughtful men as the true explanation and justification of an idea which they cherish so
devoutly, and which I hope they may not be obliged,
through the arguments of their opponents or through
their own inconsistencies, to abandon.

I look upon the Jewish nation as an abiding sign
to the Christian Church of the honour which God has
put upon national life, and of His will that the Church
should never strive to set itself up as something
separate from the nations. I look upon it as the sign
to each nation in the East or West of the law under
which it is constituted, and according to which it will
be judged. And because I believe this to be a true
unchangeable law, therefore I believe it will at last
make itself good in each case. One great central
manifestation of it may be, and I trust and believe
will be, the restoration of the Jewish Commonwealth.
And that restoration will, as I hope, be followed by
the restoration to national life, in connexion with
Christian and Catholic life, of those countries which
are now combined under the sceptre of the prophet,
separated from each other by the most violent
sectarian controversies, incapable of understanding
how they may be distinct and yet one. In a
Christian Jew a Mahometan sees what he was meant
to be; sees the truth embodied which he has been

twisting into a denial and a falsehood. I cannot, therefore, quarrel with the conviction of those who dream that Jews will be the agents in the conversion of Mahometans, and that a Hebrew nation will be the sun and centre of the Eastern world. But if no one pretends that such a result will be accomplished without great conflicts and heavy judgments, why may I not suppose that the West will, through the like process, attain to a like blessing? Why may I not suppose that the principle of Judaism will be asserted, the exclusiveness of Pharisaism be confounded, by the full development of European nations, and of their colonies in the other parts of the world, the universal Church being still the life-giving power, the uniting principle to them all?

2. But it is indeed a decisive confutation of all these hopes, if they set at nought the truth of the second appearing of our Lord, upon which the Church has been resting in her greatest troubles, and to which the Scriptures urge us so continually to look forward. I should be more sorry perhaps than most, to say a word which could weaken this faith in any mind, because it seems to me that the revival of it in our day has been one great means of removing the clouds which had hindered us from looking at Christ's Church as a Kingdom, and from connecting all individual blessings and rewards with its existence and its establishment in that character. The wretched notion of a private selfish Heaven, where compensation shall be made for troubles incurred, and prizes given for duties performed in this lower sphere—this unnatural notion, clothing itself in the language of Scripture and of

other days of the Church, but severing that language from the idea with which it was always impregnated, and connecting it with our low, grovelling, mercantile habits of feeling, had infused itself into our popular teachings and our theological books. It could not be driven out by those who merely preached the doctrine of justification by faith, for they, in their eagerness to get rid of the doctrine of human merit, seemed to take away the hope of reward altogether, and while giving a present relief to the conscience, to leave the heart and spirit without any future object after which they might aspire. If to the state of feeling which either of these forms of teaching was likely to produce, there has succeeded in any country of Europe a vague and indistinct but still perhaps a real acknowledgment of another end which men may seek after than the selfish individual end, even the end of beholding Him in whom is no selfishness, no darkness at all, of sharing the light of a common sun, of feeling a common warmth and life from his rays, the change, I believe, must be ascribed in a great measure to those who have steadfastly asserted, amidst much opposition from others, and much discouragement from the confutation of their own favourite schemes of interpretation, the doctrine that the Church is to live in the expectation of the appearance and the triumph of her Head.

But the more strongly I feel our obligation to these teachers on this account, the more I must regret, not perhaps particular crudities of opinion which may have mingled themselves with this faith, for these we must always expect, but any great central confusion which may have weakened the grounds upon which it rests, made it unacceptable to wise and thoughtful men, and given an almost unlimited licence to the speculations of those who are not thoughtful or wise. Such a confusion seems to me to lurk in the notion that the Advent, or, as St. Paul far more frequently describes it, the Epiphany of our Lord, will be the beginning of a *new* order and constitution of things. Now it seems to me that the phrases in Scripture which refer to this event positively refute any such imagination. The appearance of a light which shall shew things as they are, and before which the darkness shall flee away, the day of judgment and distinction, the gathering of all together in one, the restoration of all things, this is the language in which we are taught to express our thoughts and anticipations respecting the future. Nay, such is the language we are obliged to use, even though our own theories might suggest some other as more suitable. And what do such words imply, but the full evidence and demonstration of that which *is now*; the dispersion of all the shadows and appearances which have counterfeited it or have hidden it from view? What do they imply, but the existence of a kingdom, or order, or constitution, which men have been trying to set at nought and deny, but under which they have been living notwithstanding, and which, in the clear sunlight of that day, is shewn to be the only one under which they can live? Is not this view of the case exactly in accordance with the language of those who speak most about the second Advent, when they say that it will take place at a period of great darkness and almost universal denial? Denial of what?—if not of a truth which has always been recognised in our institutions and our ordinary habits, which men have only just found courage utterly to reject as inconsistent with their conduct and their other professions, at the moment which shall shew that conduct and those professions to have been false, the witness of conscience against them, and in favour of that which they resisted, to be true? Is there any shelter from this conclusion in the distinction between the *spiritual* dispensation or *spiritual* kingdom which has existed since our Lord's first Advent, and the outward visible kingdom which shall be established after His second? If by the words outward and visible it be meant that something less spiritual is in reserve for the time to come than for the time which is; that now we are living by faith, that then we shall live by sense; that now we recognise the highest glory in that which " eye hath not seen, nor ear heard, nor it hath entered into the heart of man to conceive;" that then we shall recognise all glory as being in the visible and comprehensible: I cannot conceive a darker or more dreadful vision than this of a millennial perfection. But if it be meant by outward and visible, that Christ's dominion will not be merely over the heart and spirit of man, over that which directly connects him with God and the unseen world, but over all his human relations, his earthly associations, over the policy of rulers, over nature and over art, then, I say, this is as much the truth now as it ever can be in any future period. This dominion has been asserting itself, has been making itself felt, for these eighteen centuries. The Son of Man claimed it for Himself when He did not abhor the Virgin's womb, when He mingled with the ordinary transactions of men, blessing their food, their wine, and their marriage feasts. The claim may have been denied at all times; it may be denied especially at the time to which we are looking forward; but that time must assert it, not as something new, but as something old; as a government which has been actually in exercise, and the ceasing of which, even for a moment, would have been followed by dreariness and death throughout the universe. Now if this be so, I think that the principle which I have endeavoured to defend in this book is not one which interferes with any sound or true apprehensions of our Lord's second coming, but only with a system which has tended to prevent men from acknowledging it; to make them think lightly of their present responsibilities, to give them a fantastic habit of speaking respecting the course of God's providence in the world, as if it signified nothing now, but was only leading to something hereafter; and which is very likely to suggest the thought, that when He has taken the power whose right it is, the Cross will not any longer be the symbol of glory and victory.

THE ROMISH SYSTEM.

With a few remarks upon the charge of underrating the guilt and punishment of Romish apostacy, I will conclude this part of my work.

A reader who has followed me through the discussions in my last and present chapters will scarcely suspect me of an inclination to look more mildly upon Romanism, when it presents itself as the sworn enemy of nations and national Churches, than when it came before us as the corrupter of creeds and sacraments.

One evil seems to be necessarily implied in the other; the same assumption which made it an uncatholic principle has made it an anti-national principle. It has perverted the idea of spiritual power, therefore it has interfered with civil power. And yet if we look at it on another side, that which we call in common parlance the Church of Rome has borne and does bear a very striking witness on behalf of the truth that Christ's Church is a kingdom, and not merely a collection of sects bound together in the profession of particular dogmas. I have never concealed this fact, for no fact ought to be concealed which concerns the history and government of the world.

But what is it that we call the Church of Rome? *I* call it the diocese over which the Bishop of Rome presides; I know no other Church of Rome than this. Certain people may have invented another notion for it, but I do not adopt their notion; if I did, I should adopt the Romish system. Now this Church of Rome, this Italian diocese, may be in a very corrupt state—I am afraid it is. I think many persons who belong to it, and who acknowledge the jurisdiction of its Bishop, would acknowledge that it is. They, therefore, must agree with us in desiring that it should be reformed. Perhaps they would agree in acknowledging, also, that the reformation is likely to be accompanied with many punishments and judgments for the sins of which its members have been guilty. The nature of those sins and the roots of them I have partly considered in this chapter. The nature of the judgments I am not competent and I have no wish to consider. They may be heavier or lighter than any other which will come upon the other portions of the Church; they may even go the length of leaving Rome a prey to some infidel power. The determining of this question is in the best hands, and in those hands we must leave it, as we may leave also the fate of the Spanish, or Gallican, or of any other Church.

But the end of these judgments, I conceive, be they more or less tremendous, will be the destruction of a false apostate system. You say that the system is part and parcel of the Church; that if one perishes, the other must perish. That is precisely the point about which I know nothing, and about which you know nothing. But this I do know, that as long as a man is alive and struggling, I have no business to say that his disease and he are identical, that the cure of the disease must be the death of the patient. Here it is that I am at issue with our modern interpreters of prophecy. I do not differ with them in that I hate the Romish system less than they do. It often seems to me that they do not hate it sufficiently; that they do not see where its extreme evil lies; that they are ready to tolerate a portion of its evil in themselves. And this want of a sufficient appreciation of its mischiefs, I discover especially in their language respecting the Latin Church. They do not seem to see that popery is continually undermining the Church, and therefore they do not feel, that the more you can persuade men to be Churchmen, the more effectually you deliver them from popery. They cry out to the members of the different Latin Churches: 'Come ye out of Babylon, and be ye separate.' Take the words as they stand in Scripture, and as they are

explained by the whole context of Scripture,
and there cannot be any more important. But how
are they to be obeyed? The common answer
is, 'By leaving the corrupt Church to which you
belong.' It seems to me that the person who does
so, is exceedingly likely to carry the Babylonian
system along with him, and to leave nothing behind
but the good elements which were mixed with it.
Whereas, he who will stay in the Church of his
fathers, maintaining resolutely that it is a Church, and
that those who have struggled to deprive it of its
distinct ecclesiastical character are his enemies, and
are to be resisted, must, I think, arrive at a deliverance from popery. He will not be delivered in the
same way in which the Protestant nations in the sixteenth century were delivered. God has a different
method for working out the freedom of His servants
in each different age; but I cannot see why it should
be a less effectual method; I hope and trust it will be
far more effectual. The serpent at the Reformation
was scotched, not killed. It could not be killed so
long as there was anything good remaining in it.
Once separate the belief of Christ's kingdom from
this system, once believe that they are not necessary
to each other, and the moral power of the papacy is
gone. What signifies it, then, if all the physical
power in the universe should for a time be granted
to it, if kings should send presents to it, if all
forms of infidelity and false worship should combine themselves with it? The Church may then with
confidence take up the language of the prophet,
"Associate yourselves, and ye shall be broken in
pieces; gird yourselves, and ye shall be broken in

pieces; take counsel together, and it shall come to nought, for GOD IS WITH US."*

* I had developed at some length, in reference to each of the different European nations, the idea which is hinted at in this section. My object was to shew, that there are at the present moment in every part of the Continent indications of a struggle which is very imperfectly explained by the phrases 'democratical tendencies,' 'dissatisfaction with old opinions,' 'commencement of a new æra '—a struggle which may indeed include all these signs or promises, but which can be very little understood by any one who overlooks the relation between Catholicism and Nationality, and who does not perceive that the history of modern Europe has been one continual effort to establish or to break that relation. I had inquired, further, whether this question has lost its application to the United States of North America, or whether there also it be not that which will take precedence of every other. But I found that I was led almost unawares into dreams of the future, which may be intended for each of these nations;—and such dreams seemed scarcely in accordance with the character of a book which aims at the discovery of that which is solid and certain. The lesson from the whole is expressed in the sad, consolatory dirge which poets of old sang, and which is now the chant of the whole Church militant,—αἴλινον αἴλινον εἰπέ· τὸ δ' εὖ νικάτω.

PART III.

*THE ENGLISH CHURCH AND THE SYSTEMS WHICH
DIVIDE IT.*

CHAPTER I.

HOW FAR THIS SUBJECT IS CONNECTED WITH THOSE PREVIOUSLY DISCUSSED.

ARE these principles applicable to our circumstances as Englishmen? If not, we may be sure that there is some flaw in them which we have not yet detected. If they are, the question how to apply them must be, above all others, important to us.

I think the young English ecclesiastical student is very apt to be perplexed with questions of this kind. 'Is our National Church, as I have often been told it is, the best in the world? Supposing it is not, why may I not go in search of a better! It is easy to talk of acquiescence in the state which Providence has assigned us. But surely there are circumstances in which a Christian must regard acquiescence as a sin. How do I know that mine are not these circumstances?'

Now were the principles which have seemed to prove themselves to us in other cases appropriate to this one, the reader will perceive at once that there is a fallacy in the statement of these questions. We have maintained that there is a spiritual and universal society in the world: that there are also national societies in the world: that the Universal Society and the National Society cannot, according to the scheme of Providence, be separated from each other, that when they are brought into conjunction, that form of character which is intended for each nation is gradually developed in it by means of the spiritual body. Can we then be called upon to prove either—(1), that there is some constitution for the Universal Society as it exists in England, which does not belong to it elsewhere, and which makes it better here than elsewhere; or (2), that the principles which unite the Universal Society with the National Society among us are not the same principles which unite it elsewhere, and that we are better for this difference; or (3), that what is peculiarly *our* National character, ought to be the character of every other nation? Evidently, no one who has any real affection for his Church or his land, will put forth such claims as these on its behalf. He will inquire whether it does or does not recognise that constitution which belongs to all mankind; whether this constitution be or be not so recognised here, as to be compatible with the distinct National Constitution; what character it is which is intended for Englishmen; how that character may be realised in its perfection, or depraved. But putting the inquiry into this form, one does not see what acquiescence can be demanded of us, which is inconsistent with the position of militant Christians. Have we lost that Universal Constitution or any element of it? We must labour by all means to recover it. Have we lost our distinct National position? We must seek it again. Are we living inconsistently with the one or the other? We must inquire where the evil is, and commence at once the work of personal reformation. The subject then upon which I propose now to enter will divide itself in the way which I have indicated. As we take for granted the previous steps of our discussion, it will not, I hope, occupy us long.

SECTION I.—DO THE SIGNS OF A 'UNIVERSAL AND SPIRITUAL CON-
STITUTION EXIST IN ENGLAND?

THERE is no difficulty in giving a direct answer to this question. Supposing these signs to be Baptism, the Creeds, Forms of Worship, the Eucharist, the Ministerial Orders, the Scriptures, no one will deny that a society has existed in England for the last twelve hundred years, of which these are constituent elements. Under all changes in the outward circumstances of the country, in its national policy, in its religious opinions, a body has dwelt in this land, which has acknowledged not one or two but all of these signs, which has acknowledged them as the conditions of its own subsistence.

But is this the only point to be considered? Ought we not to inquire whether the same import has in all times, or what import has at any particular time been attached to these signs, by the body which acknowledged them? And again, may there not be two bodies existing at the same time in this country, differing with each other, and yet both acknowledging all these signs? In that case how are we to determine which does and which does not represent the Universal Society?

I. In reference to the first question I answer, If you mean that I am to take the votes of the members of the English Church now, or at any period since it was established, for the purpose of ascertaining what the majority think or have thought about any or all of these signs, I should decline the task, not merely on the ground of its impossibility, but because, if it were possible, I should be violating all the principles which I have put forward in this book, by undertaking it. I have said, that the members of a Church will be continually losing sight of the grounds of the society to which they belong, and that permanent institutions are given us for the purpose of witnessing against our tendencies to degeneracy, and of enabling us to obtain, in each successive age, a clearer view of the Divine purpose and order. On the same grounds, I must protest against any attempt to ascertain the principles of the English Church, by comparing or balancing the opinions of its most eminent writers. For I have urged, that permanent creeds and institutions are our preservatives against the particular judgments and prepossessions of these writers. But if there be among these signs any one which has so far a peculiar character, is so far distinctively English, that it may be taken as expressive of the mind of the English Church itself, by that I am most willing it shall be tried. Now a Liturgy is of this kind. I have shewn how remarkably it is the sign of a universal society. Yet it is equally true that each nation has always had its own Liturgies. To this, therefore, there is a fair appeal. But how shall the appeal be made? Why may I not read my own opinions into the Liturgy as well as into any other book? Undoubtedly I may. And therefore, the fairer way of getting at its meaning is to receive it from others, especially from those who have attacked it. Let us try this course.

1. Again and again the English Dissenters have complained of our formularies, because they assert in what seems to them such plain and direct language, so solemnly, so habitually, the principle that a baptized man is to regard himself as regenerate, a child of God, an heir of the blessings of the New Covenant. 'It is idle,' say these Dissenters, 'to pretend that by leaving out a few words in your form of baptism, you would remove this dreadful plague-spot from your Church. Supposing that were possible, think what a monstrous delusion you have been propagating in such solemn moments for so many generations. What, thrust out such words privily in this nineteenth century! They ought to be extirpated amidst groans and confessions of sin, for having mocked God and ruined the souls of men. But if you did thrust out the words, the spirit of them goes through all your other services. You tell the same story to the children whom you are catechising; you declare to them that they are members of Christ and children of God. Nay, every confession and every prayer in which you call upon adults old in sin to engage, turns upon the same principle. You invite them to confess and to pray, as if they were children of God, and as if the Spirit were still with them.'

That these charges are constantly preferred against us everyone knows. I ask, are they not true? Has any apologist for the Liturgy, who agreed with the Dissenters in their theological principle, been able to refute them? And is it not very painful to think that we should be using equivocations and double meanings, at a time when we are professing to address the most awful prayers to Him who is Truth?

I may affirm then, not from any conclusions of my own, but on the authority of those who are most opposed to me, that the idea of Baptismal Regeneration is the idea of our Liturgy.

But is this connected with the idea of an *opus operatum?* I think the question has already been answered. The Dissenter perceives, everyone who thinks perceives, that the whole of our Liturgy is constructed upon the principle that the men who engage in it have not lost their baptismal privileges ; that the sin which they confess is the sin of not having owned God as their Father, of not having remembered His covenant, and therefore, of not having walked in His ways ; that they ask to be restored to the enjoyment of a position with which their lives need not have been and have been at variance ; in one word, that the sacrament is not believed to have conferred on men a temporary blessing, but to have admitted them into a permanent state, which is at all times theirs, which they are bound at all times to claim, and by which they will be judged.

I know that we have apologists who can defend us from this imputation as well as the other, by dint of ingenious special pleading. They say, 'All this language presumes the existence of discipline ; we have undoubtedly lost our discipline, but we are not therefore to lose our prayers.' How, not to lose our prayers ? We had better lose anything than go on in direct mockery of God. If the want of discipline makes the prayers false, if there are not half a dozen persons in any congregation who would dare to say they have not lost their baptismal purity ; and if those nine or ten be the very persons, who one may be sure cannot join in these prayers, or in any prayer but that of the Pharisee, how can we have courage to practise such profaneness, because, at some time or other, we hope to get a discipline which shall cut off the majority of those who now call themselves Churchmen? But does our Liturgy give the slightest sanction to the notion, that the most complete restoration of discipline would make these prayers more true than they are now? Why then in her 'Commination Service' does she not announce the doctrine of the *opus operatum?* Why does she not say, there, 'You have been made members of Christ once, but the privilege is gone, the blessing is exhausted; you have resisted the Spirit, He is striving no more with you; recover the gift, if possible, by penitence and prayer?' Why in this service, as much as in all the rest, are men called to repent, on the ground of their being children, though rebellious children; on the ground of the will of God, that they should turn from their wickedness and live?

2. Thus far I have spoken of Baptism. The view which the Liturgy takes of the Creeds, is sufficiently evident from the mode of their introduction into it. They are made parts of our worship; acts of allegiance, declarations by the whole congregation of the Name into which each one has been baptized; preparations for prayer; steps to communion. The notion of them as mere collections of dogmas is never once insinuated, is refuted by the whole order of the services.

3. In speaking of the Eucharist, it is safer again to refer to the language of opponents. Again and again we have been told that the idea of a Real Presence is distinctly implied in our Communion Service; that at all events the words must convey

this impression to any ordinary person; that they are such as could not have been written by anyone who held the simple Zuinglian dogma, and cannot be used with comfort, nay, without a sense of pain and contradiction, by anyone who feels it to be the true one. And yet, though there may be constant admonitions respecting the spirit in which this sacrament is to be received, the faith and repentance which are the preparations for it, the danger of a careless and unworthy treatment of such mysteries, is it not evident at the same time, from the earnest exhortations to partake of it, that it is looked upon as a common blessing, as one to which all men have a claim, as one from which it is a perilous responsibility to exclude any, whose open sins do not shew that they have excluded themselves? The English Dissenter, regarding this ordinance as the right of a few who can give an account of their feelings, and experiences, and change of mind, is continually denouncing our service for its manifest departure from the maxims upon which he acts. On the one hand the Eucharist is spoken of in such awful language, as it seems to him must have been borrowed from periods of pure superstition; on the other hand, there is the strangest notion of it, as if it were a bond of fellowship for the whole universe. 'One would suppose,' he says, 'from the phrases you use, that you look upon this sacrament as the very opening of the kingdom of heaven, and yet you treat it as the proper preparation for the most vulgar and earthly employments. Sometimes you seem to fancy it possible, that men should eat the flesh and drink the blood of the Son of Man by partaking of these elements, and yet you can admit persons to be partakers of it who would have very great difficulty in explaining themselves respecting the most ordinary propositions of the Christian system. By your carefulness in restraining the administration of the sacrament to a particular class, one would suppose that you regarded it as a Jewish sacrifice, or as something yet more wonderful. And yet you speak, at the same time, of the sacrifice of Christ, once made upon the cross, as full, and sufficient, and satisfactory.'

Meantime, it is not pretended by any person, be he friend or foe, that a single passage exists in this service which favours the notion that the presence of Christ is connected with a change in the elements. Whoever adopts that notion instantly becomes dissatisfied with the eucharistic part of our liturgy, proclaims it to be cold, heartless, dead, etc. In like manner, whoever believes the Eucharist to be a sacrifice in any sense which implies that the sacrifice of Christ upon the cross is less complete and finished for all mankind than it has been supposed to be by the strongest Lutheran or Calvinist, also denounces our Liturgy as departing from that idea which the Mass, in other portions of the Latin Church, embodies. By the confession, then, of all it regards the feast as the highest Christian privilege, as the most complete reality; not because it works a change in our Christian state and position; not because it brings one before us who is habitually absent from us, but because it enables us to enter into the fulness of our Church life, into that truly human and divine fellowship, which Christ, by His incarnation, His death, and His ascension, has claimed for all whom He is not ashamed to call His brethren.

4. This being the case, the communion service in our liturgy interprets the rest of our worship. Throughout, it is the worship of a body, of a family. It is open, and has been subject, to all the objections which the defenders of extempore prayer can raise against any form as belonging to mankind in general, and not to our nation and our family, to our particular circumstances, except so far as we can connect them with the knowledge of God and of His purposes to our race. On the other hand, it is open, and has been subject, to the objections of those who think that worship is cold and dead, if it lead us from the visible to the invisible, if it claim the privilege of approaching at once through the one Mediator the throne of the Absolute and the Infinite. It proscribes nothing; it does not affirm how much or how little of the sensible may be useful in assisting us to reach that which is beyond our senses. Human agency and help it distinctly recognises as the appointed and ordinary channel through which the blessings of Him who was made flesh descend upon His Church, and through which the prayers and praises of His Church ascend as a united sacrifice to Him. But it does affirm, that all sensible helps, and all human agency, lose their meaning and become positively evil when they are converted into ends, or when they impair the belief that the whole Church is admitted into the holiest place.

5. It is impossible to separate this subject from that of ministerial orders, as it is expounded to us in our ordination and consecration services. Part of the complaint against these has been considered already. Only those who have received presbyteral

ordination are allowed to administer the Eucharist or to pronounce absolution. 'Now,' argue the Dissenters, 'you may say if you will, that the words πρεσβύτερος and ἱερεύς are different; and that you affix the former, not the latter, to the second rank of your ministers. But is not the refusal of these particular offices to the lower order a distinct and significant recognition of the principle, though you may not express it by a name? If your Church felt as we do about the sin of appropriating these names to men, would she have dared to approach so very closely in her acts to such an assumption? Would she have proceeded habitually upon a maxim, which must at least convey the impression, that she thinks it no assumption at all?' I leave those who please to answer these arguments; to me they seem irresistible. Nor am I better able to clear our services of the charge of distinctly and formally connecting the gift of spiritual powers with ordination; of distinctly encouraging and urging her ministers to believe, that they have the Holy Spirit committed to them for the work of the ministry. I do not complain of anyone who performs the office of a minister in our Church, and yet believes that he possesses no such power. I should no more wish to exclude him from his office on that account, than I should wish to depose a magistrate who did not understand the extent of the powers which the laws invested him with. Each may be using that which he does believe is his, very far more honestly than I am using that which I believe is mine. Each is far more honest than he would be if he merely acknowledged the words without attaching a meaning

2 B 2

to them. But still the words are there; and I think he cannot complain of me for taking them in their plain sense; for saying that, little as I enter into their force, little as my conduct corresponds with them, there are very few which I have ever heard, that I could bear less to part with, or that I more feel I must learn to understand by acting upon the conviction of their truth.

With the continual allegation of Dissenters, that in spite of many tendencies to the contrary opinion in some of our divines, ancient as well as modern, our Liturgy recognises the Episcopate as the root of all the other orders, and supposes it to contain them all within itself, I can as little quarrel as with either of the former. They seem to me to have made their point good. And I cannot find that any answers which have been made to them amount to more than awkward though ingenious evasions.

But where are we to find the doctrine of the vicarial powers of ministers in any part of these services? Where are we to find one single hint that the Presbyter absolves or administers the Eucharist, that the Bishop exercises his own functions or that he ordains others, as the minister and delegate of one who is absent from his Church? Those who adopt this opinion begin at once to exclaim against our services, as containing the most cold and unsatisfactory recognition of the mighty authority with which the Priest and Bishop of the New Testament are endowed. They feel it absolutely necessary that he should clothe himself with other attributes, in another mystery, than any which the English Church recognises in him. The self-same language which offends the Dissenter as containing such high and profane assertions of a perpetually derived and renewing power, is that which contradicts this notion of an inherent power.

6. Lastly, we come to the Scriptures. Here the intention of the Liturgy seems remarkably evident. The Scripture is adopted into our worship, the service explains the lessons, the lessons explain the service. The Bible is read partly as a continuous history, the history of God's revelation, and of the Church's growth and expansion; partly in connexion with our communion—the epistles of the New Testament expounding to us the law of the Spirit of life, the Gospels, the image after which the Spirit would form us. This is precisely that relation between the Scriptures and the Church, which I endeavoured to set forth in the former part of this book. The Protestant Dissenter says that we set aside the Bible, though we read more of it in any one month in one of our Churches than he reads in two years in any of his meetings; and though our reading of it is continuous, his casual and arbitrary. The Romanist says that we set aside the authority of the Church in the interpretation of Scripture, though we make it a formal and habitual part of the services, in which the mind of the Church is expressed.

II. 1. I think, then, I have answered the question as to the meaning which the English Church puts upon the signs which it has in common with other Churches, fairly and legitimately. Another question was, how we can determine between two bodies, both existing in this country, and both possessing these signs, which may and which may not fairly call itself Catholic. If our previous statements have been true, this question is also settled. A body acknowledging itself connected with the Church in all previous ages by the bond of sacraments, of creeds, of worship, of ministerial succession, has the *primâ facie* marks of Catholicity. Should any other body standing aloof from it put in a claim upon the same grounds to be Catholic, it is bound to show the reasons of its own pretension, and the reasons upon which it rejects the former pretension. Those reasons must be the same which we have considered already. We are not Catholic in the opinion of the Romish body which resides in this country, because we do not acknowledge the *opus operatum* in Baptism, the new creeds of Popes, Transubstantiation, in the Eucharist, the existence of an intermediate agency between Christ and His members on earth, the vicarial authority of ministers, the existence of a Universal mortal Bishop, the right of the Church to hide the Scriptures from the Laity; in one word, because we do not acknowledge that system which appeared to us, before we entered upon English ground at all, to be anti-Catholic. The Church in every land exists under the condition, either of professing this system, or of protesting against it. Its existence is not denoted by the Profession or by the Protest, but by the Signs to which the profession and the protest refer. If the Romish body say that it stands in certain notions *about* sacraments and about orders, and not in its sacraments and in the orders themselves, that declaration is a practical renunciation of its claims to be a Church. We say that we protest against these notions, because they are incompatible with the acknowledgment of Christ's Spiritual and Universal kingdom.

2. But since we have seen that the confessions in different Protestant bodies have (contrary to the intentions of their compilers) greatly interfered with the simple recognition of the facts contained in the creed, and that the Romish confessions sanctioned by the Council of Trent, and by Pope Pius IV., interfere with it yet more; we are bound to shew whether there is anything corresponding to these in the Church of England, any addition made upon its own authority to the admitted formularies of the whole Church. Till we are satisfied on this point we cannot, I conceive, rightly understand our own position in reference to the other portions of the Church.

Now it appears that in the sixteenth century, we as well as the Protestants and Romanists on the Continent, drew up a set of dogmatic articles, and that these have continued to be the test of orthodoxy for those who take orders in our Church and for those who are studying in at least one of our universities, ever since. Seeing then that there were different systems at that time in vogue, and that the object of different religious bodies in making confessions, was to identify themselves with one or other of these systems,—for example, the Genevan body thus identified itself with the Calvinistic system, the Romanist bodies with the Tridentine system,—we must desire to know how far these articles of ours identify us with any of them. One remark has been made respecting them, which is not unimportant for our present purpose, that they carefully avoid any intrusion upon the ground occupied by the old creeds. They do not take the living forms of the creeds, they constitute a set of distinct dogmatic propositions; they would be ridiculous if introduced into worship; they are not intended for the majority of the laity; they belong exclusively to the student. But these observations respecting them would be of little worth, if it appeared that they inculcate upon the teacher a certain theological system alien from the spirit and temper of the creeds; for this system he will communicate to those who hear him.

How stands the case? We have seen that there is one main characteristic of the Calvinistic system as a system. It makes the fall of man the central point of its divinity: it treats the incarnation, and all the facts which manifest the Son of God to men, as merely growing out of this, and necessary in consequence of it.* On this principle that very spirited confession which was drawn up by the Scotch preachers for the use of the Kirk in the sixteenth century, is constructed. The first Article is on the Trinity; the second, on the Fall; then comes the explanation of the existence of the Church or Kirk, as grounded upon the predestination of certain individuals in this fallen race to eternal life. There cannot be a finer or better model of a purely Calvinistical confession than this one; nor any which illustrates more completely the direct opposition between the idea of the Genevan system and the idea of the old Catholic Creeds. We have seen again that the Lutheran had a very different conception of Chris-

---

* A reader may ask, What then is meant by a Supralapsarian? I answer, not a person who supposes the union of *mankind* with its Creator to be an idea anterior to that of the fall, but a person who thinks that the redemption and salvation of certain individuals out of mankind is the highest end of all God's purposes, for the sake of which the fall itself was permitted and ordained.

tianity from this, a great desire to make the incarnation of Christ the centre of all his thoughts, and to use the Apostles' Creed as his symbol: of such a disposition the Augsburg confession is a satisfactory testimony. But we have seen, also, that in his eagerness to assert conscious Justification as the one great principle of divinity, he was driven back upon the same ground as the Calvinist; he was forced to start from the evil root, in order that he might explain the process of restoration. And thus, as I remarked before, systematic Protestantism became identical with Calvinism, until the Arminian form of it was developed, which is little more than a contradiction of Calvinism, little more than a denial of the principle that the will of God is the originating cause of all good in man.

Now if anyone will turn to our Thirty-nine Articles, he will perceive that the first Article being upon the Trinity, the second is upon the Incarnation, and that the first eight Articles relate to truths directly connected with the being of God, to His manifestations of Himself, to the Scriptures as expounding them, to the Creeds as illustrating and interpreting the Scriptures. When this Catholic foundation has been laid, we proceed in the ninth Article to the fall of man, and then to all those questions concerning free-will, justification and election, which were occupying men's minds in the sixteenth century. On all these points it seems to me the language of the Articles is as distinct and definite as it can be. The Calvinistic and Lutheran *principles* are plainly and distinctly asserted, there is no hint or prophecy of Arminianism; the Romish system in every point wherein

it is opposed to the distinct affirmations of the
Reformers, on the subject of God's will and man's
faith, is repudiated; that is to say, the system
of Romanism is rejected in the Articles from the
ninth to the nineteenth, just as the system of Calvinism, or pure Protestantism, had been repudiated
by the Articles from the first to the eighth. The
principles of the Reformation are asserted in the
one division, not as necessary qualifications, but as
indispensable conditions, of the great Catholic truths
which had been asserted in the other. And so, to
whatever cause we owe it, this has been the result
of these Articles; they have been thorns in the side
of those who have wished to establish an English
theological system, fashioned out of the materials
which either Romanism or Calvinism supplies; they
have encouraged persons of all sects and schools to
hope that their principles, in some sense or other,
might be contained in them, or by some process or
other extracted out of them, or, at all events, not
positively denied by them; and yet there is no sect
or school, when speaking its sect or school language,
which, if it were honest, would not confess that there
are clauses and passages in them which it would be
glad to be rid of; that a small omission, or addition,
of a 'not' would often be very acceptable to it; that
it would like exceedingly, if not to remodel them, at
least to subjoin to them on all occasions a commentary
of its own.

I conclude this head with remarking, that if
our observations respecting the true meaning of
Quakerism, of Calvinism, of Lutheranism, of Uni-
tarianism, be accurate, the ideas and principles of each

of these bodies are expressed in the forms of our English Church; only the systems which they have grafted upon these, and which have separated them from each other, are rejected. The idea of man as constituted in the divine Word, of a Kingdom based upon that constitution, of a Spirit working to bring him into conformity with it, of a perpetual struggle with an evil and sensual nature; this is the idea of Quakerism, and it is the idea of our Liturgy in every one of its forms and services. The idea of a divine Will going before all acts of the human will, the primary source of all that is in eternity, and all that becomes in time, to which everything is meant to be in subjection, which can alone bring that which has rebelled into subjection, to which every creature must attribute all the motions to good which he finds within him, the primary direction of his thoughts, the power of perseverance; this is the idea of Calvinism, and it is the idea which is implied in all the prayers of our Litany, which is formally set forth in the words of our Articles. The idea of man struggling with his own evil nature, discovering in it nothing but a bottomless pit of evil, grasping at a deliverer, finding that in union with him only is his life; that he is strong only in his strength, righteous only in his righteousness ; this is the idea of Lutheranism, and it is the idea which is involved in all our prayers and Creeds, which our Articles reassert in logical terms. The idea of a unity which lies beneath all other unity, of a love which is the ground of all other love, of Humanity as connected with that love, regarded by it, comprehended in it; this is the idea which has hovered about the mind of the Unitarian, and which he has vainly attempted to comprehend in his system of contradictions and denials: this idea is the basis of our Liturgy, our Articles, our Church.

SECTION II.—DOES THE UNIVERSAL SOCIETY IN ENGLAND EXIST APART FROM ITS CIVIL INSTITUTIONS, OR IN UNION WITH THEM?

To this question the answer is unanimous.

The English dissenter affirms that the Church is embodied in the State; it is an Act of Parliament Church. The modern civil Ruler says, that the State is impeded in all its operations by the Church; the Sovereign is crowned by the Archbishop, the Bishops as a body take part in the deliberations of Parliament; above all, the greater part of the education of the land is ecclesiastical. The Romanist affirms that the Church has no pretensions to be called a Catholic body; it is a national body. There can be no doubt, then, that the ecclesiastical and civil institutions are united, and this by bonds which it must require some violence to break. But when did this union take place? How was it brought to pass? Who were the contracting parties to it? On all these questions history preserves a profound silence. It records no meeting of Sovereigns and Bishops to adjust the terms of the fellowship; it fixes no date at which the Church began to say it would acknowledge the State, or at which the State said it would acknowledge the Church. So soon as we find the Church in the land, we find her doing homage to the civil powers, such as they were, which ruled the land. So soon as the Church begins to exercise its own peculiar influence, the civil power begins to feel that influence, and to be moulded by it.

Then indeed we meet with records of transactions between these two bodies, each of which is perceived to have its distinct representative, and its peculiar object, though neither the representatives nor the objects are defined by any formal line of separation. But these transactions are not for the purpose of establishing a covenant on the part of the State, that it will protect the Church, or on the part of the Church, that it will do certain services for the State; far rather they are attempts by each, either to reclaim a portion of its own province which it supposes that the other has invaded, or to conquer a portion of that province of which the other has hitherto had peaceable possession. They are such transactions as presuppose a real, though a yet imperfectly understood *relation*, not such as could have been produced by a compact, or had the least tendency to create one. The Church affirms that it has a right to assign the powers and jurisdiction of its own Bishops; the State maintains that Bishops as well as the rest of its subjects must acknowledge its paramount authority. The Church affirms that it has a spiritual government altogether distinct from the civil government. The State says that the minister of the Church must submit like other men to its laws and its tribunals. Every impartial and thoughtful reader of our history feels that there is a right and a wrong in each of these pretensions; that Becket must have been contending for a principle, that Henry must have been contending for a principle. The resolution of our annalists generally to choose favourites, and to nickname opponents, the eagerness of young readers to arrive at a positive conclusion about every matter in dispute, the obvious injustice of those (so called) fair critics, who try both parties by the standards of their own time, and of course condemn both, acquitting and exalting only themselves and their own wisdom, may hinder us from acknowledging at once and in terms, that we are under deep obligations to these opposing champions, and that a higher power was working out its ends by the help of both; but we all feel inwardly, that this is the case; we all unconsciously express our conviction that it is so in one set of phrases or another. And we feel also in a remarkable way, that the history of these struggles is, if not the history of England, yet the heart and centre of it, whence more light is thrown upon the records of the conflicts between Kings and Barons, Normans and Saxons, the old orders and the new, than they throw back upon it. Those who have learnt that the science of politics is not comprehended in the theory of representation, that in order to understand what representation means, we must first know what there is to represent, have perceived that in these civil and ecclesiastical disputes lies the inward secret which we have need to investigate before we can trace its working on the surface and in the external machinery of Society.

So it was before the Reformation. And what was the Reformation itself? Its opponents of both classes say, that it was merely a national movement. 'Henry not Cranmer was at the root of it. There was more of politics in it than of religion.' I should not use such language; I do not understand their distinction between politics and religion. But I believe that in their meaning they are right. The most obvious peculiarity of the English Reformation seems to be this, that it was a movement originating with the Sovereign and not with Theologians. And therefore it was not a new movement, but one of a series of movements. Not only the Constitutions of Clarendon, made in the days of a rebellious Sovereign, but the statutes of præmunire, passed in the time of some of the most orthodox, some of the greatest persecutors of Lollardism, had attempted to cut off the correspondence of the Church of Rome. The difference in the reign of Henry VIII. was simply this, that a large body of the Bishops and Clergy had been led by their religious feelings to desire that this correspondence should be broken off; to feel that the English Church could not maintain its own position unless it became strictly national; unless it abandoned that subjection to a foreign bishop, which the State had always wished it to abandon.

And what has been the state of things since the Reformation? It is this : a number of bodies or sects have gradually grown up in the country, which have affirmed that the principles of Protestantism were not asserted with sufficient boldness at our Reformation. We stopped short, it is said, at a certain point. We retain much of the papal system, which the other protestant nations have thrown off. On the other hand, the Romanists have felt that the English Reformation was more fatal to the maxim upon which they were habitually acting than the Reformation in any other quarter had been. There was a hope that men might renounce a new system of opinions and adopt an old one. But a Church which had affirmed the principle of nationality, which had come to an understanding with the Sovereign of its own land, was, to all appearance, utterly incorrigible. The most earnest and intelligent Jesuits who came over perceived that this was a condition of things, which must be changed, not merely by preaching, but by plotting; many of them believed that the best hope of the restoration of the papal power lay in the triumph of those sects which professed a more vehement Protestantism. Another curious point deserves to be noticed: the Puritan body was, as I have said before, essentially Calvinistical. Calvinism was the principle of its life. It was the feeling that the English Church was not founded upon the Calvinistical idea which gave occasion to the earliest Puritan movements. And yet we imported the anti-Calvinistical doctrine, which the Puritans afterwards identified with popery, from one of the purely protestant countries of the Continent. Nay, further, it was not till we had a Scottish King upon the throne, a King bred under Presbyterian preachers, that we had any connexion with this Arminian system at all. It is to this King that we owe a very marked change in our position. Elizabeth had troubled herself as little as possible about systems of opinion; she had merely endeavoured to assert her position as a national Sovereign. James could only look upon every question as a schoolman and a pedant. He had, indeed, one living practical feeling; he had been disgusted with the Presbyterian preachers, and had found that their power practically interfered with his. But he had no sense of sympathy or connexion with our Church; he only wished that the Episcopalian *system* should prevail against the Presbyterian. And this system, with whatever belonged to it, was to be

established in Scotland, and maintained here, by the
efforts of the State. Both in Scotland, therefore, and
in England, the feeling that there is a spiritual power
distinct from and higher than the mere State power,
was called forth. In Scotland this spiritual feeling
connected itself with the national feeling. The
people revolted against the notion of a prelacy which
was imposed upon them by England. Here, the
mixture of spiritual with national feelings in the
Puritan produced some strange anomalies. The body
in the Commons' House which had most sympathy
with Puritanism were occupied in maintaining the old
forms of the national constitution against the royal
prerogative. The Puritan clergy were raising their
voices *against* old national and ecclesiastical forms, and
maintaining the rights of the spiritual man. Mixed
with these assertions, however, one can perceive in
them from the first a desire for a more formal and
systematic divinity than had ever existed in England
before. At length they triumph, and it is their business
to realise as well as they can their three objects, of
upholding the liberty of the subject, which had been
asserted by the Long Parliament; the superiority of
Christians to outward forms, which had been maintained by their preachers against Laud and the Bishops;
and, lastly, the all importance of a peculiar theological
system. The first attempt issued in the establishment
of a military despotism; the second led to the rise
and independence of the different sects which revolted
from the stern Presbyterian government and sought
to maintain freedom of conscience; the last effort
was embodied in the deliberations, decrees, catechisms,
committees of triers, of the Westminster Assembly.

It is a grievous thing that English Churchmen should, from their prejudices and partialities, refuse to study the history of this remarkable period simply and fairly, looking at it from all sides and all points of view, and labouring to do justice to the feelings of all the parties who were concerned in it. For it is when thus considered, and not when warped into an apology for some ecclesiastical hero, or into a sentence of condemnation upon his opponents, that it illustrates and makes manifest the essential relation between spiritual and civil life, and the impossibility of destroying that relation by any efforts of ours, however unfriendly and uncomfortable we may make it.

The Westminster Assembly had done their best to establish an uniformity of opinions; that wherein they had left their ministers free, was in their modes of worship. The opposite principle had been the one hitherto recognised in England. The bond of national fellowship had been supposed to be the bond of worship; men who had books and leisure might occupy themselves with the study of opinions. I do not know how far the Episcopal clergy at the Restoration were aware that this was the question at issue between them and their opponents; possibly they looked upon it merely as a question whether the nation should adopt a more or less comprehensive system. But if so, their old habits were stronger than their theories; the State felt that it could not trouble itself about shades of opinion, but that old forms of worship were practical and general, and there was One over us who saw further than either statesmen or churchmen. At all events, this was the result. The Act of Uniformity in Worship was the substitute for the efforts at a dogmatic uniformity which belonged to the genius of Presbyterianism. The immediate effect of that measure was the separation of the Puritan clergy from that which was now again recognised as the national Church. Then began various stupid efforts on the part of the State to silence them, or to coerce them into a union, mixed with various royal experiments at a general liberty of conscience which should include Romanist as well as Protestant Dissenters. The resistance to these marks the strong sense of the people and of the Parliament that Romanism was something anti-national. This feeling was strong in the minds of the seven Bishops who refused to read James's declaration. They believed that the act of the King was, as it proved to be, suicidal. Several of them could not, however, follow out that principle to what seems to me its legitimate consequence; that when the King did commit his act of legal suicide by deserting the country, he was as one lying under a sentence of deposition from God Himself, for having violated the covenant by which he held his power. The Convention Parliament took that pious view of the matter, and accordingly inquired, not what person they might by their own power or in conformity with the people's will choose into his place, but who seemed to be designated to the office by the providence of God.* At no period, I think, was the religious character of the English State more distinctly asserted than at this; and at no time was it more important that it should be asserted. For now was beginning that change in

* See the celebrated passage in Burke's Reflections, wherein he replies to the sermon of Dr. Price upon the subject.

the habits and feelings of men, here as well as elsewhere, to which I adverted in Part I.; the change, I mean, from the notion of government as grounded upon deep mysterious principles, to the notion of it as the result of mere commercial arrangements—of some imaginary artificial compact. That this change has been productive of very mischievous effects to the Church and the nation of England, I shall have occasion presently to remark. That it has led to any legislative Acts which involve a formal or a virtual violation of the union between the ecclesiastical and the civil bodies, I believe is a notion which could only have become prevalent through this very habit of mind. We have supposed the Church and the State to be knit together by some material outward terms of agreement: we do not know what they are; they may be that the State shall not recognise any persons as its subjects who are not Churchmen; in other words, that it should ignore facts; they may therefore be violated by Acts of toleration, repeals of test laws, emancipation of Romanists. I do not express any opinion about the policy of one or other of these measures; some of them may have been inexpedient measures; they were all, I should conceive, defended as well as attacked by many feeble and imperfect arguments. But I do think that it requires something far deeper and more subtle than any such measures, to destroy a union which has cemented itself by no human contrivances, and which exists in the very nature of things. By carelessness, ignorance, faithlessness, immorality, we may undermine our national life, and to these perils it is continually exposed. But the Acts of our legislators when they are evil, are in general but reflexes of something which is evil in the national mind, and which legislators cannot correct. And in general they are better than could at all be expected from the tempers of those who passed them, or of us who criticise them. Oftentimes the very errors which are in them, and the mischievous consequences to which they lead, may become our teachers, and may be far more profitable to us than the success of our opposition to them could have been. And therefore I am naturally led from the consideration of this subject, to that which I proposed next to consider.

SECTION III.—WHAT IS THE FORM OF CHARACTER WHICH BELONGS ESPECIALLY TO ENGLISHMEN? TO WHAT KIND OF DEPRAVATION IS IT LIABLE?

FROM what I have said already, it will be evident to the reader that I believe the first thoughts of men upon this subject to be well founded. 'You Englishmen are such mere *politicians*,' this is the ordinary complaint which foreigners make of us. 'Alas! how exclusively we are devoted to *politics*,' this is our continual groan concerning ourselves. The proofs of the position are manifold—none more striking than those which are supplied by men who are determined that *they* will at all events be exempt from the national disease; that they will be artists, philosophers, mystics —anything but politicians. Watch them well, and you will see how utterly impossible it is for them to realise their dream; how continually some speculation about the organisation of society, some practical effort to remodel it, mixes with their high and serene contemplations; how fierce and restless the contemplators become, from the very effort to keep themselves from all contact with the fever and restlessness which they suppose to be inherent in the English character, and which they know are in their own. Other cases there are, of another kind, which confirm the same fact still more remarkably. I have known persons who possessed no practical talent whatever, all whose attempts at action were of the most ludicrously and painfully abortive kind, who, if they tried to realise some fine conception of their own, were sure either to render it contemptible by their failure, or else very soon to run into one of the old ruts from which they had been labouring with all their might to extricate themselves. And yet such Englishmen as these, who, if they have any gifts at all, seem to be exclusively endowed with those which are most un-English, feel themselves just as much compelled to be political and practical as their countrymen. They find it impossible to think unless they can in some way or other connect their thoughts with action, and despairing of any such alliance in their own persons, they try whether they may not at least be able to point out a method of action to others, aspiring to no other fame than that of the whetstone;

> "acutum
> Reddere quæ ferrum valet, exsors ipsa secandi."

But though these arguments are very decisive, I cannot but think that there are others which are more cheering. Why do we turn to the literature of the reign of Queen Elizabeth as to that which most represents the genius of our nation, as that which most

shews of what we are capable? Why but because in
every department it was more historical, more political,
than it has been at any time since. Look at our
drama, how it draws its highest inspirations from the
old records of our national life. See how needful it
was even for the allegorical poet, the singer of 'Fairy
Land,' when dealing with his twelve moral virtues,
and the battles of the inner man, to interweave a
history of Prince Arthur, and to confound the image
of Gloriana with that of Queen Elizabeth. With all
their dreams about poetry, and scholarship, and philosophy, how evident it is that the deepest and most
earnest thoughts of Sidney and Raleigh were occupied
with policy and politics! What nation may not be
able to shew profounder works in exegetical or dogmatical divinity than we? Who can hold our countrymen pace, when they fashion their minds to the
consideration of the laws according to which God has
formed heavenly, and human, and natural creatures?

Hooker's work is the specimen of a class, though
certainly the highest specimen. And when one
considers it, and the whole life and character of the
man who wrote it, I think we must feel how very
little excuse lies in that habit of mind which God
has bestowed upon us, for any defect in meekness and
gentleness, in superiority to the low notions and canons
of this world, in converse with the hierarchies of
heaven. I do not wish to exalt this form of character
above every other; I cannot tell whether it is better
or worse than that which belongs to Frenchmen or
Germans; I know only that it is ours, and that it is
capable of being expanded into that which is most
noble, as well as sinking into that which is most base.

We ought to contemplate it in both conditions, that we may not separate hope from humiliation, that we may know both our responsibilities and our temptations, and that we may be able to honour the good when it is mixed with the evil which lies nearest to it. Of that charity we have need in every part of our history. It is impossible not to observe a tendency in the English Reformers of the sixteenth century to a kind of diplomacy which one does not like to perceive in holy men, and which it is very easy to represent as pervading the whole of their characters, and explaining the meaning of their acts. Presently after you find them suffering with a constancy worthy, their detractors say, of heroes,* we have been used to believe and think, of martyrs. The political bias of their mind did not, I fancy, tend on the whole to lower the tone of it, to bring them more helplessly into contact with outward things, or to give them less faith in the invisible. Its main effect was to lead them to think of Christ's Church, as a Kingdom rather than as a system : in the dust and bustle of affairs their strong conviction that this kingdom was a reality and not a metaphor may have led them to forget that it is the type of all kingdoms, and is not moulded after the maxims of any even of those which confess it, and do homage to it. But in silence and

---

* Wherein lies the distinction between a hero and a martyr? I should presume in the feeling of the first, that he is acting by some power and energy of his own; of the latter, that he has to depend upon that strength which is perfected in weakness. We may safely appeal to the discourses and letters of our Reformers in prison, to decide which feeling is most characteristic of them.

suffering, this thought gave a fixedness and substantiality to their faith, which even the most devout schoolmen are seldom able to attain. They knew that it was a Person in whom they were believing; in the hour of trial and death they looked directly to Him, and not to any dogma or system of dogmas, for strength and consolation.

That this way of considering the Church is an eminently English one, became evident in the time of the civil wars. It might be said to characterise every class of thinkers. It was at first less marked in those among whom one would expect most of it, I mean among the Episcopalians; for the systematic tendency had become very prevalent through the influence of James I., and Laud especially seems to have contracted it. His faults were far more those of a schoolmaster* or a collegian, than of an arrogant and usurping politician. And these faults made him especially unable to deal with the energetic national impulses of that period. But the sense of the Church as a kingdom returned to the Episcopalians in their hour of humiliation. It is this which prevailed in the mind of Jeremy Taylor, above all other views. In spite of his learning and his fondness for casuistry, he could not bear to contemplate Christianity as a system. He would look upon it as a life, but then it was a life connecting itself with an order, and realised in that kind of dependence which a subject pays to his sovereign, rather than that which a pupil renders to his master. Therefore one may trace a curious point of sympathy between him and the most extreme mystics and spiritualists of that

* Mr. Carlyle has made this remark in his Lectures on Hero Worship.

age; all spoke of a divine kingdom, none could be content with any language which did not import it, or with any acts which did not endeavour to realise it. Even Milton, who was as a star, and dwelt apart, was in the last age of his life as much as in the first, dreaming of a polity. All men might be kings and priests in his commonwealth, but kings and priests they were to be, not professors and doctors.

But we must look at another side of the picture. When the feeling of spiritual life and spiritual government decayed, as we saw it did decay, in the latter part of the seventeenth and the beginning of the eighteenth century, one may fancy what an effect must have been produced upon a people, whose political feelings were the deepest which they had. Our literature could not separate itself from our social life. It was a mere mockery and pretence when it tried to throw itself into some Arcadian condition of things. It had always been real and homely, and such it must continue to be. But if all realities had become conventions, if what was homely had become base, we need be at no loss to understand the necessary limitations of our best, and the fearful debasement of our worst literature during the period between the Revolution in England and that in France. The degradation of our professed statesmen, the loss of all high ends in their policy, the maxims and practices which have made Sir Robert Walpole's name and administration immortal, are all equally explicable. Still there were indications of English strength, and of the direction which that strength naturally takes. In the physical world, men are busy, either about the mechanism of actual things, or about God's laws and order. Either study was most fitted to the truest and noblest part of our character, and here therefore there were true and worthy results.

But the commercial activities and the scientific discoveries of this age were gradually concentrating an immense population of human beings in our cities. Who were caring for these? The Church possessed some prelates of high and even comprehensive views, many humble and sincere pastors in its rural districts; many men capable of thinking vigorously respecting the moral constitution of individuals and of society. In general however, its habit of mind was too well expressed in the theory of Warburton respecting the alliance of the Church and State; in the practice of sending bishops to Ireland for the sake of supporting the English interest. It apparently possessed the means of influencing the aristocracy; but the aristocracy was commonly infidel. It should have been able through its less exalted members to have reached the heart of the trading classes, but they were chiefly under the influence of dissent; it seemed not to be aware that the new class of poor men was coming into existence. Undoubtedly they were members of the National Church who first went forth to evangelise the mining and manufacturing districts; but their movements were regarded with anything but sympathy by the rulers of the Church; no pains were taken to give them a right direction. Humble and quiet men in country parishes disliked them because they were opposed to the order and regularity which had been always associated in their minds with the idea of religion; to others they were odious because they appealed to feelings which were dormant in themselves, but which were found to exist in their flocks. Then came the French Revolution, with its terrors and warnings. The clergy began to feel themselves less mere parts of an obsolete machinery existing for some unintelligible purposes; more necessary to the being of the commonwealth. The aristocracy began to acknowledge them in that character. Their scepticism vanished, and they spoke of religion and its teachers with much respect, as exerting those influences of fear and hope, which could alone make property and government secure. Such was the new tone which the character and patronage of George III., and the dread of French disorganisation, rendered popular. One cannot call it a very elevated tone. So long as the war lasted, it was mixed with much that was generous and patriotic in the upper classes of laymen; the portion of the clergy who shared in it became active magistrates, careful of their domestic and relative duties, zealous in defence of that which seemed to them old and English. With these useful dispositions were connected a tendency to maintain customs and practices, simply because they did exist, and could allege some moderate prescription in their favour; an acquiescence in the maxims of society even when they seemed to be at variance with the higher morality; a great impatience of enthusiasm and mysticism, and all that cannot be at once brought under the rules of existing convention or obvious expediency; a suspicion of any great efforts of active virtue and self-sacrifice; a feeling that the Church is bound to sympathise with the aristocracy, and to overlook its sins, for the sake of preserving good order among the people; a strong sense of the service which subjects owe to their rulers, without any corresponding sense of the service which rulers owe to their subjects; an inclination to assert the privileges of clergymen, chiefly by treating it as a rudeness that any infidel notions should be broached in their presence; great anxiety for a State encouragement of religion on the ground that otherwise it was not likely to thrive, or to enlist fashion and the opinion of the world on its side; a vehement dislike of dissenters, as disturbing the quietness and regularity of society, and as introducing something of vulgarity into religion; a certain anger and restlessness at the discovery of any new doubts respecting the English Church or Christianity, which could not at once be removed by an application of the arguments used on behalf of Establishments in Paley's Moral Philosophy, and of the Gospel in his Evidences.

Now the spirit of this State Churchmanship was evidently the spirit of an age of our national Church, not of the Church itself. That continued to express itself in the Liturgy; and when it required a dogmatical language, in the Articles. The younger and more active members of the Church soon became conscious of the contradiction. They began to seek for some SYSTEM which should be a refuge from the dreariness of political Anglicanism. What they have found is our next inquiry.

CHAPTER II.

MODERN ENGLISH SYSTEMS.

SECTION I.—THE LIBERAL SYSTEM : THE EVANGELICAL SYSTEM : THE HIGH CHURCH OR CATHOLIC SYSTEM.

1. 'SEE!' exclaims the liberal, taking his view of this English orthodoxy from that side on which it presents itself as the antagonist of change and improvement, 'see what a hopeless class of people these old pillars of the Church are! How can it stand if it is to be supported by such maxims as these? Is not everything moving about us, and can we determine to remain stationary? Opinions upon every subject are undergoing revolution, and we think that our Articles and Formularies can be kept as they are? How can you be so foolish as not to perceive that the Dissenters will grow upon us, and ultimately overwhelm us, unless we discover some scheme for comprehending them? And then, there is that body of Romanists in the midst of us; why are you determined to look upon them as if they belonged to the days of Gregory the Seventh or Innocent the Third? Why not make them your friends, by assuming that they are so? Why not throw overboard your prejudices, and enter at once and heartily into the spirit of the age?'

2. In quite other language did the Evangelical complain of the spirit which animated the members

of the old school; 'They have lost sight of all spiritual
influences and realities : a dry notion of human merit
is at the bottom of all their thoughts and teachings.
They expect men to get to heaven by being baptized,
and by leading good and respectable lives; the
principle of faith is forgotten altogether. The power
of the Gospel, as a message of peace to man, is not
felt or regarded. Another bond of union than that
of spiritual fellowship with Christ is set up; hence
holy Dissenters are denounced, ungodly Churchmen
fraternised with. Restore the doctrines of our
Articles; preach the Gospel in season and out of
season; this is the only way to improve the condition
of things among us, to remedy the mischiefs which
the indifference of the last age has produced.'

3. 'Alas!' cry those members of the English
Church who wish to be called catholics, 'miserable
comforters are ye all. It is true that our English
orthodoxy is very bad; you liberals and evangelicals
will introduce something which is a thousandfold
worse. The error of those whom you attack is, that
they thought they were members of a nation rather
than members of a Church; that they were to follow
the maxims of their own day, and not recall the
maxims of better days; that they were to look up
to the State as their guide and authority, instead of
feeling that the State has an object altogether
different from ours, that at certain happy moments
under some godly princes, it may conform itself to
our teachings, but that habitually, and at this time
above all others, it is our jealous foe, and aspires to
be our tyrant. The Church is a body which may
combine with a State, or rather, submit to it, but

which has no natural connexion with it. It has divine sacraments, an apostolic order, a power of binding and loosing; the practice and rules of the age of the Fathers are her model; to these she must be ever seeking to adapt herself. She must reject communion with the Dissenters in this country, not because they want the privileges of the State, but because they have cut themselves off from the universal Church; renouncing her orders, counterfeiting her sacraments. She must, in like manner, repudiate those Protestants abroad who have separated from and abandoned their succession; she must aspire after union with the orthodox Greeks and Latins, but must be content to wait till we or they are prepared for this union. At home we must labour to assert the worth of sacraments, to introduce discipline for the purpose of preserving baptismal purity in our children, and giving repentance to those who have lost it; of cutting off those who hold schismatical or heretical notions under the garb of Churchmen. We must stir men up to a more exact and religious life, encourage them to do good works, and to expect heavenly rewards for them. We must urge our disciples to retirement from the world, to penances and mortifications; we must preach repentance as the only way of recovering the privileges of Churchmen, which were given once, but which most men lose through sin; we must discountenance every exercise of private judgment, except in the matter of choosing teachers; we must advise our disciples to be content with probable conclusions, as all that faith requires, and bid them leave certainties to men of science.'

SECTION II.—REFLECTIONS ON THESE SYSTEMS, AND ON OUR POSITION GENERALLY.

THESE are the main outlines of the three systems which offer themselves to the deliberation of the young English theologian in the present day. He is told by the supporters of each that he must embrace one or other of them. All his attempts to incorporate them into each other have been very vain. It seems prodigious arrogance to invent a scheme of his own. He feels that he cannot fall back upon the old State Churchmanship.

This fear of arrogance is surely one which we ought to encourage in ourselves, and in every other person. If we had had more humility, we should probably have much fewer difficulties to encounter than we have. And therefore I would say, if I had any chance of being heard, Let us try by all means to be humble. And that we may not be otherwise, do not let us hastily set ourselves up to condemn any of these systems, or those who propound them. Our consciences, I believe, have told us from time to time that there is something in each of them which we ought not to reject. Let us not reject it. But we may find, that there is a divine harmony, of which the living principle in each of these systems forms one note, of which the systems themselves are a disturbance and a violation. This seemed to be the case in our previous inquiries respecting Protestant bodies and the Catholic Church; let us see whether our own national Church presents an exception to the rule, or an illustration of it.

1. How much does every true heart respond to that assertion of the Liberal, that if our Church be indeed a living body, it cannot be tied down by the system of a particular age; it must have an expansive power; it must breathe and move; it must be able to throw off the results of partial experiences; it must be able to profit by all new experiences! With what sympathy do we listen to him, when he says that the Church is meant to comprehend and not to exclude; that neither Protestant Dissenters nor Romish Dissenters should be out of the range of its sympathies, or should be prohibited from sharing in any portion of its benefits! And, now, how would he accomplish his beautiful conception? He proposes to us that we should abandon the prayers which we have derived from ages gone by, and the Articles which have come down to us from the Reformation; or he would have us adapt these to the maxims of our own time. But what if those Prayers should be the very means by which we have been preserved from the bondage to particular modes and habits of feeling, when they have been threatening to hold us fast? What if those Articles have kept us from sinking into a particular theological system, and have compelled us to feel that there were two sides of truth, neither of which could be asserted to the exclusion of the other? What if the abandonment either of the Prayers or the Articles, or the reduction of them to our own present standards of thought, should bring the Church into the most flat and hopeless monotony, should so level her to the superstitions of the nineteenth century, so divorce her from the past and the future, that all expansion would for ever be impossible? Again, how

would he accomplish his projects of comprehension?
He would take away this and that thing about which
we and the Dissenters differ, till at last he discovered
a few common principles upon which we might all
agree. But what if the peculiar doctrines and practices of each class of Dissenters be those in which
their most living feelings are expressed? What if all
plans of comprehension have failed just because the
best and most earnest men were those who saw most
the importance of that which was to be given up? If
these suppositions should be true, we must look somewhere else than to a liberal system, to produce the
effects which Liberals have dreamed of.

2. With what truth and power do the words of
the evangelicals come home to us;—that the loss of
faith was the great misery of the last age; that outward acts usurped the place of life-giving principles;
and that, therefore, outward acts were poor and dead;
that if a vital glow was restored to any part of the
Church at the close of the last century, it came from
the feeling that God had interfered on behalf of his
creatures, and was interfering on behalf of them still;
that there is a real relation between the creature and
the Creator; that there is a real power coming forth
from the Creator to succour his creatures, and to
enable them to do his will! What mighty words are
these! How important it must be, as the evangelical
says, that all men should hear them, and be brought
to act upon the conviction of their truth!

And how is this hope to be realised? Go forth
and tell men that their baptism is *not* an admission
into the privileges of God's spiritual Church; that
they are *not* to take this sign as a warrant of their

2 D 2

right to call themselves members of Christ, and to pray to God as their Father in Him. Go and tell them that they are not in a real relation with God, but only in a nominal one; go and tell them that if they are ever to enter into that relation they must bring themselves into it by an act of faith, or else wait till an angel comes down and troubles the waters; go and tell them that the Eucharist is not a real bond between Christ and his members, but only a picture or likeness, which, by a violent act of our will, we may turn into a reality; go and make these comfortable declarations to men, and mix them well with denunciations of other men for not preaching the Gospel; thus you will fulfil God's commission; thus you will reform a corrupt and sinful land.

3. What a charm lies in the words of the propounders of the Catholic system;—that there is indeed a Church in the world, which God himself has established; that He has not left it to the faith and feelings and notions of men; that He has given us permanent signs of its existence; that He has not left us to find our way into it, but has Himself taken us into it; that being in it we are under His own guidance and discipline; that we are not bound to prove ourselves members of it, by tests which exclude others who share the same privileges with us; that we are not bound to form ourselves into circles and parties and coteries; that we belong to the Communion of Saints, and need not seek for another! What good tidings, amidst all the confusions of our political parties, to hear that we are not the slaves of any of them; that we can do without the State's money, or

the State's sword; that we have powers of our own, which the State did not give nor can take away!

And as to practical matters, how evidently true we feel the assertion to be, that men ought to be called to repentance, and to do good works, and to restrain themselves, and to offer sacrifices to God! How clear it seems, that the evangelicals, though they may wish most heartily to press these duties upon their flocks, are practically unable to do so; that they cannot bid the members of their congregations generally, 'Arise and go to their Father,' because they will only allow that a portion of them may call God their Father; and because that portion of them, according to their doctrine, has already repented and turned to God; that they cannot call the members of their congregation generally to do holy acts from holy principles, because they do not believe that the majority of them have received the Spirit, from whom all holy desires and just works must proceed!

But how great then must be our confusion and dismay, when we discover that the preaching of repentance and of good works, is just as impossible, upon the Catholic system, as upon the evangelical; that the congregations of the one are to be treated practically as if they had lost their baptismal rights, just as the congregations of the others are to be treated as if they had never obtained them; that repentance and moral discipline are to be held forth as the possible means of recovering a treasure, not as the fruit of shame for the past, and precaution against the future abuse of it; that exhortations to good works, therefore, must of necessity take a selfish form, and be confirmed by selfish sanctions! After all those splendid assurances, that the Church really exists, and that it is endowed with such mighty powers, how grievous it is to find the most strange uncertainty about the terms under which she exists; whether only as a splendid dream, whereof the record is preserved in the writings of the Fathers, and which may some day be realised; or as a potentiality, which was made a fact during the Middle Ages by the supremacy of the Pope; or, lastly, as an invisible equatorial line between Romanism and Protestantism; a line, of which some dim traces may, from time to time, be discovered, with the help of powerful glasses, in our English history, but which has gradually been lost in the dark ground upon one side of it. And, finally, to men who had felt the intolerable pride, and the real slavery, of those notions about private judgment, which have been of late current among us, how painful is the discovery, that these Catholic denouncers of it do in fact justify the most extravagant, self-conceited, and unreasonable use which has ever been made of it; and only condemn it when it has lost its evil character, and is actually exercised under moral discipline and government! For what can be more subversive of all order and government, what so direct an outrage upon fact, as the assertion, that men in general are left to choose their teachers? And what so subversive of the very idea of a teacher, as the notion that he is not to cultivate the mind and judgment of his pupil, but only to pour into him certain notions of his own? The very arrogance from which we wish to deliver men, is the notion that they are not to receive the teachers, the parents, judges, pastors, whom God has set over them. The very hope we wish to encourage in them is, that if they receive humbly the light which is vouchsafed to them, it will be increased to them more and more, till they are brought into the perfect day.

And, lastly, the dogma respecting probable evidence, which the Catholic school makes the foundation of their intellectual, as the dogma of baptismal purity is the foundation of their moral, teaching, seems to contain the very virus of that scepticism which they denounce in the Liberal. The Liberal says, ' Nothing is certain in morals ; one opinion may be less mischievous or more plausible than another ; but, as to the thing which dogmatists call *truth*, sensible men, who know anything of history, have discarded the dream of it altogether.' And what says our English Catholic ?—' We admit nothing is certain in morals ; but then we do not want certainty. We are so faithful and submissive that we are content with appearances and likelihoods ; we receive what we are told by the authority which we have determined to be on the whole the best. God has not willed that we should have more light.' I appeal to the conscience of mankind against this language. Do we not mean when we use the awful name of God, ' THE BEING, He who IS ? ' If there be no certainty, how dare we take that name into our lips ? Are not the very words, ' I believe in God the Father Almighty,' an assertion that there is something fixed and eternal upon which the pillars of the universe rest ? Do not the next words mean, ' He who Is has revealed Himself to us ? We are not to live upon probabilities and plausibilities.

He who is Truth does wish that we should know the truth, and that the truth should make us free?' I do therefore say, that this system, so far as it stands upon the doctrine of probabilities, begins in scepticism, and that in scepticism it must terminate.

It will be observed that I have not charged the authors of these systems with the tendencies which they commonly impute to each other. I have not said that the Liberal wishes to substitute Rationalism for Orthodoxy; that the Evangelical wishes to establish the principle of Dissent; that the Catholic systematiser wishes to introduce Popery. My charge against each is, that he defeats his own object. As to the question how far these different accusations are true, I should be obliged in many cases to give a double answer in order to make myself intelligible. I can quite understand that each of these parties believes the clear and strong assertion of its own principle to be the best preservative against the very evil which it is supposed to favour. And I think this is a true and reasonable opinion. I think the Liberal has a right to say, 'Recognise the idea of Rationalism in the Church, and it will not assert itself out of the Church in the form of Infidelity.' That the Evangelical has a right to say, 'Recognise the idea of personal faith as the condition of Christian fellowship in the Church, and it will not assert itself in the form of Dissent out of the Church.' I think the Catholic has a right to say, 'Recognise the idea of Catholicism in your Church, and it will not assert itself out of the Church in the form of Romanism.' But while I acknowledge this, and therefore can enter into the feelings of disappointment and indignation which each in turn experiences when he finds that his purpose is not understood, I must say also, that it seems to me evident both from facts and reason, that each of these principles, when it is worked into a system, does become fairly obnoxious to the complaint of those who denounce it most vehemently. I cannot see what Church Liberalism reduced to a system is but the denial of any thing as given to men either in the shape of Tradition or Revelation ; what Church Evangelicism reduced to a system is but the denial of the very idea of Church fellowship or Unity, and the substitution for it of a combination of individual units ; what Catholicism reduced to a system is but Romanism ; that is to say, the direct denial of the distinction of National Churches, and the implicit denial of the Church as a spiritual body holding a spiritual Head. And it seems to me a false way of speaking to say that each of these systems is good in moderation, but when pushed to its extreme is bad. I do not think the system is the extension or expansion of the principle, but its limitation and contradiction. I do not see how the principle can be carried too far. I do not see how anything can be done towards the formation of the system, without introducing a seed of evil which must germinate till it produces all its natural fruits.

I have written very much in vain, if I have not yet explained why I suppose this must be the case. These systems, Protestant, Romish, English, seem to me each to bear witness of the existence of a *Divine Order;* each to be a miserable, partial, human substitute for it. In every country, therefore, I should desire to see men emancipated from the chains which they have made for themselves, and entering into the freedom of God's Church. But it seems to me, that in England we have a clearer witness than there is anywhere of our right to this emancipation, and of the way in which it may be effected. This system-building is not natural to us. We have evils which are natural to us, and against which we have to be continually on our guard. But *this* is an exotic product: one of the charges which the Liberal and Evangelical and Catholic systematisers make against our native English divines is, that they have little understanding of any systems; that they go on in a blind mechanical course, merely caring to keep their places and do their work. And yet the members of all these parties are continually giving proof, when they are not occupied with actual controversies, that they feel this maxim of "keeping their places, and doing their work," to be not a low or grovelling one; but one which their consciences testify in favour of, and to which they would wish, if they could, to conform themselves. As they become more aged and holy, more disciplined by affliction, more apprehensive of God's will and of the ends which they are to seek, it would seem as if this old-fashioned notion, which struck them as so vulgar and earthly in their youth, is more and more acknowledged to be one high in its origin, and difficult in its realisation. An old systematiser in England is a very rare spectacle indeed. There is either a gravitation into some lower region, or an ascent into some higher one; either a fall out of the middle air of speculations to our mother clods; or a clear perception that the heavenly things are substantial, and that in the solid earth and not in

the clouds we are to find the images of them. I
should be very presumptuous if I spoke to such men,
except in the language of deference and humility,
beseeching them not to make us that which they have
ceased to be themselves; not to let us fancy from
their words that they belong to schools and parties,
when we know that in their closets and in their lives
they must be renouncing them all. It it from the
ranks of young men that these parties will be recruited.
They want, as they say, principles and ideas. They
cannot move on in the line of mere practical business
and exertion. They must know why they act and
what is the end of action, or they will not act at all.
I think I am as sensible of this necessity as they can
be; and sensible, too, how little their elders are able to
sympathise in the want, or to satisfy it. Nay, I
think I can see further, that unless we who are
younger do earnestly seek after principles and grounds
of action, we must sink into the monotony of the last
century, or into a far worse state than that. I believe
the great principles, which each of these systems has
developed, have been made known to us for the wisest
purposes. But then I think that they are the sap
which is to invigorate and restore the oak trunk which
has been standing for so many ages on our soil, and
that the seedlings which they themselves have sent
forth, are of a poor, weak, tortuous growth, not
capable of resisting any tempest. I do not urge the
young English student to make light of these principles; I say he cannot with safety make light of any
one of them. All belong to him, he has need of them
all; but I beseech him to consider solemnly, and as in
the presence of God, whether he may lawfully do any

acts which imply that he adopts one of the systems in which these principles are buried, and whether he dares to fraternise with any parties, as parties, which profess them.

He will be told, of course, that to stand aloof from them is practically impossible; that to attempt it is an act of self-conceit and self-will; that he is an Eclectic or a Syncretist; that in a short time if he perseveres in his determination he will throw off his faith altogether. To the first charge he may reply, that it cannot be impossible for an Englishman to be that which it is the natural bias of an Englishman, not under some peculiar influence, to be. To the second he will answer, that instead of rejecting the instructions of his parents and teachers, he is seeking to hold them fast. Possibly they belong to a particular school. His first impulse on beginning to think, is to emancipate himself from their notions, to choose new teachers, to adopt the system which is most opposite to that of his education. Those who beseech him not to join a party say, 'By no means do this; the notions which you have learnt must not be abandoned; There is a truth in them which you must have; never let them go till you have made yourself master of it; when you are master of it, do what you like with the system; you will love those who taught it you more than you ever did; you will only not suffer their teachings to keep you separate from men whom you ought also to love.' The accusation of Eclecticism or Syncretism it is better not to notice at all; nine out of ten persons who use the words, do not know what they mean; they are merely bugbears to frighten children with; the tenth

man who does know will understand that he who
endeavours to substitute a Church for systems, must
regard with most dread and suspicion the attempt
at a complete, all-comprehending system.   Hating
all systems, he hates those most which are most
perfect, because in them there are the fewest crannies
and crevices through which the light and air of
heaven may enter.   He hates the Romish system
more than all Protestant systems, because the latter
are inconsistent and fragmentary, the former is all-
embracing and satisfactory, therefore more lifeless,
inhuman, godless.   As to the fear of his losing his
faith, when he has thrown down the party walls which
have been raised for the defence of it, he may venture
to stand the risk.   If his faith be in the doctrines
of men and not in the wisdom of God, the sooner it
falls the better.   If it be in Him whose name is Truth,
to Him be the care of it committed.   We believe that
His sentence has gone forth against systems and
parties; we do not believe that He has recalled the
words, 'None who trusteth in Me shall be
confounded.'

I am sure our responsibility in this matter is becoming more weighty every day.   I have said that these
systems are not natural to us.   But I do not mean
that they are not able to assimilate themselves with
our most characteristic tendencies.   Elsewhere the
defenders of a system may merely form a *school*.   In
England, because by constitution we are politicians
and not systematisers, they must form a *party*.   The
moment we have adopted a peculiar theory we begin
to organise.   We have our flags and our watchwords,
our chiefs and our subordinates.   All the generous

feelings of sympathy and courage, of readiness to
support a friend, of unwillingness to desert him when
he has done some unpopular act, bind us to one and
another maxim which our leaders or allies have put
forth, even though there is nothing in our own minds
which answers to it; we throw the feelings befitting
men of action and soldiers, into the defence of propositions which have been worked out by the most
dry school logic. Thus personality necessarily enters
into all our solemnest discussions. A noble symptom
of what we ought to be! a miserable effect when we
are striving to make ourselves something else! The
respectable champions on each side ask, and ask
again, why they should be treated with harshness and
malignity, for maintaining principles which they believe
in their hearts to be charitable and true. Immediately
after, their Newspapers and Reviews are seen generously
striving that no other party shall have the stigma of
being more unfair and libellous than their own. What
seems to me worse and more grievous still—all, whether
they are capable of understanding systems or not, are
expected to enlist in one of these parties, and to bear
its name. The poor must be instructed in penny
tracts to call such a man a Papist, or such a man
a Low Churchman. Our children must become
polemics before they can repeat their catechism; and
the members of that sex which exists to pacify and
harmonise society, to be a witness against our cold
logical habits of thought, to teach us the worth of
things above words, must talk about opinions, imitate
our discords, pollute their minds if not their lips with
the ribaldry which we think it a part of our Christian
duty and profession to indulge against those who are

called by the same name and partake of the same sacraments with us. Surely such a state of things must bring down heavy judgments upon our Church and land, and therefore everyone ought to consider whether he will make himself an accessory to the sin, whether he can do nothing to avert the punishment.

I am aware how much pains the defenders of party have taken, to engage the practical feelings of Englishmen on their side. They have said, ' Let theorists talk what they will, the moment we begin to act, we must associate with some men or other, and this association will assume a party character. To bid us abandon parties and systems, is only another way of bidding us hang down our hands in stupid indolence. Those who wish to *do* anything must be content to take things as they find them.' Yes, this is undoubtedly the right test; I rejoice that we should be brought to it. I leave it then to the defenders of systems and parties, to explain what they are doing *with* them. They cannot complain that their machinery is not in active operation. It may occasionally meet with a little obstruction from a certain vague impression in men's minds, that they have been commanded to love their neighbours as themselves; still they cannot be so ungrateful as not to acknowledge that it has been brought to very tolerable perfection, and of course, to very great efficiency, in this nineteenth century in our English towns and villages. Any description of its results from an opponent could not be a fair one. I will therefore confine myself to a short statement of certain modes of action which I believe are open to a person who does not avail himself of this machinery, but is content with the powers which he believes God has bestowed upon him, as a minister of his Kingdom.

1. Does such a person find himself among the members of different sects and parties—a Quaker here, a Baptist there, a Unitarian on his right, a Plymouth Christian on his left? He believes that he is a member of a polity which recognises the truth contained in each of these systems; but they have made a system out of some principle which they have torn apart from the rest; that they have destroyed that principle by its separation. He believes that there are earnest men in these sects who are feeling this to be the case, who are catching at all schemes of union because they feel it, who are angry with us because we do not enter into their sense of the necessity of a union and therefore fraternise with them; who are proclaiming the very principle upon which the Catholic Church stands, that all unity is to be in Christ, and that intellectual notions and opinions ought not to divide men from Him. There is therefore a practical renunciation of the sect principle, as something which is no longer tenable. There is at the same time a very furious desire to maintain it as against the national Church. The reasons will seem to him to be these. First, the Church has put itself forth merely as an English Church. Its character as a Catholic body, as a kingdom set up in the world for all nations, has been kept out of sight. Secondly, in the reaction against this tendency, it has taken a negative, *i.e.* a sectarian, form. The idea of the Church, as a united body, has been put forth, chiefly to shew the wickedness of those who have separated from it. Its episcopacy and its

sacraments have been looked upon chiefly as exclusive of those who have them not. Above all, the spiritual character of the Church as deriving its life from its head, a character which the Dissenters are especially disposed by their profession to recognise, has been disjoined from the institutions which embody it. Men have been asked to receive these institutions merely as such, and then to hope for spiritual life through them. Little attempt has been made to prove to them that the institutions are themselves living portions of the divine kingdom. A person therefore who has entered into these convictions himself, will not despair of seeing all the true hearty Dissenters gradually receiving them also. He will not be impatient to force any notions of his own upon them. His desires will be to meet their feelings and to enter into them. He will be most anxious not to destroy any thing which they have received or learnt; to confirm them in their feelings of affection and reverence for their fathers; to strengthen in them by all means the hereditary affections, which their doctrines respecting private judgment so much impair. He wishes to preserve all the faith which they have from the destruction which is threatening it; to unite their faith with that of those from whom they are separated; to make them integral members of the body from which they fancy that it is the object of our pride and selfishness to exclude them. What the result of such a method may be, is in God's hands, not ours. At all events other methods have been tried and have failed; this has not been tried.

2. Or does the Churchman I am supposing find himself in one of our awful manufacturing districts?

Of course, the sense of his own utter inadequacy to
deal with the mass of evil which he meets there is the
first which will take hold of him, and will grow stronger
every day. Yet he is there, and he knows that there
is One who cares for this mass of living beings infinitely
more than he does. Nay, his own coldness and heart-
lessness will continually remind him that if he is to
care for them at all, the feeling must be communicated to him by Him who often seems to these
unhappy creatures utterly heedless of their sorrows
and complainings. And then he has the consolation
which the Athenian orator found when he reflected
on the reverses of his countrymen, and the resistless
march of Philip. 'If we had done such and such
things and they had failed, we might despair; we
have not done them, therefore let us hope.' A Church
which was looked upon, and almost looked upon itself,
as a tool of the aristocracy, which compared its own
orders with the ranks in civil society, and forgot that
it existed to testify that man as man is the object of
his Creator's sympathy; such a Church had no voice
which could reach the hearts of these multitudes. The
Liberal proclamation which says, 'Teach them; impart
to them a few of the things that we know,' was more
genial and humane. But there are thoughts ever at
work in these Englishmen, in these human beings,
thoughts quickened by hunger and suffering, which
such instruction could not appease. More impressive
far was the speech of the Methodist and the Evangelical: 'You have immortal souls, they are perishing;
oh! ask how they may be saved.' Such words spoken
with true earnestness are very mighty. But they are
not enough; men feel that they are not merely lost

creatures; they look up to heaven above them, and ask whether it can be true that this is the whole account of their condition; that their sense of right and wrong, their cravings for fellowship, their consciousness of being creatures having powers which no other creatures possess, are all nothing. If religion, they say, will give us no explanation of these feelings, if it can only tell us about a fall for the whole race, and an escape for a few individuals of it, then our wants must be satisfied without religion. Then begin Chartism and Socialism, and whatever schemes make rich men tremble. Surely, what the modern assertors of a Church system say about the duty of administering active charity to these sufferers, of shewing that we do not merely regard them as pensioners on the national bounty, but as fellow-men for whom we are to make sacrifices—surely this language is far more to the purpose. Surely if acted upon even imperfectly, it must produce most happy effects. But how would the proclamation to our Chartists and Socialists, that they had baptismal purity once, and that they have lost it now; that they must recover their ground by repentance, by prayer and fasting; that they must submit to discipline, and be deprived of privileges which they never exercised nor cared for; how can such a proclamation as this meet any of the confused, disorderly notions which are stirring in their minds, or set them right?

On the other hand, if the new and unwonted proclamation were to go forth, 'God has cared for you, you are indeed his children; his Son has redeemed you, his Spirit is striving with you; there is a fellowship larger, more irrespective of outward distinctions, more democratical, than any which you can create; but it is a fellowship of mutual love, not mutual selfishness, in which the chief of all is the servant of all—may not one think that a result would follow as great as that which attended the preaching of any Franciscan friar in the twelfth century, or any Methodist preacher in the eighteenth? For these are true words, everlasting words, and yet words which belong especially to our time; they are words which interpret, and must be interpreted by, that regular charity, that ministerial holiness, those sacraments, prayers, discipline, of which the Catholic speaks. They connect his words about repentance with those of the Evangelical, making it manifest, that nothing but an accursed nature and a depraved will could have robbed any of the blessings which God has bestowed upon us all. They translate into meaning and life all the liberal plans for the education of adults and children; they enable us to fulfil the notion, which statesmen have entertained, that the Church is to be the supporter of the existing orders, by making her a teacher and example to those orders respecting their duties and responsibilities; by removing the hatred which their forgetfulness of those duties and responsibilities is threatening to create in the minds of the lower classes.

3. But a Churchman, such as I have supposed, would be both compelled by his circumstances, and urged by his principles, to change these convictions into action, by enlisting all the wealthier inhabitants of his parish in different services and occupations for the benefit of their inferiors. I am unwilling to enlarge upon this subject; first, because my practical

ignorance makes me unfit to offer any suggestions upon it; and, secondly, because I am certain that our English political wisdom, guided by Catholic feeling, is already doing much in many parts of this land, in the accomplishment of such a design. I must, however, refer to it for the purpose of remarking, how the notion, that party organisation is necessary, is at once explained and refuted the moment we aim at an ecclesiastical organisation. It is explained when the truth, that no man is meant to work alone, which is the truth that is implied in this strange maxim, is made the principle of our action. It is refuted; for we find how infinitely freer from friction a society is which is held together by sacramental bonds, and is moving under the direction of an appointed pastor, than all societies constructed upon a party model, or acknowledging a party motive, ever have been or ever can be. For the one seeks to preserve all existing ranks and relations, the other sets them all aside. The one is continually endeavouring to understand how the middle classes may be brought most to act upon the lower, so as to be their guides and not their tyrants; how the upper classes may be brought to act upon the middle, so as not to be their fawning slaves and at the same time the betrayers of their consciences at elections, cold and distant and the objects of their servile imitation at other times; how each portion of the community may preserve its proper position to the rest, and may be fused together by the spiritual power which exists for each, the minister of all, the creature of none. The other confounds all orders, and yet does not the least diminish their mutual repulsion, or make them feel that they have a common object. Above all, the Churchman is ever longing to discover how the handmaidens of the Church may be brought to do her the services which they alone can do, without departing for a moment from their own true estate, as wives, as sisters, as mothers; how the whole sex may be an order of Sisters of Charity; and how, in each particular neighbourhood, this order may be at work in lowliness and meekness, softening and healing the sorrows of the world. The partisan acknowledges no difference of vocation in man and woman; all are to be equally feverish and restless; careful about many things, unfit alike for quiet contemplation or regular activity.

4. Again, let us suppose our Churchman in Ireland, amidst a population, the majority of which acknowledge no relation to the body of which he is a member; how would he feel, and how would he desire to act? Would he not think thus within himself?—'When Anselm came over from his Norman convent to be Archbishop of Canterbury, and his victorious countrymen thought that he of course would look upon the old Saxons of the soil as they did; he told them plainly, that a Churchman acknowledged no distinctions of race, and that his vocation was to be the friend of the poor and distressed wherever he met with them. And these principles, of course with great exceptions and deviations, were acted upon by a large portion of the Norman bishops and clergy. What was the effect? We grew up to be an English nation. The Saxon serf felt that he had a portion and a right in the soil; he recollected the sounds of his native language; he began to speak it; in due time the conquerors and the conquered became one.

If our Churchmen had but acted upon this principle
in Ireland; if they had but said to the English
settlers,—We will have nothing to do with your
Orange lodges and your hell-fire clubs, except to
discipline and restrain those who belong to them;
we are come over as protectors of these Celts; we are
to raise them out of barbarism; to speak to their
Church feelings and their national feelings; to call
forth both together :—if these had been our maxims,
how many problems, which perplex the statesman at
this day, might have been solved long ago! But that
phrase, *The English interest,* was continually present
to the minds of the statesmen who sent out our
Bishops, and though they might often stumble by
mistake upon a noble rebel to their commands, they
sought diligently for men who should forward their
own narrow policy. What has been the consequence?
The national feeling in Ireland has strangely and
unnaturally associated itself with that Romanism
which is the foe of all national feeling. The Irish
look upon our Church as a Saxon Church, and they
actually fly to Rome to give them an Irish Church.
But even now at the eleventh hour, if better and
truer feelings of our position are rising in the minds
of statesmen, may not the Church be the means of
carrying them out? We have tried what the mere
preaching of Protestantism will do in Ireland, and so
far as it has been earnest and sincere, it has not been
in vain. But still it has not touched the hearts of
Irishmen; there has been a resistance to it, not
merely in their bad feelings but in their good. State
liberality has been tried. So far as it has been the
token of kindness and sympathy, perhaps this too has

not been in vain. Still all must acknowledge that it has done very little; most men think that a fair proportion of evil has been mingled with the good. But if there be a sympathy between the Catholic and National principle, if they cannot really exist apart, why may we not begin to speak to the national sympathies of Irishmen; to speak to them as members of an *Irish* Catholic Church; to declare that every Irishman ought to look upon himself as a member of such a Church, and not of any other Church, Saxon or Romish; to make it manifest by acts, that we hold our revenues for the good of the whole land, and that it would not gain anything but misery by the confiscation of them, or by the extirpation of those who possessed them?' Such thoughts, I say, are likely to arise in the mind of an Irish Churchman, who enters into the principles I have endeavoured to develop. They may be very crude, but still they may be the germs of acts which neither the State nor the Church will have reason to complain of.

5. To one who feels the importance of the Protestant principle, and that its true home is in the Catholic Church, it must needs seem a strange providence in respect to England, that she should have on one side of her a nation in which Protestantism has tried to exist nakedly and exclusively; on the other side, a nation which wishes to be Catholic by being Romanist. Each experiment is, I think, very decisive, but each is connected with sins which we have need to confess and deplore. The utter insufficiency of Presbyterianism to support a national life has been surely proved by the example of Scotland. But we began with setting up our episcopacy as if it were

an English thing. We gave the Scotch people the notion, that their own kings were coming back to reduce them into an ecclesiastical province of England, and the religious as well as the national spirit rose against such a pretension. Now, it would seem as if the episcopalian body in Scotland had the opportunity of shewing, that they are neither members of a religious sect nor tools of England. They have existed for many years without any State patronage; their chief fault has been, that they have not sympathised with the feelings of the people, that they have stood too much upon their ecclesiastical dignity, that they have seemed too much mere anti-presbyterians. But if, in the present crisis of Scotland, they will consider earnestly, that they exist as witnesses, not of a system but of a Church, not of certain notions about episcopacy, but of episcopacy as part of the constitution of Christ's spiritual kingdom; they will find, I think, that they may exercise a quiet and soothing influence over that ferment of Scotch feelings, which all State contrivances have been so utterly ineffectual to allay. They will not, I hope, look with proud aristocratical contempt upon the earnest cry which the people have sent forth to be freed from civil dominion. They will not, I hope, indulge in mocking allusions to the proud language in which Presbyterianism used to assert that it was free of this control. They will acknowledge that spiritual freedom is most essential to the life of a nation. They will labour to shew, that the Church, rightly and truly constituted, is able to humble the lofty and to exalt the lowly; that the tyranny which Presbyterianism granted to its aristocracy at the time

of the Reformation, is the tyranny against which its
sons are groaning now; that its boast of being a
Church for the poor has ended in a sadder separation
between the poor and the rich than has almost ever
existed in any country. Here again I am suggesting
no projects or plans to Scotch Churchmen. I am
merely urging them to consider seriously the indications of God's will, and to desire that they may act
in accordance with it.

6. The lessons which we have derived from the
history of our connexion with Scotland and Ireland
(I have spoken before of those which are suggested
by the circumstances of our old colonies in North
America) cannot surely be lost upon us when we go
forth to plant new settlements on the other side of
the globe, or when we are inquiring how we are to
deal with those which we possess already. Every
circumstance of their position and of ours seems to
say, ' See that you do not merely establish an English
kingdom in those soils; if you do, that kingdom will
not be a blessing to the colonists, to the natives, or to
the mother country. See that you do not merely send
forth preachers in your ships to tell the people that all
they have believed hitherto—if they have believed
anything—is false, and that we hold a doctrine which
sets it all aside. See that you raise up in the midst
of them what they shall feel to be as real a kingdom
as the one which is presented to them in the persons
of governors and judges; a kingdom which does not
only deal equal justice to natives and to settlers, but
which claims both alike for its citizens, endues both
alike with its highest privileges; a kingdom which
comes to subvert nothing, but to restore that which

is decayed and fallen; to adopt into itself every fragment of existing faith and feeling; to purify it and exalt it; to cut off from it only that which the conscience of the native confesses to be inconsistent with it; to testify that wherever there is a creature having human limbs and features, there is one of that race for which Christ died, one whom he is not ashamed to call a brother.

In such countries as New Zealand and Australia, such a testimony as is borne by the establishment of a Christian kingdom of peace and righteousness is everything ; for there, of course, only the rudest and most incoherent spiritual theories and speculations will be found to exist. In India the case is altogether different; yet there, more than anywhere, is it needful that the signs of a spiritual kingdom should be introduced, that Christianity should be regarded as something more than a fine theory. For how did the simple tenets of Mahomedanism prevail over the complicated creeds and philosophies of the Hindoos but because the former came forth in the shape of an organic society, and the latter were only forms of thought connected principally with the physical universe? The Christian Church ought to understand the positions both of the Hindoo and the Mussulman, in respect to the strange masses of feelings and opinions which are exhibited in the traditions of the one, and to the struggle after consistency and unity which are visible in the actual history of the other. Would that the supporters of Indian missions had taken this ground when they were assailed by the cowardice and indifference of the merchant-emperors thirty years ago ! Would that they had been able to reply to those who had accused them of disturbing the faith of the natives, and so endangering English dominion—*No; it is your godlessness and rapacity which endanger their faith; you are making them infidels while you pretend to indulge their superstitions: we go to save their faith by delivering them from their superstitions and your example; we go, that England may not perish in that day when she shall be called to give account of the crimes which you have committed.* But it was not fully understood at that time that Christianity was anything else but a sect, or a collection of sects, sent into the world to displace Pagan and Mahomedan sects; therefore, the years which have followed have produced their natural effect, and we have now to deal for the most part with a generation of open or disguised infidels. Still the good men of that day, guided by a higher wisdom than their own, were led to ask strenuously of the English legislature, that a Bishop might be sent out to them. They felt that they wanted a Church. A heart was put into a country which had hitherto only been directed by wise heads or skilful hands; a heart which is still beating, and which we trust may yet send a life-blood into every part of that vast empire. The issue is with God; but He has taught us by sufficiently manifest indications in what way He wills that we should fulfil our part in the work.

7. I have not yet spoken of the spirit in which we should act towards the members of foreign Churches, be they Romish or Protestant. But enough has been said in former parts of this work to indicate the course which an Englishman, who

is not tied down by systems, must strive to pursue
in reference to them. What I have been chiefly
wishing to show is, that here we have the means
of acting upon the principles which all men everywhere ought to act upon if they could; herein it
seems to me lies the blessing for which we have
to give thanks. Our Church has no right to call
herself better than other Churches in any respect,
in many she must acknowledge herself to be worse.
But our *position*, we may fairly affirm, for it is not
a boast but a confession, is one of singular advantage.
If what I have said be true, our faith is not formed
by a union of the Protestant systems with the Romish
system, nor of certain elements taken from the one
and of certain elements taken from the other. So
far as it is represented in our liturgy and our articles,
it is the faith of a Church, and has nothing to do
with any system at all. That peculiar character
which God has given us, enables us, if we do not
slight the mercy, to understand the difference between a Church and a System, better perhaps than
any of our neighbours can, and, therefore, our position,
rightly used, gives us a power of assisting them in
realising the blessings of their own. By refusing to
unite with them on the ground of any one of their
systems, by seeking to unite with them on the grounds
of the universal Church, we teach them wherein lies
their strength and their weakness; by determining
that we will be a nation distinct from all others, we
encourage each of them to be a nation distinct from
us and from all others. By shewing them how our
Church life and our national life are interwoven, we
teach them that the bonds which make them one

with us are necessary to the support of that peculiar character and position which make them independent of us.

But for such tasks as these—for reconciling the different sects in our own land, for dealing with the wild feelings respecting government and society which are abroad, for bringing the different classes into co-operation, for entering into the strong passions of Scotch Calvinists and Irish Romanists, for taming the savages of the antipodes, for restoring the strange reliques of ancient civilisation among the natives of British India, for suggesting any practical hints, or giving any practical help to our brethren on the Continent; what need have we of another discipline and another spirit than that which we seem at present to possess! Shall we obtain either the one or the other by sitting still, by affirming that these tasks are too great for creatures so infirm and fallen, by waiting for some sudden inspiration? This cannot be. These works are set before us; in one way or other, we are trying to carry them on, and must carry them on. The necessity is laid upon us; the only point to be considered is how we can support it. Do we tremble at the great efforts of thought which are presupposed in these outward undertakings, the careful studies in history, ecclesiastical and civil, the acquaintance with the powers and the distinctions of words as the signs of thought, the intimacy with the symbols which nature and art have furnished to the mythologist, the patient toil with which these must be weighed in our minds before we can cast ourselves into the feelings of other men, while yet we do not lose our own? Assuredly this is required of us, not the whole of each student—for the Church is one body, and hath many members—but something of every one, and the habit and disposition of all. But there is nothing in all this to stagger the countrymen of Bacon and of Newton. Study is painful and intolerable to Englishmen if they cannot connect it with action. They cannot pursue it for its pleasure or its comeliness; make them feel that there is an end in it, that it is necessary for their business, and they will be as diligent slaves in the reading of books as in the making of roads. Our systems and our parties have confused us in every direction; they lead us to fancy that all things are moving round in a weary circle, or are imprisoned in lifeless notions. At the same time they tempt every man to suppose that he is to be everything, and to know everything, and to do everything; for he feels that if he has not the whole of his system before him, each part of it becomes mischievous and false. And he cannot trust other men to do their work while he does his own; for he feels that he belongs to a party rather than to a Church, and therefore he has no security that each person has his order and duties assigned to him. Thus we are at the same time indolent and over-diligent, ignorant and encyclopædic. Once break this spell, and we shall again begin to connect our specific studies with a general humanity, and so at once preserve their limitations and make them universal.

But there is another and the more serious subject. I have spoken of a different *discipline*, but we need a different *spirit* in order to that discipline. Not a different Spirit from that which we received in our

baptism, but an altogether different one from the
spirit of party and of selfishness, which we have
allowed to enter into us and possess us in our manhood. To exorcise this, that the other may really
inform us and rule us, should surely be our first
object. And we cannot drive it out of others until
we have striven that it may be banished from ourselves. If we, who form the clergy of the land,
believe that we are its heart, we must suppose that the
purification of the body generally depends upon our
purification; we must feel that every evil which we
call upon others to repent of has its origin and root in
us, and that we must repent of it first. I fear that
the habit of apologising for our institution, when it
has been ignorantly attacked by those who know
nothing of its meaning or its blessing, may have
operated injuriously upon our lives. We have defended the arrangements of Providence and the order
of the Church, till, unawares, we have begun to defend
ourselves, who have so grievously sinned against those
arrangements and that order, and have hindered men
from perceiving what they are. For this fault, if we
have committed it, we must wish to make amends;
since we must know that there can be no national
confession or national reformation, if we, who ought
to be the foremost in both, as having the most to
answer for, are trying to make excuses for ourselves,
hiding the evil which we are inwardly conscious of, or
imputing it to circumstances, most of which are very
favourable to us, none of which ought to be our
masters.

But if shame and humiliation are needful for
English clergymen generally, they must be espe-

cially needful in those who have presumed to speak of
our sins, and to offer any suggestion for our amend-
ment. It is too probable that they would have known
nothing of the evil of systems and parties in others if
they had not felt it in themselves; nay, that the irri-
tation of the beam in their own eye has made them
more eager to detect the mote in their brother's eye.
I have in this book attacked no wrong tendency to
which I do not know myself to be liable. I hope I
am conscious to a certain degree, though very insuffi-
ciently, of the danger I am in of substituting the
denunciation of it for the practical correction of it in
the only sphere over which I have any control. I am
not ignorant, also, that the hints which I have offered
in opposition to systems may, themselves, be turned
by myself or by others into a system; and that neither
its weakness and inconsistency, nor the insignificance
of its originator, may prevent it from connecting itself
with some new party. I believe that some of whom I
have spoken in this chapter began to fulfil their
mission with as sincere a desire that their words
might never become the symbols of a faction as I can
feel now. I do not therefore, confide in myself. But
since a school, which should be formed to oppose all
schools, must be of necessity more mischievous than
any of them; and since a school, which pretended to
amalgamate the doctrines of all other schools, would
be, as I think, more mischievous than that, I do pray
earnestly, that if any such schools should arise, they
may come to nought; and that, if what I have written
in this book should tend even in the least degree to
favour the establishment of them, it may come to
nought. On the other hand, if there be any thing

here which may help to raise men above their own narrow conceptions and mine, may lead them to believe that there is a way to that truth which is living and universal, and above us all, and that He who is Truth will guide them in that way—this which is from Him and not from me, I pray that He will bless. 'Let all thine enemies perish, O Lord;' all systems, schools, parties which have hindered men from seeing the largeness, and freedom, and glory of thy kingdom; 'but let them that love thee,' in whatever earthly mists they may at present be involved, 'be as the sun when he goeth forth in his strength.'

NOTE ON THE ATHANASIAN CREED.

As I have spoken in my article upon Creeds only of two, it may be supposed by the reader, that I have some reason for objecting to the third. Had I felt such objections I should have stated them openly, and not left them to be discovered by inference. There would be little courage in acknowledging them. The number of those who reject this Creed may not be so great as it was in the last century, but it is still large, and composed of persons respectable for their learning, their piety, and their influence. Those who are most strong in defending it will find so much fault with my opinions on other subjects, that I should not be at all likely to conciliate them, by professing an agreement with them upon this.

I omitted to speak of the Athanasian Creed, merely because it did not concern the subject I was treating of. Its formula is not, 'I believe,' but 'Quicunque vult.' It has never been connected with Baptism. It has never been used except as an occasional service in any Church; its antiquity, though venerable, is certainly below that of the others. Evidently, therefore, its merits or its defects stand upon a different ground from theirs. I will now endeavour to explain why the ordinary objections to it seem to me of little weight, and wherein I believe its value consists.

The complaints against this Creed are chiefly two. 1. That it is not consistent with the Nicene, which asserts so clearly the idea of filial subordination. 2. That it is at direct variance with the command, 'Judge not, that ye be not judged.' If I believed either of the allegations to be true, the authority of no Church upon earth could induce me to use this formulary. But the more I have considered them, the less reason have I found in either of them.

1. The passage in the Athanasian Creed, which seems to some to interfere with the doctrine of the Nicene, is that in which it is affirmed, that Christ is equal to the Father as touching His Godhead, inferior to the Father as touching His Manhood. Here we are told, 'it is signified, that the subordination of the Son to the Father is

connected with His human nature. Whereas, according to the doctrine of the other Creed, which Bishop Bull has so finely developed, the subjection which was manifested in our Lord's acts when upon earth was really involved in the very idea of His Being; that flesh which He took could not in any sense change the law of His existence, but was the medium through which it was shewn forth.' I cannot doubt the truth of these remarks. The words, 'Not I, but the Father,' seem to me to be the key to the mystery of our Lord's self-sacrifice, that is to say, of His innermost life; how, then, can I think them other than the expression of His own very Personality? But it is implied in what I have said that the *fulness* of the Godhead was in the man Christ, that He was the perfect God. The very objection which we are considering rests upon the ground, that our Lord's acts, as a man, would not be a complete exhibition of Himself, if we might regard them as only belonging to His assumed nature. But, if this be the case,—if we need to express two truths, one, the perfect and complete Godhead of our Lord; one, His subordination as a Son to the Father; each necessary to the other, each practically unmeaning without the other:—why may we not look at the union of humanity to the Divinity, as that which supplies us with the language for both? The idea of subordination apart from all inequality, exists in the very nature of the Godhead; it is brought out and expressed through the inferiority of Manhood to Godhead. The Sonship of Christ is the type and ground of the relation in which the human stands to the divine. What then more complete and beautiful than the language of the Old Church upon this subject?

Do we not feel that if we had only the Nicene Creed—if a new heresy had not called forth another exposition—we should have been in great danger of losing our apprehension of a truth, from having but one imperfect form of language to unfold it in? Nay, do we not feel that as the Apostles' Creed, without the Nicene, would lead us into the danger of thinking only concerning the relation in which the Divine Being stands to *us*; so the Nicene Creed without the Athanasian, would still lead us to think merely of *divine relations*, without remembering that there is an absolute ground visible in them and through them?

2. But the charge of uncharitableness is one which is far more popular and intelligible than that of which I have been speaking; perhaps, therefore, I may venture to meet it in a popular way. We are commonly asked such a question as this: 'Though you may be able to explain away these clauses by ingenious sophisms in your study, do you not feel when you are reading the Creed in your Church to the people, that you are not uttering the kind of words

which you would wish to utter, or acting in the kind of spirit in which you would wish to act, when you read the seventh chapter of St. Matthew's Gospel, or the thirteenth chapter of the first epistle to the Corinthians?' I can only answer this question for myself; but I doubt not there are hundreds who can say, with a perfectly clear conscience, what I say now. To the best of my knowledge and recollection, I never have felt tempted while reading this creed, however I may have felt tempted at other times, to indulge one hard thought about the state of any man who is living now or has lived in former times. I do not think that the creed calls upon me to do this; nay, I think that its awful language forbids me to do it. I dare not ask myself who has committed the fearful sin, of 'confounding the Persons and dividing the Substance,' which it denounces. It may not be the man who has used the most confused and heretical forms of expression; it may not be the man who has even seemed to the Church to be most self-willed and refractory; it may be the man who is resting most contentedly in his orthodoxy; it may be myself. Nay, have I not a witness within, that every wrong act which I have done, or wrong thought which I have cherished, so far as it has diminished my sense of the distinction between truth and falsehood, right and wrong, has been of the nature of that sin which I describe by the words 'Confounding the Persons,' and has brought me into the danger of committing it; that every self-willed, unkind, schismatical act or thought has been of the nature of that sin which I describe by the words 'Dividing the Substance,' and has tended to bring me into it? For this creed takes me into another region altogether from that of words and names and forms of the intellect, though it makes use of those words and names and forms, for the sake of correcting the abuses which they have produced, and as signs which may shew me my way to deeper truths and principles. It is my own fault if I stay in the outer region, and do not let the Church guide me into its inner circle; it is my own fault if I do not warn others, and warn myself, of the connexion between eternal truths and principles, and that 'doing good' or 'doing evil,' to which, as the creed declares in its last articles, eternal life or punishment are appended.

But why do I wish to retain this creed, seeing that some may use it amiss for the condemnation of their neighbours, and not for good to them or to themselves? I answer, that if I parted with it I think I should not help the cause of charity, and should do great injury to the cause of truth. The language of the Old Church may sound stronger and fiercer than that which is common in our day, but it is grounded upon the words, 'This is life eternal, that they may know

Thee the only true God.' The bottomless pit which the fathers really dreaded was that of Atheism, the state of the human spirit left without God. I believe the more we return to this idea the more of inward charity we shall have, the more we shall understand our glory and our perils, the more we shall have of common hopes and common objects; the more we shall be free from vulgar selfish desires, and from superstitious fears. I could not give up this creed without saying, that the meaning and principle of it belonged less to this time than to former times. Whereas, I believe that they belong more to our time than to any time. For this, it seems to me, is the question which is in debate now. Are we to behold the unity which has its deepest and most real ground in that name of God which this creed speaks of, informing all society and all nature; or are we to see everything broken, divided, unharmonised; a dark form of self-love, embodied in some visible tyranny, above us, and a gulf of utter nothingness beneath us?

THE END.

CHARLES DICKENS AND EVANS, CRYSTAL PALACE PRESS.